Paola Viganò

The Biopolitical Garden

Spaces, Lives and Transition

To Paolo and Adriana

Table of Contents

Acknowledgements

For their help, support, and presence over the years, I would like to thank Alessio Tamiazzo and Tommaso Pietropolli, as well as all the collaborators of Studio Paola Viganò, in particular Simona Bodria, Etienne Schillers, Bertrand Plewinski, Morvan Rabin and Qinyi Zhang, for nourishing the projects presented in this book with their ideas and for their patience with me.

I would also like to express my sincere thanks to the students who have contributed to these adventures in various ways: Noélie Lecoanet, Anna Karla de Almeida, Elena Calafati and Elvira Pietrobon, PhD students at the EPFL Lausanne and at IUAV Venice, and Roberto Sega. I am grateful for the many opportunities I have had to present and discuss the main assumptions of this book. Each of these moments has been meaningful to me. Finally, I would like to thank Cristina Bianchetti for her friendship, attentive reading and support of the book.

INTRODUCTION

Fig. 1
Renaat Braem, Linjstad (Linear City), residential block, collage, 1984 (Strauven 1985).

Spaces. Towards a New Biopolitical Project

"The metaphysical and methodological commitment of modern Western urbanism is towards conceiving the project of the city and the territory as being part of a vaster biopolitical action". " Bernardo Secchi[1]

The book and the project

In his last paper on European urbanism and its tradition, Bernardo Secchi takes up Michel Foucault's biopolitical hypothesis and extends it to modern urban planning and design. Secchi considers the entire European tradition of city design as part of a "broader biopolitical action" and committed, consequently and in terms of the construction and transformation of space, to keeping a population alive, along with that population's protection, education and emancipation. Modern urban planning is aligned with this commitment, developing a profound reflection on space that it imagines, designs, and transforms.

Today, however, we cannot refer to the limits, inadequacy and modesty of contemporary urban design to the ambitious project of modern urbanism, nor the lack of visions and decisions capable of solving the problems posed by cities and territories in transition. There are myriad reasons for this—cultural (radical criticism of the project proposed by modernity), political (the abandonment or fragmentation of the reformist project that fuelled it; the increasingly deep divide between different strata of society), and ecological (the environmental crisis and rarefaction of resources). This doesn't mean that the space we inhabit and its design have lost their biopolitical connotations. On the contrary. In a context of radical change, space, life and design once again resume their full depth of expression.

These aspects raise at least two important research questions. The first: what broader biopolitical action is the project of the city and territory conceived within today? The second (if this action does not seem satisfactory or even convincing): how can the design of space help shape a biopolitical action of substantial emancipation, and what themes and strategies could define it?

This book begins with an urgent call to rethink the city and the territory project (in transition) as a biopolitical issue. The first question is addressed by taking up some of the fundamental spatial concepts that have inspired modern and contemporary design, concepts with a high biopolitical content, and emphasising the permanence and inertia in current urban design practice and the debate surrounding it.

1. (Secchi 2014). See also (Cavalletti 2005).

The second question—what themes and strategies define or could define an affirmative biopolitical action—opens to a few contemporary experiments and experiences reframing the role of space and spatial design in a condition of social and ecological transition. The hypothesis is of a possible new emancipation and coexistence project. Space is understood here as collective capital, support and agent. These are essential interpretative keys, I believe, to adapt our lives to acutely changed conditions.

First Part
Spaces: Space Function, Space Nature, Social Space

To discuss contemporary design as a biopolitical issue, I have considered three types of space, examined them in depth and deconstructed them. They represent powerful aspects of design discourse that have given tangible form to the space of modern and contemporary living in the form of influential paradigms and, at the same time, tangible spatial experiences. Each type of space proposes a different idea of freedom, coexistence and the individual/collective/social/nature relationship. Each proposes an original aesthetic, which unambiguously differentiates it from the others, and a new hypothesis of spatial continuity.

The three spaces cohabit within the existing city and are part of it, just as they still feature in the debate about its future. They interest me because they are sediments of ideas that have passed through and shaped the contemporary city, albeit with different characteristics in different places. Their deconstruction allows ideas and practices to emerge that persist and operate within the city design and habitable space, continuing along paths that are still open or, on the contrary, measuring their unbridgeable distance.

Second Part
Space and the biopolitical project

The spaces dealt with in the first part do not disappear, the topics do not dissipate. In the second part, some categories such as collective capital, support and agency highlight the complexity of our relationship with space: a *subject* space. They define a transition that is not only epistemological but ontological and ethical, driven by a few fundamental fields of reflection pertaining to the spheres of biopower, deep ecology and emancipation. Through this conceptual matrix I tackle the role of space within a hypothesis of "affirmative biopolitics" (Esposito 2004).

Architecture and urban planning are certainly concerned with life, but the frequency with which life is referenced in discussions and projects varies a great deal over time. Before the arrival of this new wave of concern for life, dramatically marked by new pandemics, ecological, political and social crises, there were other controversies at the core of architecture and the city project. Only a few decades ago, a linguistic turn, accompanied by the use of metaphors that read the city as a text, marked postmodern thinking.2 Architecture was thought of as an autonomous field that could respond to itself and for itself, drawing on its own references and internal history. Manfredo Tafuri's "definitive" criticism in *Project and Utopia* (Tafuri 1973) of the unfounded ambition of architecture and urbanism to change the world certainly contributed to this retreat. In more recent decades, the frequency of terms and metaphors referring to life in urban and territorial design discourse has increased dramatically, to the point that it is no longer possible to avoid their impact and not question their meaning. Beyond the ecological crisis and the new awareness that has arisen around it, this semantic thickening highlights the complex relationship between space and life; between bodies, populations, space and power; and its centrality in the present and future of the city.

Third Part
The biopolitical garden, projects

The third part opens with an exploration of the second question posed at the start of this introduction through the hypothesis of the ecological and social transition as part of a new emancipation and coexistence project. As this is not a history book, in that it does not deal with the relationship between architecture and power in the long process of city construction, it is the projects and research I have worked on in recent years that "situate" my reflections on the re-emergence of the proximity of space and life within a set of tangible experiences: their openings, aporias, potential and consequences.

These projects are based on certain antecedents: ideas, research and project experiences that have attempted to redefine the conceptual and thematic horizon of the city project. These include the design of "porous cities" (Secchi, Viganò 2011), "isotropic territories" (Viganò, Secchi, Fabian, 2016) and "horizontal metropolises" (Secchi, Viganò 2010; Viganò, Cavalieri, Barcelloni Corte 2018; Cavalieri, Viganò 2020, Barcelloni Corte, Viganò 2022). The book does not cover these themes, other than episodically, but it considers them an essential part of the construction of a new project of space. The unavoidability of the biopolitical dimension in a context of ecological, social and economic crises requires us to rethink and reformulate the figures, measures and discourses of such a project, to redefine our commitment, as intellectuals, by critically re-reading our traditional fields of action and opening up new ones.

2. For the start of this approach to urban semiotics, see Roland Barthes, "Sémiologie et urbanisme" (1967) and Michel Butor, "La Ville comme texte" (1982), in which the city is an accumulation of text, or *The Urban* Text by Mario Gandelsonas, 1991.

1. SPACES

Fig. 2
Doug Wheeler's "Sa mi dw sm 2 75 continuum atmospheric environment" was exhibited at the Guggenheim Museum in Bilbao, Spain, in 2001. Photo by Paola Viganò.

1.1 THE PROBLEM OF SPACE

Over the years I have developed an uneasy observation that grapples with design, its representations and epistemological status. The production of ideas, the capacity of design exploration to integrate and evolve a broader debate on the city and the territory, to raise good questions within a political, cultural and social decision-making process, and to select pertinent avenues for a comparison with collective expectations—these were the arguments that I felt legitimised research on the project as a knowledge production tool. This hypothesis reacted to the current marginalisation of design work; and its consequences were developed on two levels: the construction of the project (its operations, the research that goes into it) and of the space, the material practised, which the project elaborates and includes.

The book in which I collected these observations[3] ends with a series of open interrogations that lie between the *archive*, in the Foucauldian sense[4]—in this case the archive in formation of the research constructed with the design tools—and *space*, the matter with which the project deals, its manipulation and transformation. I consider the two entities, archive and space, not as mere open questions but *problems* capable of identifying, revealing, and constructing things that do not yet exist.[5] The *archive* brings out a geography of perimeters and enclosures, territories and conflicts: among them is the ongoing need to enact the research carried out with the design tools. *Space*, in the double meaning of the configuration of *mobiles* and practised places (de Certeau, 1980), is often reduced to a secondary, marginal entity: central are the procedures and processes of its production, rarely the ideas and reflections that inspire it. The difficulties in dealing with space lie in its ambiguity: in the continuous oscillation between an idea of autonomy (that of a pure and almost transcendental space) and its dispersion in the universe of practices that alone seem to make it exist.[6]

3. Viganò 2010. More in-depth reflections on this matter are developed in Viganò 2018a.

4. The universe of what has actually been said and could have been said in a certain historical and political-cultural context. Michel Foucault shifts the interest from the archive to the conditions that make it possible, and therefore to the relationships necessary for the things that were said to survive and be maintained (Foucault 1969).

5."Problema", *Dizionario di filosofia Treccani*, 2009, Treccani.it. http://www.treccani.it/enciclopedia/problema_(Dizionario-di-filosofia)/ (consulted on 6 January 2022).

6. Space, an "intricate and convoluted element" (Tschumi, 2005:35). With regard to his contradictions, Tschumi wrote: "...architecture is about two mutually exclusive terms, space and its use, that is, from a theoretical point of view, the concept of space and the experience of space." (Tschumi, 2005:18).

The *archive* is being formed. Like a mirror, through gaps and points of accumulation, it reveals the extent of the research carried out with the project means and, simultaneously, the poverty of the production of knowledge and spatial experimentation. The problem of the space, subject matter and objective of each project lies, in part, within this poverty, one of the reasons that led me to write this book.

An implicit concept

The weak status of knowledge related to the design of space and the lack of confidence in its ability to formulate original hypotheses (which reduces opportunities for experimental production and exacerbates the social question with its demand for solutions) define an initial interpretative framework. "Space as a problem" is too rarely addressed, the questions concerning it remain implicit, concealed within a broader debate on city transformation and closed to innovation. As a result, many design conception layers are completely inactive.

There are many reasons for this and they lie, to a great extent, outside of design research[7] but are partly concerned with it. The normalisation brought about by urban planning, a process that has occurred under the protective canvas of the modern *grand récit*, has created situations of automatism and inevitability capable of transforming the theory of (modern) space into "a given part of the natural world ... applied almost without conscious decision."[8] When a situation like this occurs, "theory no longer counts as theory."[9] If, as Cary Nelson has suggested, the transformation of theory into nature is a disastrous fact that overturns the meaning and role of things, its consequences concern the loss of critical distance to ideas that are now unrecognisable due to too many adaptations or are simply unsuitable to help understand today's problems. The loss of legibility of relationships that cut across space—between built objects and bodies, between crowds, groups and individuals, between public, private and common space;[10] its inclusiveness which is always at risk, and the expansion of the security devices that have characterised modern design to the point of reducing individual and collective freedoms—all of these make questions about the density and distance, closure and openness, transparency and opacity of space once again central. This is why I consider it necessary to conduct research that questions the space we live in, starting

7. The aggression of forms of neoliberal capitalism and their trust in the financial economy as absolute *drivers* of urban dynamics have marginalised the reformist project, the only one in which European urban planning was formed and within which it developed its own tools. See also Viganò 2016a.

8. Paraphrasing Cary Nelson, 1997, in *Manifesto of a Tenured Radical and Revolutionary Memory: Recovering the Poetry of the American Left*.

9. "no longer counts as theory", *ibidem*.

10. On these topics, see some of the texts by Bianchetti, 2016 and 2020.

with a simple and entirely initial assumption that space is largely, although not exclusively, still a repository of ideas and theories formed by and stemming from modern architecture and urbanism. Despite the only partial achievement of modern theories in the reconstruction of Europe after the war, and despite the criticism against them since the 1950s. It is the space created from an explicit and demonstrative biopolitical project; on which a layer of habits and of institutions is slowly deposited; which is normalised and naturalised in urban and territorial construction practices until it becomes invisible, no longer treatable: "part of nature". An implicit project and a space that over time has given rise, through opposition, adherence or criticism, to fragments of different spatial hypotheses.

The need to fundamentally rethink the modern urban planning project confronts and clashes with the persistence of many of the concepts that inspired it, invisible and immersed in practice.[11] They have become standards and rules in an almost automatic sequence of moves, techniques and procedures. An implicit project functions without clearly recognisable responsibilities, or arrestable procedures, like that of a machine whose motion can no longer be suspended, even if many of its functions and objectives have lost their meaning and justification. A "natural history", indeed, like the much more tragic one described by Winfried Sebald in *Natural History of Destruction* on the bombing of German cities at the end of World War II (Sebald 2009).

As a whole, norms, rules and techniques contain, in unspoken ways, concepts of space and time, social relations, life and living together. The material devices in which they are represented (Viganò 1999), developed during the construction of the modern and contemporary city, and their sequences implicitly affirm their continuity. Their endurance, precisely because it is implicit, must be carefully observed as it makes the possibility of a renewed reflection on spaces, rhythms, materials, measures and the densities of living together more remote. This prevents us from grasping the topicality, despite everything, of some of the cues contained in this same project, the reinterpretations/inventions that contemporary territories provide, and the depletion and transcending of their paradigms.

11. Take some of the great metaphors around which the project of the modern city is constructed, for example the green belt, and observe their permanence and evolution in contemporary projects. See Viganò 2010.

Space

Submerged by rules and parameters, constraints, laws and ideologies,[12] the city and territory design hardly ever communicate the spatial concepts that structure and inform it. There are at least two reasons for this: first, because it takes the concept of the space to which it refers or that inspired it for granted; second, because there is still no comprehensive alternative to the Athens Charter manifesto, despite attempts to emulate it. Partial answers—fragments of space—are contained in practices concerning city sustainability, a project in the making, but one that has not sufficiently reflected on the biopolitical nature of this transformation, often relying on generic and simplified images that belong to the same questioned past. From this viewpoint, attempts to leave the modern city space are almost always hybridisations of previous spatial solutions, returning to the key figures and materials of cities of the eighteenth, nineteenth and twentieth centuries (the block, the boulevard, the garden suburb...) or longstanding concepts of the green belt, transit-oriented development, taken up without the filter of a new interpretation of the contemporary spatial, ecological and social condition. It is still difficult to grasp the extent of these attempts: they are partial, because they only address certain aspects of the urban crisis, for example by focusing on open and green space, or a public transport axis, but almost never truly addressing the separation-of-functions problem, the possibility of radical reuse, or the need to rethink the home/work relationship. They are partial because when they have bottom-up project qualities, they do not allow a structural review of the problems, the adaptation of services, or public and collective space, which are just as marked and in need of a profound rethink; or, on the contrary, they do not take advantage of local energies if top-down policies are implemented.

The conception and design of space claimed as the fundamental agent of transformation is, paradoxically, little explored. Conception and design are exhausted in an endless series of modifications and variations, never fully discussed or consciously pursued, the outcome of which is unknown, while verification appears unnecessary. It is as if, after all, theories and ideas of space do not count for much, a bit like in *Ecotopia*.[13] Or as if the ecological, economic and social transition, and the biopolitical crisis we are immersed in, did not really need them, and we instead limited ourselves to a mere regulatory framework review, or a mere set of practices of self-managed and spontaneous

12. Paul Rabinow rereads a part of the history of modern urban planning and describes how over time forms and norms acquired increasing autonomy from the social spatial contexts in which they arose, reaching a level of abstraction which legitimises their alleged universalism (Rabinow 1989:13).

13. "People themselves design and build structures for their living group or enterprises with astonishing competence and imagination, often using modularized design and standard materials that by now have taken on practically the quality of folk architecture." This is the description of the disappearance of the role of expert in *Ecotopia* (Callenbach 2009, ed. or. 1975).

spatial transformation. The result is a lack of concrete experimentation and likewise a lack of critical theory capable of interacting and shaking up the "naturalisation" of rules and norms, ideas and concepts, and the abuse of common places and old rhetoric. The lack of research and experimentation, prototypes that move images of space and propose practical directions, is an important sign of this.

The concept of space is complex and polysemous. It has countless definitions on different abstraction levels and at different distances from the solid practice of places and design, i.e. from what interests us most here. It is the active and full space described by Kern during the transition from the nineteenth to the twentieth century (Kern 1983). The agent and supporting space. Long before the spatial turn in social sciences,[14] the city and its transformative events were read as stories of spaces. In *Time and Space*, Kern emphasises the shift that occurred between the nineteenth and twentieth centuries from an idea of space as an inert void containing objects to an "active and full" space. Space is no longer a negative element "among the positive elements of floors, ceilings, walls", but a positive element to be "sculpted." This shift likely resulted in the city and the events that transformed it being read as a *history of spaces*.

Space is at the heart of the urban and architectural history of Giedion and Zevi, who point to space as the protagonist of architecture. The fluid interior-exterior relationship is the key element on which the problem of the new space and a different order of things is grafted.

In *Space, Time and Architecture*, Giedion places space at the centre of history, of urban and architectural history (Giedion 1941). This is followed shortly after by Bruno Zevi, who in *Saper vedere l'architettura* and in *Saper vedere l'Urbanistica* points to space as the protagonist of architecture and urban space as an architectural cavity (Zevi 1948, 1960). Zevi names some spaces of the past: the Greek space without interior (Giedion spoke of exterior), the Roman static space (for Giedion it is interior), the space of the medieval continuum, the Renaissance perspective space, the Mannerist interrelated space, the space of the nineteenth-century city (which he does not define but judges as not particularly innovative), concluding with the open and organic space of the modern age (for Giedion it is interior/exterior, perhaps anticipated in the Renaissance with the perspective that links interior and exterior within a single vision).

14. Starting with the work of Foucault and Lefebvre, Edward Soja spoke of a "spatial turn", a turning point in the field of human sciences, in how the role of space is interpreted in the relationship between culture, politics and society (Soja, 1996).

Space is alteration, awareness of the limits of its perception in direct, physical, sensory, cognitive, kinaesthetic experiences. Modern and contemporary art thoroughly questioned the qualities of space's different dimensions, and in the 1970s research into the possibilities of manipulating space and the spectator's perception were defined and made concise, producing works that see us confronting the limits of perception within cognitive processes. These works also articulate our fascination with the construction of distinct artificial environments (the art of constructing environments) of which the audience can have direct experience (physical and cognitive, kinaesthetic), as in the work of Doug Wheeler.[15] These are not illusionist spaces, but a "perceived real experience" that increases awareness of our physical presence in a space.[16] Those artificial environments are compositional, space-device and procedural transformations and variations (Tschumi 2005).[17]

Space is political. In the 1970s, Henri Lefebvre, in *La production de l'espace*, contrasted the abstract space of capitalism (the space defined by "global networks of business and banking, by flows of energy and information", the space we now call globalisation) with natural space and its distinctive climatic and topographical traits. The latter, natural space, and its distinctive traits are reduced to materials on which the productive forces of society operate. Space is used to produce a value surplus and consumed by tourism and recreation. Like the infrastructural development of an industrial activity, the spatial organisation of cities, regions and nations increases production and facilitates the reproduction of manufacturing relationships. Critical of abstract space—simultaneously homogeneous and fragmented, pulverised by relationships of private ownership, but also a global productive force—Lefebvre was convinced that the contradictions within space would lead to a *differential space*, a space of the expression and representation of differences (Lefebvre 1974).

Space is biopolitical. The techniques of space are equivalent to the techniques of power that affect life. In this sense, doctors, priests, psychiatrists, prison guards, and of course "engineers, the builders of bridges, roads, viaducts, railways" have been and are much more technical and more essential builders of space than urban planners and architects (Foucault 2002). A great deal of literature addresses how architecture, city design and governance intersect to provide justification, beyond sheer disciplinary devices, for security conditions

15. Doug Wheeler, exponent of the "Light and Space" movement, created the "Infinite Space" installation for the first time in Milan, in the Salvatore Ala gallery in 1975. That year his *environmental projects* were bought by Giuseppe Panza di Biumo and, in 2000–2001, the "Infinite Space" installation was included in *Changing Perceptions: The Panza Collection at the Guggenheim Museum*, Guggenheim Museum Bilbao.

16. *Changing Perceptions: The Panza Collection at the Guggenheim Museum*, exhibition catalogue, p.244.

17. See also texts by Luigi Moretti collected in *"Spazio". Gli editoriali e altri scritti*, Marinotti, 2019.

that are as extensive as possible and upheld by "norms". In our case, these norms relate to the design of space, and they coexist, collaborate or conflict with other norms and social transformations. Out comes a "middle ground" of techniques and norms (Rabinow 1989:9) that have designed our ordinary space. I will return to these points in the introduction to the second part of the book.

Three Spaces

The transition from the modern city to the contemporary city is mediated by a reflection on some types of spaces that react to the previous concepts. They converge and hybridise in the city-territories of the present-day, developing new "species of spaces" (Perec 1974). My hypothesis is that, in the twentieth century, three fundamental types of space could be recognised as innovative with respect to nineteenth century cities. Each space type corresponds to a different idea of freedom, a different aesthetic, and a different idea of continuity.

An epigone of enlightened modernity, *functional space* runs through the contemporary city. It is overlapped by ideas that have partly refuted it, without contradicting it as a whole; *space nature*, mythical and acting at a symbolic, psychological, ideological level; and *support space*, which structures and designs the conditions of the infinite varieties of appropriation and transformation practices of an inhabited place. A fourth space might be added: the space that takes up the measurements, models and references of the city of the past, in its various forms, from the Haussmannian city to the English rural village. I will not consider the thinkers who have explored this fourth type of space, not because I underestimate their depth, but because the conceptual reservoir of the history of space could extend well beyond the modern Western city and likewise its palimpsest of memory. The encounter of the different spaces, their conflict, forms, hybridisation, re-invention of ideas and ideologies, has led to an extended urbanity, the reuse, completion and adaptation of which we will deal with at length. Recognising these spaces and their inertia, permanence, return, or degradation allows us to define, with good approximation, the problem of contemporary space and its design. But this condition requires renewed effort in terms of spatial imagination. Ideas of space—the concepts and metaphors on which they rely—cannot, at a time of social, economic and ecological transition, be the implicit matter of the project of the city and the territory.

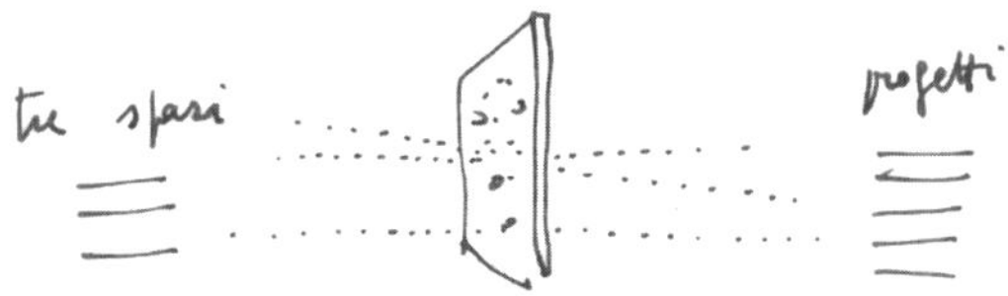

Fig. 3
Diagram of the book structure, 2022. Paola Viganò.

The first of these spaces is obviously the *functional space*, marking a break with the nineteenth-century city and created, in real terms, between the 1920s and the 1970s, including during the reconstruction of post-war Europe. This space had already come under fierce criticism by the end of the 1950s and during the 1960s, for example in the Netherlands and France, leading to an interruption in the creation of the *Grands Ensembles* at the end of the 1950s. In emerging countries, the functional city space is still a reference, albeit increasingly faded, disapproved of and far from its initial ambitions.

The second, *space nature*, is an integral part of the construction of Western modernity. Its feeling of nature was reformulated in the post-war period by hybridising the "garden city" and the functional city. Some of the most interesting examples of this type of space come from that period. It extends, in unexpected ways due to its pervasiveness and influence, to today and to many projects announced for the future.

The third, the *social space*, unfolded between the end of the 1950s and the 1970s and then seemed to disappear only to re-emerge forcefully in current debate. This space provides answers that, while still highly fascinating, do not seem to have learned from previous criticism.

The three spaces represent the greatest contribution produced by the reflection on cities and territories since the post-war period until now. They therefore deserve to be observed and understood in depth.

Functional space is dominated by the idea of the machine; it is defined within an aesthetic of order and functioning. It is the space of a functioning city, essential to a society made up of individuals who work and pursue a goal of utilitarian efficiency. Among its many projects, Ernst May's districts in Frankfurt, built in the 1920s, are still one of the clearest references of the best part of the modern biopolitical project.

The second type of space is dominated by the idea of nature; it is constructed within an aesthetic of variability and difference, fragments and the picturesque. Tapiola, a Finnish forest-city began in the 1950s, is an extreme case of this.

The third space is social; it is constructed within an aesthetic of complexity, congestion and appropriation. It is dominated by the idea of structure. Constant's New Babylon is the most radical example of this: his is the space of leisure, a civilisation that, thanks to technological innovation, escapes the need for work and expresses itself through play and the construction of spaces for relationships. Some cases that have been partially achieved, such as Toulouse-Le Mirail, were built on the same themes addressed by Constant. Le Mirail is a controversial case, but one that should not be forgotten.

The three spaces break the continuity of the nineteenth-century city fabric and seek a new continuity in which a different idea of individual and collective freedom can be expressed. Ideas about freedom[18] alongside ideas about the city (excluding traditional references to the *polis* or city-states) should probably be referred to what Foucault recognised from the eighteenth century onwards, when a "reflection on architecture as a function of the objectives and techniques of the government of societies" was developed (Foucault 2002). Whether or not this theme induced "a change in the spirit of architects, or in their techniques", Foucault stated, "remains to be proven." What remains are the liberating and emancipatory intentions, found to a strong degree in the three types of spaces, and the awareness that, once again echoing Foucault, "freedom is a practice" and not an architectural or urban planning project.

In the functional city—the first space—it is the machine that guarantees continuity, establishing unambiguous relationships of dependence and collaboration between the different parts. Freedom is guaranteed by smooth operation and its resulting order. Ernst May's Frankfurt districts are a canonical example of this. Nature and infrastructure are considered as part of the machine and its movement: nature is air, light and background, infrastructure is support and the mechanism. In Tapiola, continuity comes from the forest, which is the fundamental infrastructural element to which everything else adapts; freedom, wrote Alvar Aalto, lies in nature, in which it finds its origins and its end. In New Babylon, or in a controversial project such as Toulouse-Le Mirail, continuity is provided by an artificial infrastructure, a new nature, an extended support for the spontaneity of the individual initiative. Freedom consists of everything that the support can accommodate and allow.

In the three cases, the spatial design defines the "milieu for the regulation of a carefully modulated freedom" (Osborne & Rose 1999).

18. Meddling in political and moral questions through the theme of different ideas of freedom in relation to space should not sound excessive or out of place. Rather, it underlines the unjustified absence of attention to the role of space and its design as the constructors of different conditions of freedom. In this sense it would be interesting, and perhaps also important, to read the three spaces using the two categories of negative liberty and positive liberty used by Isiah Berlin in the inaugural lecture of the chair of political theory at Oxford University in 1958 (Berlin 1969). As is known, a very important debate developed after this lecture, reconstructed by Carter and Ricciardi in *L'idea di libertà* (Carter, Ricciardi 1996).

Fig. 4
The three spaces: Ernst May Haus, Frankfurt (website https://ernst-may-gesellschaft.de/mayhaus) 1927-1928; Pentti Ahola, patio houses (website https://www.hs.fi/kaupunki/espoo/art-2000008595030.html) 1962-1964; Tapiola; Université du Mirail, Toulouse, 1966-1972, Photo Paola Viganò.

Tapiola, New Babylon, Frankfurt.... they do not have the primacy of the ideas represented in them, nor are they always innovative spaces; they are, however, real and mentally exemplary places of accumulation and deposit, sometimes an amassing of the multiple and heterogeneous ideas that take shape within them and which are transformed into spaces that converge, lap and collide in the present-day city. They are the sediments of a long process that has been produced in different ways in different territories.

The three spaces are influential biopolitical devices and we still make use of their images, concepts and metaphors. I propose a reinterpretation of them that relies on an analysis of the biopolitics that fuelled and generated them. The project interrogates anew this store of socio-spatial imagination, to ask questions that are somewhat different from those that besieged them in the past; to denaturalise their order so as to understand them more deeply; and to discuss their relationship to policies concerning/for life.

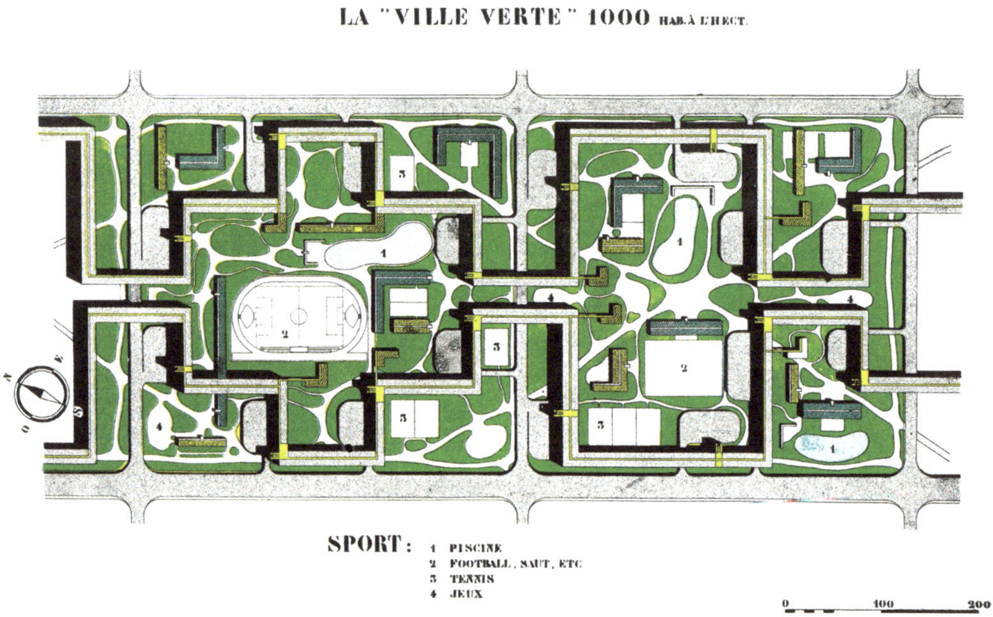

Fig. 5
Le Corbusier, La «Ville Verte», 1000 habitants/hectare, 1930 (Flc).

1.2 SPACE FUNCTION

The first type of space is dominated by the idea of the machine functioning and manufacturing efficiency. It constitutes the conceptual and formal basis to which, due to opposition, adhesion and integration, the next two spaces react. The discourse on the functional city involves positions, movements and research paths.

Experiments: Three moves

In the early decades of the twentieth century, in the Netherlands, Vienna and Frankfurt, districts and parts of the city were created that would take on an exemplary role in the European debate. According to Carlo Aymonino, the urgent need of a solution to the housing problem established, among other things by studies on poverty and sanitation, shifted the topic of urban design from the city as a whole to the city's parts and specific housing-related matters (Aymonino 1965). The city expanded with the addition of discreet elements, becoming a place of discontinuity, separation, heterogeneity and estrangement.[19]

In a fitting reading of the gradual opening up of the block in the twentieth century, Panerai, Castex and Depaule distinguished three main movements (Panerai, Castex, Depaule 1977). The first (explored in south Amsterdam by Berlage between 1901-1905 and 1914-1917 and in Vienna in the Karl-Marx-Hof [1100 metres long, 1382 apartments]) concerned the expansion of the block and the search for repeatable methods of collective living. The Amsterdam experience is one of the references used by CIAM as an example of governmental administration and architects working together to improve living conditions.

The second move refers to the opening up of the block. The principle of "satellite towns" (under the strong influence of Unwin and the concept of satellite suburbs) was explored in Ernst May's districts in Frankfurt, built between 1926 and 1931, where *Siedlungen* were proposed as alternative facts to the nineteenth-century city. We can suppose that the collection of satellite towns[20] in Frankfurt were to be connected by a network of roads, green corridors and belts similar to the ones that appeared, for example, in Eliel Saarinen's constructs for Helsinki in the early twentieth century. May's

19. On this point, in addition to Foucault's research, see Secchi 2000 and 2005.

20. Between 1925 and 1926 Ernst May developed a regulatory plan framework for Frankfurt based on *trabantenprinzip*, the development for satellite towns influenced by Unwin and by Karl Scheffler's text *Die Architektur der Groszstadt* (1913). May had already used this framework in a competition for the Wroclaw plan of 1921, accompanied by the motto "satellite".

framework can still be recognized in an image of present-day Frankfurt: among the "satellites" that Karl Scheffler accepted "as the only positive and non-contradictory solution to the questions that the city asks itself" (Grassi 1975:18), large swathes of open space create new green and urban continuity. The relationship between satellite and green areas is not only functional and ecological, but also definitional for new spatial and architectural features.[21]

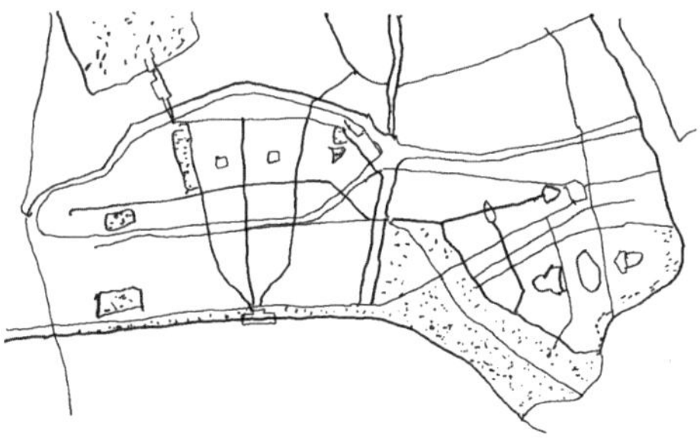

Fig. 6
Left: Redesign from H. P. Berlage, Amsterdam Sud,1901-1905/1915. Paola Viganò.
Below: Redesign from Karl Ehn, Karl Marx Hof, 1926-30, Heiligenstadt. Paola Viganò.

21. Giorgio Grassi gave a shrewd interpretation of the role of open space in the construction of a city's architecture, a relation that links designs such as that of the Nidda Valley, Niddatal. Again linking *Trabantenprinzip* to an idea of *embellissement*, rather than functionalist thinking, Grassi on the one hand lost sight of an important relationship which I will cover under "Functionalism" below, and on the other established and clearly confirmed the architectural unity between built complexes and open space: "From an architectural perspective, in the classical city, the main function of these green areas related to the buildings, villas or palaces they belonged to, the monuments to which they were related, was to be an inseparable part of their architecture...". For this reason, starting with the *Siedlungen* project along the river, Grassi reconstructed the fragments of a genealogy that links the building of districts along a stretch of open space for the purpose of interrupting the continuity of the city to the example of the large villas of the past or the complex of gardens of the Belvedere and Schwarzenberg palaces in Vienna (Grassi 1975: 29-30).

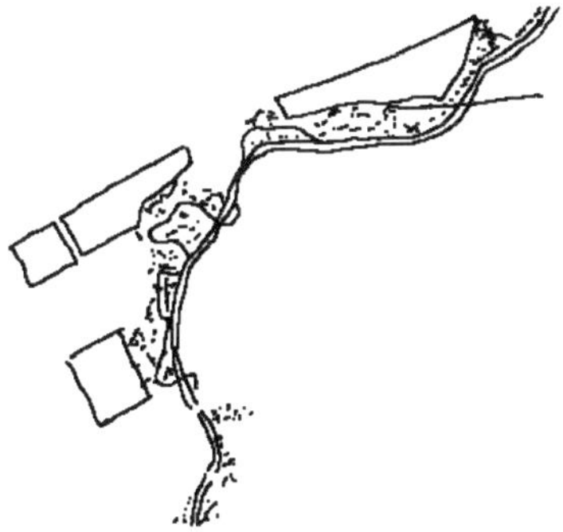

Fig. 7
Sketch of the Siedlungen along the Nidda in Ernst May's Frankfurt. Paola Viganò.

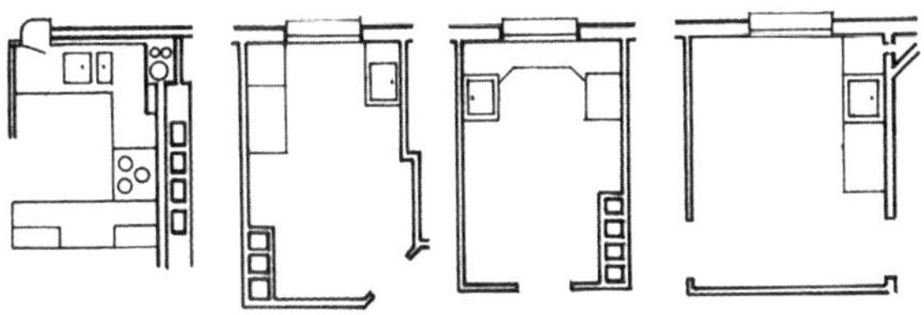

Fig. 8
Genealogical table: 1947, Unité d'Habitation de Marseille, Atelier le Corbusier et Charlotte Perriand, 1920-1930; kitchens typical of Paris, 3 types: economical, intermediate and medium rent (Clarisse 2004).

Before the imperious choice of "tall houses" established at CIAM "Rational methods of construction. Low, medium, tall houses", debated in 1930 in Brussels, Frankfurt's districts experienced different gradations of space which, by being private and individual, and crossing thresholds, became public and collective. The choice, in Frankfurt's *Siedlungen*, to build almost exclusively low single-family homes with gardens; the serial nature of the settlements, rigorously anchored to the heliothermal axis; and the construction of sequences of public and private spaces in which the role of open space turns out to be fundamental, define their main characteristics.

The buildings still maintain a relationship with the road even if it is not traditional, as for example, in the Praunheim (the principle of *Zeilenbau* used for military camps offering the simplicity and repeatability required by industrial production methods). The Frankfurt kitchen, social services, roof gardens and parks designed by Leberecht Migge (Haney 2010)—here the intention is to demonstrate the use of the assembly chain for "social-democratic" purposes.

The research on *Existenzminimum*, presented at the second CIAM held in Frankfurt in 1929, concerned the search for a biological and not economic minimum and the development of new ways of living together, comparing radical ideas of shared spaces. Gropius spoke at the conference envisaging "a new era of cooperation and common law" that would replace "the era of individualism of the 19th century and the rule of money". This transition according to Gropius, unlike the Frankfurt policy, would be from the single-family house to the apartment and shared house. The evolution of the traditional role of women in society is outlined in the dimensions of the new domestic workspaces; the *dom-kommuna* in the Soviet Union proposed they be entirely surpassed. "Floating somewhere between socialism and social welfare" wrote Aldo Van Eyck about the CIAM's activity (Mumford 2000). For Manfredo Tafuri, in *Project and Utopia*, the *Siedlungen* of Berlin and Frankfurt were built up residential areas that contradictorily evoke "built utopias" rather than interventions that qualify as a new urban dimension of the city; they are often an ideological display of a theoretical "working-class city" that takes the form of an *ethical city*, a city of physical and social hygiene, a city of *social peace* (Tafuri 1973).

The third move stemmed from the idea of a new type of space, definitively and radically different from the previous city: the Ville Radieuse of Le Corbusier which was proposed as "modern" and "revolutionary".

In 1930 a competition was announced for a decentralized socialist *garden city* for 100,000 people on a site of 15,000 hectares situated 37 km from Moscow, understood as a city of *loisir* for workers who would rest on their weekly day off (a vast proletarian model clinic). Strong opposition arose between urbanists (supporters of collective settlements of limited size and shared services) and disurbanists (who proposed linear settlements of individual isolated homes scattered along transport lines).[22] After the competition Le Corbusier was asked for his opinion. He lashed out against the disurbanists, claiming that density is the only guarantee of an economic, social and cultural life (*élites* inhabit the big city). Starting with his design for Ville Contemporaine (1922), Le Corbusier proposed a high-density core and living spaces in green areas. The Soviets, interested in his criticisms, presented him with a long questionnaire on the future of Moscow: his *Réponse à Moscou* (8 June 1930), composed of 66 pages and 21 drawings, was the first formulation of what would become Ville Radieuse.

22. Anticipating, according to Eric Mumford, Wright's *Broadacre City*, 1935.

Space and society: Two positions

Speaking about the modern city, and the modern movement city project, is not easy. There are many approaches and stories about it and the "functional city" in particular. They come together to form a discourse[23] that links the architectural form to positive urban and social transformation.

This discourse established a relationship between the form of architecture and the form of society which the modern movement, heir of the nineteenth-century reformist tradition and vanguard of the considerations on welfare developed between the two wars, and above all after the Second World War, interpreted taking two different approaches. The first, which hypothesized the need for political change starting with the collectivization of land ownership, was supported by the ABC group, formed in 1924 in Basel, and Mart Stam. Architecture can change the world, as long as the world changes; architecture gives shape to change what has occurred, it is a form of its representation. Kenneth Frampton, in the preface to Eric Mumford's book *The Ciam Discourse on Urbanism, 1928-1960*, recalls CIAM's statement at La Sarraz in 1928 which remarked on both the link between architecture and the general economic system, and the need for a collective land use policy: "The idea of modern architecture includes the link between the phenomenon of architecture and that of the general economic system. (....) Town planning is the organization of the functions of collective life; it extends over both the urban agglomeration and the countryside (...) The chaotic division of land, resulting from sale, speculations, inheritances, must be abolished by a collective and methodical land policy. This redistribution of land, the indispensable preliminary basis for any town planning, must include the just division between the owners and the community of the unearned increment resulting from works of joint interest."[24]

The second approach, which theorises the capacity of new architecture to improve living conditions irrespective of the political context, was obviously promoted by Le Corbusier. Unlike the extreme wing of the CIAM, Corbu throughout the 1920s sought to apply the lessons of Taylor and Ford to cities and architecture. Like Ford, Le Corbusier claimed that, since the code of mass production is neutral, it should be possible to apply it within different regimes and types of government. The physical design, which using the elementary composition method adhered to the assignment of separate programmatic functions to distinct geometric volumes more than to political actions, could

23. With regard to the modern movement, Eric Mumford took up the Foucauldian conception of discourse as a linguistic field in which concepts are established, a field that defines what can be said and what cannot be said within a certain spatial and temporal context (Mumford 2000).

24. CIAM's initial statement, in Conrads 1970.

have made a real improvement to living in the industrial city. "Architecture or revolution" wrote Le Corbusier in *Vers une architecture* (1923).[25]

Was it an overestimation of the role of architecture and its design in society, a loss of sense of proportions, or an attitude of profound cynicism?

The hypothesis I put forward and attempt to explore is that it was something different, and that Le Corbusier's attitude, like that of others committed to the same programme, was instead guided by in-depth research on the minimization of labour effort in an attempt to define "work" differently from the Marxist sense. Work was instead a conquest of new freedom. Being modern meant conquering a new form of freedom: being free, not so much from work, but from the effort of work.[26]

The ambition to minimise effort implies minute attention to the use of space, distances, rhythms and functionality. The disciplinary aspect exercised on the body and the individual and the social regulation of the population become central; some important lines of research deal with them starting with the development of an idea of normality and better hygienic conditions. The first approach, the construction of a new normative dimension, requires, to achieve standardisation, a definition of normality and efficiency that includes a definition of what normal is not. The presence of air and greenery, i.e. hygienic and healthy conditions for all citizens, is what makes it possible to keep a population, understood as a workforce, alive—this is the second major research approach.

Both themes are part of a long history that belongs to Western modernity, but they took shape and extended globally with the industrial revolution and its impact on the construction of a new city: the modern industrial city.

25. 1913 saw the first application of Fordist methods in Detroit. The Taylorist organisation of production, based on the mechanization of production processes achieved through the introduction of assembly lines and standardization of the final products, finds one of its most ironic and cruel representations in the film *Modern Times* by Charlie Chaplin, released in 1936. The streamlining process also included a clear separation between the organisers and those who perform the work (scientific management).

26. Labour and work contain two traditional characteristics of work: *occupation*, which brings suffering and fatigue (in French *labeur* is *charge*, labour and *travail* derives from the Latin *tripalium*, an instrument of torture with three stakes); and *creation*, implementation, not necessarily in opposition to leisure time, *loisir*. See the insistence on (alienated) work as punishment in Hegel and Marx.

Lines of research: Normal, normalized

It was this first research topic, and not a generic positive intention, that gave rise to the conviction that architecture is capable of improving the world. In other words, social and political reformism through architecture acts at the level of great detail in which different bodies enter into relationships and collide. Through resistance from and to a specific type of space, bodies are educated in the modern sense. Georges Canguilhem dedicated his reflection to two terms—*normal* and *normalised*—which were introduced into the French dictionary in the mid-eighteenth century (Canguilhem 1966) and signalled a new concern for the well-being of a population. It is this concern that justifies and legitimises biopolitical action (Rabinow 1989:10).

On the other hand, the La Sarraz declaration also states: "The idea of 'economic efficiency' does not imply production furnishing maximum commercial profit, but production demanding a minimum working effort...". The reference to Taylorism is clear, but perhaps a broader interpretation of the terms "economic efficiency" or "minimum working effort" is necessary, capable of revealing the freedom that derives from research on the minimisation of effort and the consequences for spatial relationships between humans, movement and objects.[27]

Rudolf Laban, in *Modern Educational Dance*, which appeared in 1948 but accounts for the research he carried out before the Great War (Laban's dance notation was published in 1928), combines research on the new forms of dance (modern or free) with the educational application of these studies. During the Second World War, in England, he collaborated on time and movement studies to improve productivity in the industrial sector during wartime. For Laban, the modern vocabulary of movement and physical effort represented an opportunity to rethink the notions of rhythm and dance "*pour les adapter à un usage économique du rythme, visant à obtenir le meilleur rendement possible. (...). Contrairement aux experts de l'étude sur le temps et le mouvement, Laban refuses d'utiliser une technique basée sur le chronomètre pour accélérer les mouvements des travailleurs.*" Here moments of rest, distraction, and the simple linking of gestures are fundamental to production and its efficiency (Preston-Dunlop 2003:145-146). The book he published in 1947 with F. C. Lawrence, an industrial consultant, has the eloquent title *Effort* (transformed in the 1974 edition to *Effort: Economy of Human Movement*).

27. In the same period Kropotkin wrote: "Political economy, as it gradually emerges from its semi-scientific stage, tends more and more to become a science devoted to the study of the needs of men and of the means for satisfying them with the least possible waste of energy—that is, a sort of physiology of society. But few economists, as yet, have recognised that this is the proper domain of economics, and have attempted to treat their science from this point of view. The main subject of social economy—that is, the *economy of energy required for the satisfaction of human needs*—is consequently the last subject which one expects to find treated in a concrete form in economical treatises." (Kropotkin 1901, from the preface to the first edition of 1898).

Fig. 9
School of Laban at Monte Verità, 1914- 1917.
©fondazione Monte Verità, Fond. Harald Szeemann.

For Laban and for the city of the modern movement, the efficiency of effort was not just the product of faster movements; rather it consisted of an improved and more effective relationship between movements, in the equilibrium between effort, stress, relaxation and rest which brings novelty and new awareness to the actions carried out in everyday life. More recently, this has also been recalled by François Raffinot: "*Dans la danse, l'espace n'est au fond qu'une Économie du flux (flux externe en interaction avec les tensions et détentes internes des corps). Dans les catégories de Rudolf von Laban, le flux et l'espace sont traités comme deux régimes différents*" (Raffinot, 2014).

The Frankfurt kitchen designed by Margareet Schütte Lihotsky in 1927 was inspired by train kitchens;[28] Laban's notation was published in 1928 and

28. Research carried out by Margareet Schütte Lihotsky continued and backed up previous research in the US by the Beecher sisters, particularly Catherine Beecher, in the second half of the 1800s, which led to the elimination of the central table, the introduction of the continuous worktop and ultimately to the reduction of a space still designed for hired help. Also important was the research of Christine Frederick, who taught domestic science and whose work was translated and published in 1924 by Bruno Taut; Lilian Gilbreth, an engineer who in the 1920s, initially with her husband, used diagrams and models to study in Taylorist terms the reorganisation of movement in the kitchen space; and Paulette Bernège, founder and president of the Ligue d'organisation menagère in France, who was invited to the CIAM of Frankfurt in 1929 dedicated to *Existenz minimum* (Hayden 1981) see: Eleb, Debarre, Debarre-Blanchard 1995; Clarisse 2004.

 a photo of Laban's free dances in Ascona dates to 1914.[29] The reduction and simplification of a housewife's movements in the kitchen, like the simplification and reduction of the pathways inside housing in Alexander Klein's famous plans, translate in the city into a simplification and reduction of the urban spatial complexity of the past through the separation of flows, the elimination of obstacles and possible conflicts, and the transparency of the space. The minimization of routes, in diagrams by disurbanists, upsets the organisation of the living space.

The effort-relaxation-rest equilibrium is ensured by the introduction of the *loisir* space within the city. In profoundly different ways from the nineteenth- and early twentieth-century city in which the role of the public park was to counterbalance factories and pollution, the large green carpet equipped for sport, games, the treatment and relaxation of the body and spirit in the modern city emphasises, in its continuity, the complementarity between effort and relaxation. The city of the modern movement blatantly contributes to the construction of a new *routine*, inspired by minimum effort, the creation of a new effort-relaxation-rest rhythm and its repetition.[30] The reduction of effort achieves the narcotizing effect described by Richard Sennett: "Navigating the geography of modern society requires very little physical effort, hence engagement; [...] Both the highway engineer and the television director create what could be called 'freedom from resistance'" (Sennett 1994:18). The design of spaces that eliminate effort, obstacles, and the need for commitment expands to the general de-sensitizing carried out by modern space. It joins the search for socially comfortable conditions of division and distancing of what is different, using infrastructure design to divide wealthy and less wealthy neighbourhoods, or to position schools in the centre to avoid the intrusion of the other, the stranger. To continue down this track would lead us astray....

The fear of the abnormal and abnormality, on the other hand, shook and anguished the late nineteenth century: "*elle a été formée en corrélation avec tout un ensemble d'institution de contrôle, tout une série de mécanisme de surveillance et de distribution...* " wrote Foucault in *Les Anormaux* (Foucault, 1999:307). Abnormals are enclosed within three categories that include legal-juridical issues and of succession: the human monster, the individual to be corrected to whom all the different institutions of *redressement* are dedicated; the *onaniste* around whom familial and parental responsibility for the child's upbringing is redesigned;

29. The ambiguities, limits and openings of Laban's experience at Monte Verità and Monte Verità's more general relationship with the themes of the *Lebensreform* that spread in Germany and Switzerland in the mid-nineteenth century are retraced in Schwab, Lanfranchi, 2001.

30. See in Richard Sennet, 1999, *L'uomo flessibile*, the fine chapter "Routine." See also in Jeffrey Eugenides' *Middlesex* (2002), the chapter "Henry Ford's English language melting pot" on the tale of River Rouge, the invention and development of the assembly line.

and the form of the modern mononuclear family which emerges from the rural patriarchal or extended bourgeois form. The architects of the modern movement conceived their neighbourhoods, their houses and their open spaces for this family.

Degeneration is one of the key words of the nineteenth century. It inspired the Catholic doctor and psychiatrist Bénédict Augustin Morel with a general theory of degeneration published in 1857,[31] which, for at least half a century, influenced thinking about the city and was only challenged by psychoanalytic interpretations of perversions and neuroses that, in the early twentieth century, reduced the distance between healthy and sick people. According to Morel, human perfection is jeopardised by bad habits and the unhealthiness of the environment, and this causes human beings to degenerate. The environment plays a negative role.

The idea of decline is addressed by many thinkers, from Marx to Darwin, Morel to de Maistre, and the idea of the degeneration of modern society and race in relation to urbanism and the new complexity of urban life was one of the fundamental positions assumed by psychiatry in the nineteenth century. The mentally and physical weak subject emerges, producing a shift from vice to illness as personal guilt.[32] The protagonist of the novel *Looking Backward, 2000-1887*, for instance, awakens after 130 years of sleep to the Boston of 2000, where he visits schools and measures the improvement of living conditions: not only the physical condition of the young Bostonians, but "insanity, for instance, which in the nineteenth century was so terribly common a product of your insane mode of life, has almost disappeared, with its alternative, suicide." (Bellamy 1888).

Adolphe Quetelet, a mathematician and statistician[33] influenced by Laplace and Fourier, worked for the Belgian government on the numerical consistency of crimes and constructed statistics on crime and mortality that

31. Bénédict Augustin Morel (1809-1873) *Traité des dégénérescences physiques, intellectuelles et morales de l'espèce humaine et des causes qui produisent ces variétés maladives*, Paris 1857.

32. "The 19th century is a 'degenerated' century wrote Mantegazza, and Nordau. Darwin, Bernard, Lamarck, Buffon, Comte, Buchez and Flourens; the bishop of Chambéry and de Maistre provided the psychiatrist Morel with the ideological basis for developing the degenerative theory of mental illnesses, seen as an indication of a negative action of modern civilization, which by reflex damages the central nervous system, thus supporting organisms that are weak and therefore unable to face the 'struggle for life'." (Roccatagliata 2002). The modern and industrial civilisation, with its sprawling and anonymous spaces, is the greatest cause of the degeneration and weakening of Western society. Even in *La scienza in cucina e l'arte di mangiar bene*, published in Florence in 1891, Pellegrino Artusi dedicates a chapter to "Cooking for weak stomachs", which "has come into fashion,' and one on cooking for "paper stomachs." He claimed: "It is not easy to indicate with scientific precision which foods are most suited to an individual weakened by the years, disease, overindulgence or weak by nature...", (from the Rizzoli edition, Bur, 1993, p.479).

33. Adolphe Quetelet was born in Ghent in 1796 and died in Brussels in 1874. In the text *Sur l'homme et le developpement de ses facultés, essai d'une physique sociale* (1835) Quetelet, who had also developed an obesity index, described his idea of the average man as a central value, the basis for measuring human characteristics.

had a significant and controversial impact on the debate opposing freedom and social determinism. Quetelet aimed to define the average physical and intellectual characteristics of a population: the average man. The problem arose when the abstract concept of the average man became, for Quetelet, a real-ideal man, as if nature aimed to create him and any deviation from the average should be interpreted as an error.[34] In physical and moral terms, a citizen appeared to be less strong and resilient than a peasant.

The paradox of the average man has recently been taken up in some Swedish research that develops a critique of the increasing weight of lobbying and image strategies impoverishing the actual contribution of citizens to political choices.[35] Bent Hamer's film *Kitchen Stories* (2003) is a good representation of the excesses produced by the markedly positivist attempt to make movement within Swedish kitchens more efficient. Here too, the logic of less effort inspired the study of movements made in old kitchens by elderly Norwegian bachelors. Observers sent from Sweden transcribed trajectories, times and sequences in their notebooks, but failed to maintain the required detachment by showing the surreal side of the whole research.

Clearly, the insistence on the normative aspect and standardisation not only relates to the disciplinary society but has also been an instrument of democracy and the extension of living quality to the masses. In Walt Whitman's verses, "the average man of to-day"[36] is at the heart of the society of modern space.

34. In Bellamy's book, for example, the statistic is the science that allows us to organise the industrial army and the production of goods.

35. Sweden is a country that has the longest and most continuous series of statistical data on the population, forming the basis of the Tabellverket of 1749. "The notion of an "average citizen" – that is, a fictional person supposed to statistically represent a larger group of people – has been one of the most influential ideas in the construction of the Swedish welfare state. By incarnating the modern project's dream of translating a complex reality into a rational and transparent model, statistical averages have laid the very foundation of the Swedish art of social engineering." The research project *The Average Citizen*, exhibited at the Fourth Biennial of Contemporary Art in Frankfurt in 2002, was inspired by low participation in political processes, including electoral voting, and from the ever-increasing weight of the media to question the possibility of a different democratic model starting with the registration and diffusion of an average point of view. www.theaveragecitizen.org

36. "I was looking a long while for a clue to the history of the past [...] It is the life of one man or one woman to-day – the average man of to-day,...". Walt Whitman, "I was looking a long while", from *Leaves of Grass*, 1900 (first edition 1855).

Lines of research: In the air and in green areas

In the air

The goals of an airy, sunny, walkable and extendable city inspired a long process that led, from the mid-seventeenth century onward, to the first London squares (Bloomsbury Square, 1661) and boulevards, to changes in the compact fabric of the *ancien régime* city.

The condemnation of the city's ills anticipated the industrial revolution: eighteenth-century doctors boasted of how healthy life was in the country where there was contact with nature, sun, air and fresher food. There are countless literary spin-offs of this theme: for example, in *Mansfield Park* (1814), as in other novels by Jane Austen, the physical and moral healthiness of village life is contrasted with that of the city. In the gardens and parks of country villas the term *improvement* caught on; according to J.H. Plumb this is the most widely used term in eighteenth-century England: there were many efforts to improve "landscapes, gardens, agriculture, science, manufacture, music, art, literature, instruction, both secular and religious."[37]

All this evolved, at the beginning of the twentieth century and above all after the First World War, into a search for a new way of life that was no longer, as in Le Corbusier's "new man", an elitist one. From the start of the century up to the inter-war years, functional space was developed in a large number of experiments linked to reformist and social democratic thinking. These touch all scales of living, as shown by the example (a micro-history within the great history of the modern city) of the open-air school (Châtelet, Lerch, Luc 2003). Mobile classrooms in the woods emerged as a solution for sickly children who were weak, it was said, because of malnutrition and an urban environment devoid of parks and playgrounds. Other events, like the British fighting in the Boer War (1898-1902)[38] or the Dutch in WWI, revealed the weaknesses of different armies. To assess and correct the situation, the British government formed a commission for physical deterioration, while in the Netherlands the Child Protection Office was set up to develop bodily and moral resistance. In a short time, the "classroom in the woods" went from being a remedy and form of education for sick children to being proposed as an ideal school for all children.

37. J.H. Plumb, *The Acceptance of Modernity*, in Neil McKendrick, John Brewer, J.H Plumb, *The Birth of a Consumer Society: The Commercialization of Eighteenth-Century England*, Europa Publications, London, 1982, cited in note 1 of chapter VI by Kathryn Sutherland to J. Austen, *Mansfield Park* (1814), Penguin, 1996.

38. Andrew Saints recalled: "Une statistique mémorable révéla que sur 11.000 volontaires originaires de la région de Manchester, 8.000 durent être renvoyés; des 3.000 restants, les deux tiers ne convenaient que pour la milice et non pour les unités de combat." *Premiers jours de l'ecole de plein air anglaise* (1907-1930), in Anne-Marie Châtelet, Dominique Lerch, Jean Noël Luc, edited by, *L'ecole de plein air*, cit.

Fig. 10
Open-air school, St. James's Park, 1934. ©Westminster City Archives.

From the early years of the century, *Waldschulen* spread in Germany. In 1904 in both Berlin, Antwerp and the Kempen region, the first open-air schools for tubercular, anaemic and weakened children from poor neighbourhoods were opened among sand dunes and pine trees, spreading to other parts of Northern Europe and the United States. Given the improvements made, in 1931 the Second International Congress of Open-Air Schools in Brussels proposed that all new schools be designed as open-air schools. From holding lessons on roofs to the development of clothing suitable for winter outdoor classes and lightweight furniture that the pupils themselves could carry into the woods, the certainty was that it would be possible to improve mankind by improving its living environment, as argued by the theorists of nineteenth-century reformism Robert Owen, Patrick Geddes, and Fréderic LePlay.

In an evolutionary approach to ways of transforming the city, open-air classrooms can now be reinterpreted as one of the "dead ends" in the construction of the modern city, an urban material that, after having been highly successful throughout Europe and beyond, almost disappeared, but not without leaving clusters of ideas that have had a lasting influence on how the architecture of schools, kindergartens and, more generally, living spaces is conceived. The advent of antibiotics (penicillin was discovered in 1928) quickly made the methods and practices used during this experience appear outdated and crude. The fact is that the rooftop kindergarten of the Unité d'habitation in Marseilles, completed in the early 1950s, or the entire roof terrace of the *redents* of the Ville Radieuse, imagined as a large beach of fine sand, are not only expressions of Le Corbusier's personal intuition, but evidence of his attention to the most progressive educational techniques of his time, which led, inter alia, to the creation of Duiker's open-air school in Amsterdam in 1930.

Fig. 11
Jean-Marie Grégoire, Roof terrace of the Unité d'Habitation of Marseille, acrylic painting on canvas, 70 x 70 cm. ©Jean-Marie Grégoire.

In green areas and in nature

The space of the functional city breaks with that of the nineteenth-century city, which had already absorbed the new green spaces (boulevard, public park, park system).

In Le Corbusier's sketches, the open space appears extremely vague, generic, often indicated by icons representing trees, lawns, water and mountains. The presence of this green and undifferentiated surface in Le Corbusier's drawings was questioned by Emile Aillaud, who in the mid-1950s designed the large Courtillières and Grande Borne districts in Paris: "*Parce qu'un Le Corbusier végétarien a un jour inventé la prairie, on a mis de la prairie partout. Elle désagrège la notion de ville. Aucune ville au monde n'a jamais, en dehors des parcs, eu du gazon.*"[39]

The meadow between the Villa Savoye and the forest is an idealised, or rather typically ideal representation of nature; humans must build a new relationship with it that is expressed in modern architecture and urban planning (Menin, Samuel 2003). The tree is a magnificent symbol which Le Corbusier used, for example, in the Esprit Nouveau Pavilion or reduced to a graphic symbol as on the title page of an edition of *Ville Radieuse*.

39. Emile Aillaud cited in Vv.Aa, *La ville à livre ouvert, Regard sur cinquante ans d'habitat*, La Documentation française, Paris 1980, p.143.

Le Corbusier's sketches depict a generically interpreted "nature" in which the new city (and in particular the pure function of living) is immersed. In views from the outside, the interpretation of open space as a large open-air gymnasium in which to regenerate body and spirit prevails; in views from the inside towards the outside, there is a direct relationship between the home and nature. If we compare these images with Renaissance perspective representations, like Fra Carnevale's *Annunciation* cited by Sarah Menin and Flora Samuel (Menin, Samuel 2003), we will notice that the sequence has been simplified with the loss of the cultivated space, understood as the intermediary space between the home and nature. That is, one of the three landscapes described by John Dixon Hunt (Dixon Hunt 1993 and 1996) is missing: between the garden-third nature and the untouched, wild, first nature.

In actual fact, the simplification is even greater: in Renaissance paintings, there is also a closed open space, sometimes the inner garden enclosed by walls in which there is a window from which the boundary can be seen; or the public space within the city, also closed, defined by solids and from which the other landscapes can be viewed—a landscape from which to view the others, again one of the three landscapes. Richard Neutra's beautiful villas in the American desert are, together with Le Corbusier's sketches, perhaps the most radical representation of the reduction of unbuilt space to "Nature", albeit tamed by sports fields and the loss of the three landscapes.[40] The reasons that lead to cultivated space being removed from representations of living space certainly include functional separation (agricultural space as a space for work, to be kept apart from living space, even when it is a backdrop) and the transformation of agriculture into a large-scale industrial activity, as early as the mid-nineteenth century in connection with the establishment of the chemical industry (which was therefore no longer a healthy activity but a polluting one).

While the garden is still an intermediary between nature and accommodation, in the reduced forms of the double-height loggia of Le Corbusier's Unité d'habitation, or as the photos of the Esprit Nouveau Pavilion show (paradoxical evidence of the influence of Fra Angelico's or Piero della Francesca's paintings [Menin, Samuel 2003]), what is produced is the reduction of nature to an icon of itself (the large green carpet as domesticated nature, the wood or the desert as an evocation of the wild space governed by humans). It is the idea of a return to origins to counterbalance technological progress or, more realistically, the expression of technological supremacy and arrogance to overcome the fear of nature's manifestations. This important new aspect in the construction of the modern space project, the loss of the second nature,

40. Neutra's *American Lawn Desert House* appears to be limited by an improbable lawn that reproduces the closed space of the garden.

should not be understood in the sense of its rejection, but of the establishment of a different spatial order, a different man-nature relationship that requires new representations. Architectural objects are detached from the ground and do not alter its characteristics; the landscape surrounding them is dominated by vegetation, it is a pre- or post-urban landscape.

It is certainly not a first attempt to provide a representation and therefore a domesticated translation of the idea of nature as wilderness. Timothy Nourse's eighteenth-century treatise, *Campania Foelix: or a Discourse of the Benefits and Improvements of Husbandry* (1700), describes the three regions of the Pleasure-Garden: in the third, Grove or Wilderness, Natural and Artificial are joined to the extent that they produce the feeling of being in real wild nature, the Wilderness.[41] In this sense, John Dixon Hunt's complaint about the loss of the representative capacity of the garden after the eighteenth century seems to disregard the immense evocative capacity of the large modern green space as an expression of a specific feeling of nature. A great unitary representation, the green carpet of the city of the modern movement, a garden as extensive as the entire inhabitable space, is the logical embodiment of the feeling of nature that ran through romanticism, hygienism, utilitarianism and symbolism. At the end of the nineteenth century, the image of Paradise Lost no longer coincided with the garden, but with the rediscovery of a wild state of flowers, trees and shrubs[42] in which a different kind of human being moved and performed their exercises.

41. This is how John Dixon Hunt starts the essay "The Garden as a Cultural Object", citing a poem by Wallace Stevens, "Anecdote of the Jar" : "I placed a jar in Tennessee,/ And round it was, upon a hill./ It made the slovenly wilderness/ Surround that hill./ The wilderness rose up to it,/ And sprawled around, no longer wild. (in *The Palm at the End of the Mind*, edited by Holly Stevens, New York, 1972, p.46; cited in *The Garden as a Cultural Object* (Dixon Hunt 1991).

42. In "Ensauvager nos jardins", Claire Margat (2004) takes up some texts by Octave Mirabeau who in *L'Abbé Jules* (1888) describes a garden allowed to become wild once again to keep nature intact and to provide a place for education and exercise. In *Le Jardin des supplices* (1899) Mirabeau places his imaginary garden in China and criticises the French school of horticulture: "*Les Chinois sont des jardiniers incomparables, bien supérieurs à nos grossiers horticulteurs qui ne pensent qu'à détruire la beauté des plantes par d'irrespectueuses pratiques et de criminelles hybridations. Ceux-là sont des véritables malfaiteurs et je ne peux concevoir qu'on n'ait pas encore, au nom de la vie universelle, édicté des lois pénales très sévères contre eux.*" (Mirabeau 1991:182, cited by Claire Margat 2004). In the same issue of *Carnets du paysage*, "Le retour du sauvage dans les parcs publics: un nouveau jardinage", Gaëlle Aggéri and Pierre Donadieu (2004) reflect on the relationship between the idea of differentiated management established in the last decade of the twentieth century and the tradition of the Anglo-Saxon wild garden (in particular, the work of William Robinson in the late nineteenth century continued in the gardens of Gertrude Jekyll).

Functionalism

During the twentieth century, and also within the functionalist position, several ideas and philosophies of space came up against each other: from the pure transcendental and spiritual space linked to German culture to the English pragmatic space.[43] In the construction of the modern city, the biological metaphor became a concept, indeed a system of concepts, in continuity with a positivist approach that refers to biology and biological evolutionism as a cognitive grid through which to interpret and design reality. From Herbert Spencer to Émile Durkheim and his *De la division du travail social* (1893), to Bronislaw Malinowski and Alfred Radcliffe Brown, ideas about evolution, functionalism and the functional system permeated the social and urban debate (Turner, Maryanski 1979). The possibility of being able to interpret the whole of reality, including aspects concerning the city and its design, on the basis of evolutionist and functionalist theory, constructed a new conceptual grid that drove the process of the modern city: its trust in the separation of activities; disciplinary *redressement*; the improvement of living conditions by minimising effort, homogeneity and standardisation; growth by discrete nuclei immersed in greenery and in the new relationship with nature. The deepest references to the space of the functional city were found in this sphere, and not only in the one most practised by critics and historians *à la* Pevsner (1936). They informed its rhetoric and slogans, the attitude towards the existing city and the need for the *tabula rasa*, confident in the prototype and the possibility of inventing a different future.

43. As Franz Marc wrote in *La seconda vista* about the poverty of the British utilitarian approach (Marc 2007).

Fig. 12
Single-family patio houses and gardens in Tapiola. Built between 1955 and 1957 (Tuomi, 1992).

1.3 SPACE NATURE

Functional Nature

Several times while observing the ground drawings of the Ville Radieuse or, again, observing sketches by Hilberseimer or Alvar Aalto, I wondered about the reasons for these representations; and, above all, I wondered what the "emptiness" of the modern city was actually made of and, finally, in what sense this "emptiness" had to do with the functionalist approach or, better, if there was any continuity between the form of the open space and the idea of function. More broadly, this reflection led me to question the possibility of interpreting modern and pre-modern urban space by underestimating the importance of the ideas and forms of representation of open space. In other words: understanding the city requires us to address different planes of thought at the same time, well beyond the simplified figure-ground relationship. As yet there is no history of the city and of the territory that stems from dealing with the most important aspects of each plane and each point of view in parallel.

To a limited extent, and taking the field to be that as defined by Le Corbusier's sketches[44] or by the images of the Villa Savoye, my reasoning starts with the observation of something missing, something removed from the picture, and is followed by the hypothesis that the current interpretation of the "green" surfaces contained in the drawings of the architects and urban planners of the modern movement—the "green area" as a device for separating functions and function itself, a space of *loisir* and recreation equipped for different ages—is still insufficient to clarify the reasons for its presence. There are other reasons that broaden our understanding of its role and that once again lead back to functionalism.

A utilitarian and functional emptiness

As I have already written, my impression is that keeping separate the two reflections that have always guided the construction of the city and the territory, the urban-architectural one and the landscape one, makes it very difficult, if not impossible, to have an in-depth understanding of the reasons for modern space, and much more besides. Much has been written on this subject in recent years, but something can still be added.

44. Charles Jencks, 2000, *Le Corbusier and the continual revolution in Architecture*, in particular the third part "Back to Nature".

Fig. 13
Vallingby New Town, 1999
(Web gardenvisit.com).

While Constant, as we will see in the next chapter, pitted the city of play against the utilitarian city, it is perhaps worth seeking to understand more fully in what sense the "emptiness" of the modern city possesses the characteristics of functional and utilitarian space. An English neologism, *utilitarian*, introduced by Bentham in 1781 to describe his new philosophy of the general interest, was immediately used, as it is today, in a pejorative sense, far from the philosophical objectives that Bentham proposed.[45] Some years after the publication of *An Introduction to the Principles of Morals and Legislation* (1789) Humphry Repton, in his treatise *An Enquiry into the Changes of Taste in Landscape Gardening* (1806), supported the utilitarian and functional principle in the organization of the park and garden.[46]

45. "*...la reconnaissance, comme critère du bien et du mal, du « plus grand bonheur pour le plus grand nombre, chacun comptant de manière égale*" (Bentham, 1789). *Vocabulaire européen de philosophie*, p.1334 (Cassin 2004). As J.S. Mill attempted to specify in *Utilitarisme* (1881), the attempt is to find a moral principle capable of substituting opinion, special interest and power, and which distinguishes between good and evil. In this sense "*L'utilità è collettiva o non è*", ibidem p.1335.

46. "...park and gardens as a convenient extension of the social space of their houses are typical of the Reptonian philosophy. Fanny Price's admiration of the Grant's shrubbery ('it would be difficult to say whether most valuable as a convenience or an ornament' (p.174), and the musing on change and memory which it gives rise to, share Repton's confidence that good design makes a social and moral appeal to the understanding.", note 2 to chapter VI by Kathryn Sutherland to J. Austen, *Mansfield Park* (1814), Penguin, 1996.

An extension of the social space of the home, a useful and functional space for many individual and collective practices, useful also because it is productive: the functional green area is charged with all these meanings. In addition, the "functioning" of natural space in an ecological sense is one aspect that has not yet been sufficiently explored. It is not only the idea of ecological connection that is developed and used in many functional city projects, starting with the plan of Jansen's Greater Berlin (1910)[47] or Saarinen's Greater Helsinki (1918), and it is not only the important role of some landscape architects such as Leberecht Migge in the design of the most interesting German *Siedlungen* of the 1920s (Haney 2010). It is a more profound turning point in the conception of space and the role of nature in the modern city that participates in ways entirely consistent with functionalist ideology, with the idea of building a different society inspired by the functionalist and evolutionary paradigm.

The reconstruction of nature

The most important experiences in the construction of the modern city, the Swedish Social Democratic City, in particular the constructions in Stockholm in the 1930s and the projects related to Van Eesteren's Amsterdam Plan, are linked to this turning point. The functionalist park aims to express the new social system by using a new idea of nature.

The Swedish park in the late nineteenth and early twentieth century was influenced by the German tradition of undulating paths and horticulture, in turn a reduction of the tradition and simplification of the English park. It was botanists such as Rutger Sernander (1866-1944, also a geologist and archaeologist) who reflected on the need for a green space, a park, more in keeping with the forms of the existing landscape. The Stockholm School (Andersson 2002) was formed around the idea of returning nature to the city, which would greatly influence the design of modern European open space. The School's achievements follow two fundamental approaches. The first strongly concerns places, the identification of their possibilities and the exaltation of their potential. The internal and specific conditions of each site are exploited "with emphasis and simplification." The second pertains to comfort, recreation and pleasure: in this sense the park is utilitarian, an asset for the greatest number of people considered as equals. For Erik Glemme, chief designer of the Stockholm Parks Department from 1936 to 1956, or Holger Blom, urban planner and director of Stockholm Parks from 1938 to 1971, the social programme of the park is as important as the natural one and reflects the conviction that the city is a profoundly democratic institution.

47. According to an entirely modern approach, Jansen introduced principles of functional organisation into the design of the city as a system of social, technical and biological functions. See: Borsi 2015.

The difference between the English park and the functionalist park was thus stigmatised: if William Kent could write "all Nature is a Garden", referring to Horace Walpole (mid-eighteenth century), then for the Swedish functionalist movement of the 1930s "all gardens are Nature." This quotation also helps to clarify the previous one with regard to emphasis and simplification. The Swedish functionalist park recreates the characteristics of the regional landscape within the city in marginal places and in reinforced (emphatic) ways; it reconstructs nature where it no longer exists and reconstructs it through its archetypes: the rocky terrain of the archipelago, the pine forest, simple landscapes reconstructed within the city.

This concludes the season of the park as horticulture and as a collection of species and starts the season of the park as a reconstruction of nature within the living space, no longer separated from it. The third of the three natures described by John Dixon Hunt, the garden, also disappears in this process. The green space infiltrates the city and does not establish any distance with it, it becomes an integral part of the urban fabric[48] and an active space in which many of the practices of its inhabitants take place.

The forest interprets a new role in the design of green space, made possible in Sweden by the profound sense of nature that pervades Nordic culture in which the forest is a place to inhabit and not to flee from, calmer and safer than the city.[49]

In the parks of Fredhäll (created between 1936-1938) in the centre of Stockholm and Norr Mälarstrand (1941-1943)—a strip only 15 metres wide along Lake Mälaren which the inhabitants of Stockholm consider a preserved natural area within the city but is instead the result of a nature reconstruction project—a new idea of a functional city is represented in an ecological and spatial sense.

The representative function of the park is not lost in modern design, especially in the most interesting and conscious experiments such as the creation of the Amsterdam Wood, a central element of Van Eesteren's plan, on land conquered by the sea and transformed into a new nature.

Jacobus Pieter Thijsse, a biologist, born in Maastricht in 1865 (Woudstra 1997), concerned with the conservation of the last remaining natural areas and a proponent of the natural garden, profoundly influenced Van Eesteren and Mulder's design of the Amsterdam Wood (Daalder 2003). Dutch culture did not

48. As the title of Andersson's essay eloquently clarifies, the original contribution made by Swedish culture for the development of the space of the functional city is "the explicit utilization of a natural landscape as a garden or a park...", (Andersson 2002:13).

49. The etymology of the word *forest* in Swedish, wrote Andersson, means "something that rises up from the ground" and not "a land beyond civilization" as in Latin etymology. The forest which provided the wood for heating was seen as a friendly place. "The forest, as a concept, in fact, stood as an equivalent of the garden, since it satisfied many of the criteria by which a garden is normally defined." (Andersson 2002:14).

appreciate the wilderness at the end of the nineteenth century: the last clearing of native forests dates back to 1870, land reclamation drastically reduced marshy areas, and Niftrik's 1866 proposal for a park system in Amsterdam was rejected. Thijsse, without coating his research with ideological colourings of the kind increasingly seen in Germany in the same period, together with Heismans, embarked on a long process of reconnaissance, which included a review of the remaining natural elements and the publication of the magazine *Living Nature*, which popularised the subject. He developed the idea of *Instructieve Plantsoenen*, an educational park to be created in every city so that all citizens could experience nature (Woudstra 1997).

With Berlage and the plan for Amsterdam South the discussion about the design of a structure of open spaces was opened up for public debate. Thijsse wrote articles in which he called for not only the creation of parks, but also a large forest south of the city. This idea was included in the new Amsterdam plan, after the city was expanded from 2,100 to 17,500 hectares in 1921. An amendment to the *Woningwet* extended the plan to cover not just residential areas and streets, but also green areas. A *Boschcommissie* set out the requirements for the new park, first seeking references in other countries (as the plan for a new recreational wood was wholly original in the Netherlands), clarifying its fundamental social role, and prescribing, under Thijsse's influence, the use of native plant species at the 1:1:1 ratio of meadow, water, wood. With input from Jacoba Mulder and J.L. Smit, and the support of J.T.P. Bijhouwer (chairman of the Society of Dutch Landscape Architects, who introduced the slogan "back to nature and native art"), the urban planner Cor Van Eesteren created the first large modern green space project (the final design dates to 1935). The approach that guided its construction combines the functional principle (the different programmes in the park) with attention to ecological functionality. Not only was the park shaped by the different activities taking place within it, but also by the plants that contributed to the land's reclamation, with its drainage system relying on all existing and man-made water features, from ditches to streams, reservoirs and lakes, allowing biological processes and biodiversity to develop.

A reinterpretation of the English park, the *Amsterdambos* has been called "the definitive democratic city park of the twentieth century"[50] and it is one of the most important expressions of a functionalism that is both ecological and spatial.

Underlying the two modern space projects is the idea that an ecosystem "functions" and that ecosystemic functions are to be related to its constituent parts, their role and quality and their effects on the ecosystems themselves,

50. Alan Tate, cited by Remco Daalder 2003. See also http://www.amsterdam.info/parks/amsterdamse-bos/history/

 concepts derived from authors such as Darwin and Charles Elton.[51] The possibility of constructing new natures and open, green spaces in which to live is exemplified in some experiences that started in the 1950s and continued in the following decades.

The Forest Town

The influence of the garden city model in the debate on the city of the future, the sustainable city and the ecological transition, is still enormous today. Despite the criticism it has received over time, it is still a key reference in the contemporary discourse about the city, displaying a conceptual resilience that, as always, urges further investigation. In the context of this book, its being understood as a biopolitical space makes the garden city model an exemplary case of modern economic, social and corporal reform. Much recent literature has sought to reveal the thick biopolitical layer embedded in its design. The ideology of the natural healthiness of the countryside, or of nature as a source of health, wealth, and knowledge, is set against urban degeneration and the weakening of the nation, even to the point of legitimising the choice of material types and architecture (Clevenger, Andrews, 2017).

Tapiola, a garden city, a suburb set in a green area with architectural housing, is a forest city founded in the 1950s in Helsinki. Its architectural and environmental quality is extremely high and widespread; it is a monument and has its merits and flaws. It is also a contemporary placc of living, inhabited as one inhabits a monument. Present-day Tapiola is different from the city built in the 1950s and 1960s: imagined in the post-war period in a context of scarcity—in terms of housing, economic resources and materials—it is now incorporated into one of Finland's most vibrant and wealthy areas, the city of Espoo, of which it represents only a very modest part.

The architectural and urban culture returns to observe Tapiola on a cyclical basis, each time asking what Tapiola has to teach us, as was literally the case at an important seminar in Helsinki in 1967. On that occasion, the forest city received harsh criticism, and during the 1970s and 1980s it was represented in a number of interventions that denied a particular, but fundamental aspect of Tapiola—its space.

Since then, architectural and urban planning culture has become interested in Tapiola on several occasions: to criticise it in the late 1960s, to

51. Charles Darwin, *The Origin of Species* 1859; Charles Elton, 1927, *Animal Ecology*, *New York*, *Macmillan Co.*

Fig. 14
Tapiola Town Plan, 1968. Espoo City Planning Office. (Tuomi, 1992).

deal with it as heritage,[52] and fifty years later to remember its foundation in 1953.[53]

Today, Tapiola survives its own myth and bears witness to a time when daily life had taken on a heroic dimension. Returning to Tapiola today means investigating an experimental, innovative space and retracing an important episode in a long tradition of reflection on the "Reverse City" (Viganò 1999).

52. Icomos, "Dangerous liaisons. Preserving post-war modernism in city centers", Conference 15-17 February 2001, Helsinki, Finland, in particular see the text by Mustonen Tapani, "Tapiola's eastern suburbs - conservation in practice".

53. The conference that accompanied the celebration of the fiftieth anniversary was entitled: "Roots and seeds of the Garden City". www.weegee.fi/tapiola50.

Fig. 15
Eliel Saarinen, Bertel Jung, organic decentralisation pattern of Greater Helsinki, 1918 (Saarinen, 1958).

Fig. 16
Otto Meurman, plan of Käpylä, 1920-1925. (Tuomi, 1992).

Antecedents

At the turn of the century, European models spread to Finland. The influence of Sitte, first, and then of Unwin and Hegemann, emerges in the work of Bertel Jung, Helsinki's first town planner from 1908. In 1918 Eliel Saarinen and Jung prepared a grand plan for Helsinki: the entire peninsula on which the city stands was conceived as a large metropolitan area consisting of a ring of satellite towns around the existing city.[54] A network of voids and open spaces that at a new scale reconstruct a different concept of urban continuity. This network overlaps the territory without denying it, but integrates it into a model that Saarinen defines as organic decentralisation.

In Finland in the first decades of the twentieth century, many projects were inspired by the idea of the garden city located along railway lines, clusters of isolated houses, often built of wood, forming villa towns. Jung, Lindgren and Sonk designed Eira, a villa town, on the Tehtaankatu Hill which was to become the prototype for a residential suburb surrounded by greenery. Between 1920 and 1925, the garden city of Käpylä was created in Helsinki, designed by Birger Brunila and Otto Iivari Meurman, a professor of town planning, theorist and lead planner of Tapiola. In Käpylä, small prefabricated wooden houses in a green area, designed by Martti Välikangas, combined "the English idea of the garden city with the traditional Finnish wooden city and the most popular models of the Swedish small house industry..." (Nikula 1993:125). Even in the first functionalist district, the Olympic Village, built in Helsinki between 1939-40 to a design by Hiding Hekelund and Martti Välikangas, the different types of accommodation and open spaces are situated within the grounds with great attention paid to natural elements.

Forest town

The expression "forest town", introduced by Alvar Aalto in the 1930s, was used in the 1960s to criticise the organic, anti-urban approach of Otto Meurman, the creator of Tapiola. It was Aalto's plan for Sunila (1936-1938) that came closest to the idea of the forest town, proposing the use of forests and rock outcrops as places to live. The forest town is characterised by its adaptation to the landforms and the idea of modular urbanisation that would allow housing and the city to grow over time, adapting to the needs of its inhabitants: "... the internal nature of architecture is a fluctuation and development that suggests natural organic life."[55]

The idea of the city as organic and of the architect-a-scientist also appeared in his writings from this period: cells divided into distinct groups,

54. Paolo Sica described Saarinen's plan as the first application of the idea of a city garden to a large city (Sica 1985).

55. Alvar Aalto, "The influence of the construction and materials on modern architecture", conference held in Oslo in 1938, passage cited by Nikula 1998; see also Menin, Samuel 2003.

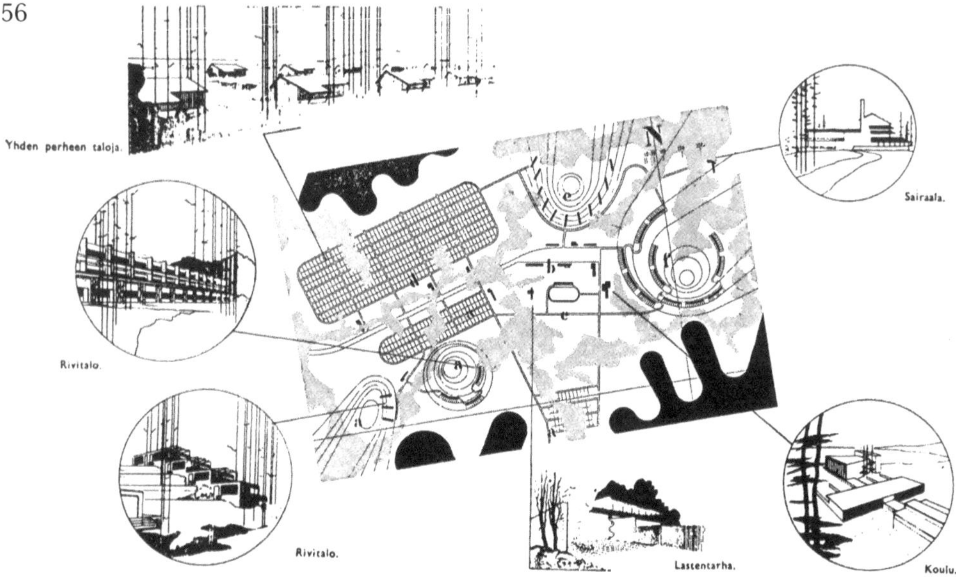

Fig. 17
Alvar Aalto, an American town in Finland, diagram, mid-1940. (aa. vv. 1994).

freely composed, and communicating with each other could give rise to a settlement pattern extended to the whole of Finland.

Both Meurman and Aalto, the former influenced by Mumford, whose *The Culture of Cities* was translated into Finnish in 1947, the latter by Wright and Mumford, used the biological metaphor that had been so successful in the architectural and urban planning debate in the 1920s and 1930s. What distinguished their positions from contemporary continental American and European ones was the local strongly anchored in the Finnish tradition of living. Modernity is not opposed to tradition,[56] but it establishes a continuity relationship with it that runs through the scales of the project: from a rural idea of the city-village, embedded in and accompanied by the overarching elements of the Finnish landscape, to an interest in light prefabrication and the use of wood in buildings. In Meurman's simplification, the city is an organically growing tree; in Aalto's words, the city built after the Second World War is not so much a larger city but is now part of the countryside.

56. The idea of tradition as a complex series of digressions proceeding from the past along "lines of force whose results work in the direction of the future" is also supported by the Finnish CIAM group, formed at the 9th Congress in Aix-en-Provence and made up, among others, of Ahola, Blomstedt, Siren, Ervi—all designers of Tapiola. The citation is from Aulis Blomstedt, "Julkinen rakennusja traditio" (Public building and tradition), in *Arkkitehti-Arkitekten* 9-10/1953, cited by Marja-Ritta Norri 1994.

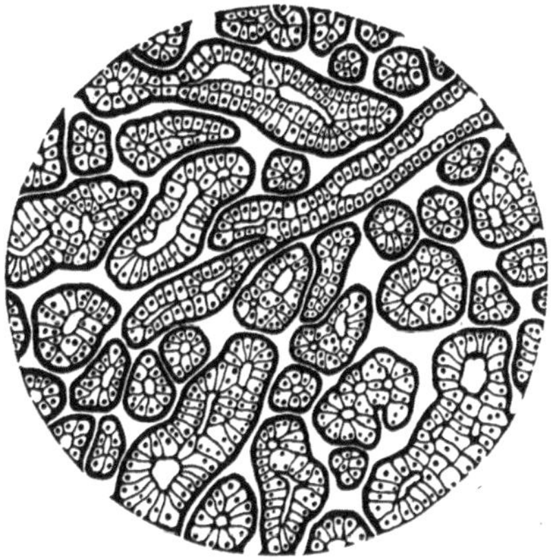

Fig. 18
Eilel Saarinen, cellular tissue: microscopic «community planning», 1943, (Saarinen, 1958).

With Saarinen, Aalto, and Meurman, an idea of the city emerges that does not fear the discontinuity[57] of the built fabric, and this conviction lasted for the first half of the twentieth century until coming up against harsh reactions in the 1960s. In the long debate that countered advocates of opposing models of the city during the twentieth century, the question of the discontinuity of urban space was unduly superimposed on that of urbanity, as if a biunivocal link united the two terms *city* and *continuity*; as if the social, cultural and economic relations that characterise urban life could only take place in the proximity and continuity of buildings.

The forest town is a discontinuous city. In research carried out at MIT between 1940 and 1941 ("An American City in Finland"), in many respects similar to Tapiola, Aalto imagined placing some housing clusters around a service core, introducing different settlement principles. What emerges from the drawings is the relationship between the buildings, the ground and vegetation. The houses are not separated from the ground; it is the conformation of the ground that organises them. The forest is transparency and a filter; it does not hide, but articulates the depth of the visual field. It is not a residual quantity, but a fundamental element of variation in the seriality of the organising principle of the grid. The principles of the forest town can be found in the plan for the company town of Imatra (1947-1953). Jussi Rautsi wrote that Aalto's plan—free, flexible and immersed in the forest—was not well used, betraying the unity planning and design imagined by Aalto (Rautsi 1988:15; Anderson, Fenske, Fixler, 2012).

The emphasis on flexibility, fluctuation, and the free development of architecture and the city pushed Finnish architects and urban planners—in

57. Taking up some of the topics raised by Unwin in the competition for the first garden city in Letchworth. I refer to the chapter Reverse City in *La città elementare*, 1999.

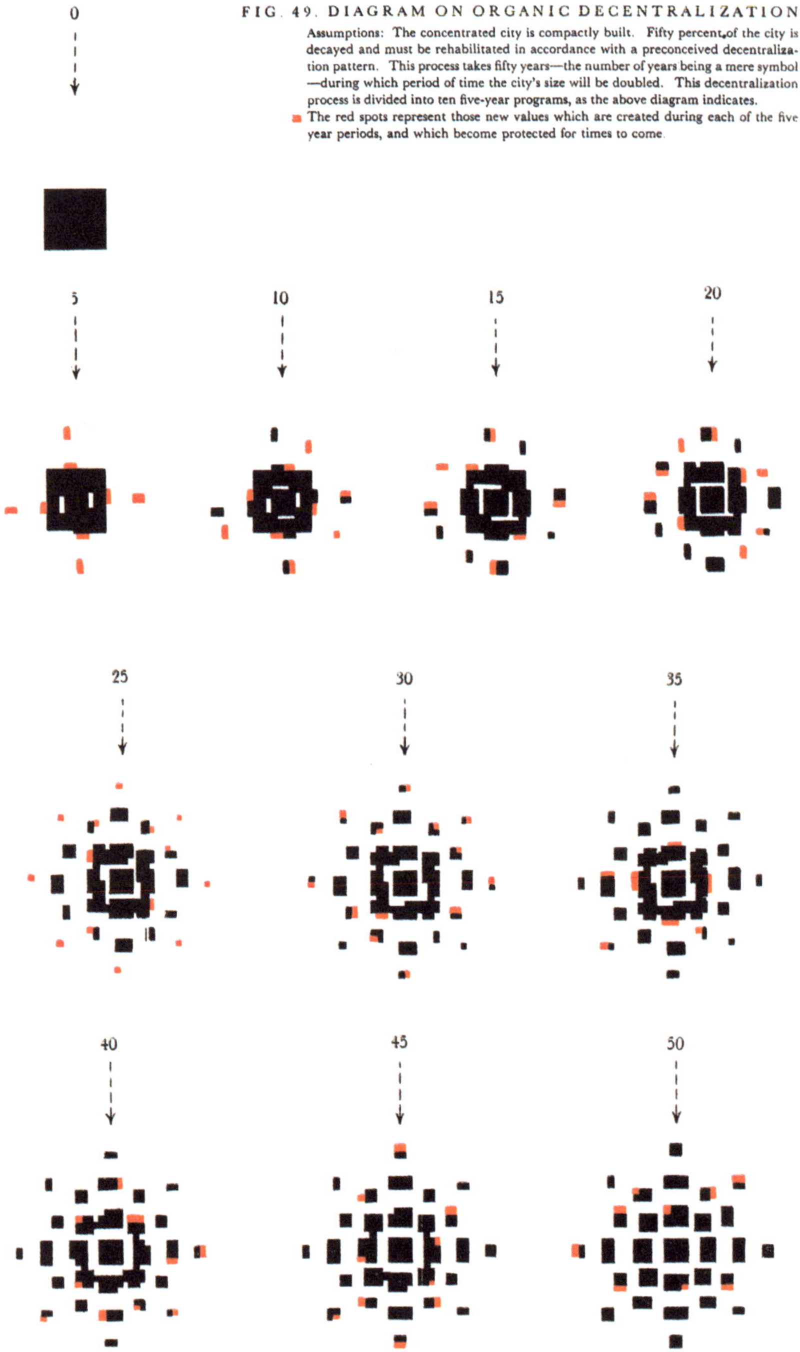

Fig. 19
Eilel Saarinen, diagram on organic decentralisation, 1943. (Saarinen, 1958).

the interwar years and at the time of reconstruction—towards innovation and experimentation, away from the established urban models and models introduced by European functionalism in the 1920s and 1930s.

Fragmentism and reverse city

...I am an empty room,
around me the cardinal points
and snow-folded trees:
cold, cold, empty.
But on my hand rises everything I loved -
the yard, the roses, the flowerpot house,
perfection:
a house like a capsule: quiet seeds
with death and motion in their tissue...
Eeva-Liisa Manner, from *Counterpoint*, 1992 (or. 1956)

The American city in Finland, like Hilberseimer's studies on Chicago and in general the projects of the modern movement, interprets the grid in a centripetal way, breaks its continuity and entrusts the connection between the different objects to other elements. In Albert Pope's opinion, the interruption of the mesh, its reduction to a comb-like structure, or ladder, has made a decisive contribution to the contemporary city's loss of legibility and urbanity (Pope 1996).

Tapiola is a fragment in the Helsinki metropolitan area consistent with a group of ideas that spread in Finland between the 1910s and 1950s through Eliel Saarinen, Alvar Aalto, and Otto Meurman, which were constantly re-proposed even in different urban situations and later taken up by other authors such as Erwin Gutkind.

In *The City* of 1943, Saarinen, who by that time had been settled in America for many years, emphasised the need for the decentralisation of the city starting with a microscopic observation of natural phenomena, of the "natural realm" which gives rise to "the existence of individual cells and the correlation of these cells into cellular tissue." The picture captions accompanying the text define a healthy cell tissue in terms of "microscopic 'community planning'", whereas diseased tissue becomes a metaphor for "microscopic 'slum growth'" (Saarinen 1958:9-10). The possibility of expression of the single individual, the single form, and the importance of the correlation between cells and between individuals are the two key concepts of Saarinen's organic urbanism, accompanied by the imagery of a cell biologist, the influence of which can be recognised in Team X's architectural structuralism and in early hints of cybernetics. Saarinen used the organic metaphor when, for example, he compared the streets to arteries in the human body that the urban planner must open up to the territory so that: "...both the city and the population can spread themselves toward the country—toward air, light and nature." (Saarinen 1958:149). The dispersed city that Saarinen re-proposed was the pattern of decentralisation for greater Tallinn in Estonia in 1913 and greater Helsinki in 1918: a new city of fragments that seem to float in the void, in practical terms connected by road networks, green spaces and lakes. The fragment formation process is narrated by the organic decentralisation diagram that shows the systematic and stubborn introduction of discontinuities into the existing urban fabric, exploiting degraded and declining areas and introducing new ones. Over a sufficiently long period (Saarinen symbolically spoke of 50 years) the city acquired a new form, which was open and unstable, dispersed and discontinuous. Its shape was very similar to that of the present-day city. Each fragment was defined and perfect within itself, just like Tapiola.

Tapiola

These early cues and the milieu outlined above allow us to connect with the story of the design and construction of Tapiola. At the end of the Second World War, the ideology of the Finnish forest city was wedded in its extreme versions to the rejection of urban life and to the exaltation of health and morality by those outside it. The Tapiola project, in which the theories of Otto Meurman (a pupil of Saarinen and exponent with the latter of the movement defined as the "social city", Deland 2001) came to fruition, and was strongly supported by Heikki von Hertzen who headed the Finnish Population and Family Welfare Federation. The aim of the foundation was to promote dispersed, healthy and diverse settlements.

In the pamphlet "Homes or Barracks for our Children" published in 1946, von Hertzen pointed to traditional urban situations as negative; and among Helsinki's neighbourhoods, he singled out Käpylä, designed by Meurman, as a good example. An interdisciplinary team was set up for the occasion, involving urban planners, architects, landscape architects, engineers, home economists, sociologists and lawyers.

In 1945, Meurman drew up a plan for 12,000 new inhabitants in Hagalund on land that was later purchased by the Finnish Population and Family Welfare Federation. The idea was to establish a new garden city made up of residential cells on the outskirts of Helsinki and connected to it by a tram line. Some routes used during the First World War for artillery transport provided the layout for the new roads. Their location in the first development unit, to the east, was one of the last parts of the project to be defined. The need to minimize costs meant that passing over rock beds was avoided, and the roads were therefore placed on sandy strips, allowing for easy passage. According to Meurman's plan, the side strips were to belong to the community.

Fig. 20
Otto Meurman, model of Tapiola, 1945. (Tuomi, 1992).

In 1952, Arne Ervi, Viljo Revell, Aulis Blomstedt and Markus Tavio were involved in designing housing and certain parts of Tapiola. The group also played a leading role in the post-war reconstruction programme[58] and was interested in experimenting with prefabrication processes and building standardisation. The relationship with Meurman marked a generational leap: the architects, influenced by the work of Le Corbusier, counterposed the romantic idea of low houses in the woods with the use of multi-storey buildings, new landmarks in the landscape. Meurman, writes Riitta Nikula, "thought a good town could be built by organising basic everyday needs in a sensible way" (Nikula 1993:140), and it was this very adherence to the everyday, the lack of emphasis, the care in the choice of location, and attention to the microclimate that were heavily criticised from the late 1960s onwards.

The need for smaller homes and a reduced number of terraced and detached houses envisaged in the first part of the project led Meurman to resign, as he did not agree with the choices and changes made. His role was handed over to Martti Välikangas, the designer of the wooden houses in Käpylä. After Meurman's resignation, in 1954, Aarne Ervi proposed moving the main

58. The serious and urgent problem concerned the 400,000 Finnish exiles from Karelia, which had become Soviet.

Fig. 21
Russian map of Hagalund (future Tapiola), 1900.

Fig. 22
Map of Hagalund (future Tapiola), 1943.

road that was to cross Tapiola from north to south to along the eastern edge, which would avoid traffic near the residential areas.

These and other changes left the first part of the settlements without local roads, an aspect that was later criticised and justified the use of settlement layouts organised by a clear orthogonal grid. In 1954, Ervi himself won the competition for the centre of Tapiola, inspired by Le Corbusier's St. Dié and the civic centre model of English-style new towns. A covered square, a shopping centre, offices overlooking an artificial lake—Ervi responded to criticism about the lack of density in the centre of Tapiola by saying that he had tried to maintain the atmosphere of the garden city and flexibility for future interventions. During the 1960s, the idea was that Tapiola could become a more important regional centre and, at the same time, that the areas surrounding Helsinki should be more densely populated. The winners of the 1967 competition to extend the centre (Juutilainen, Mikkola, Kairamo, Pallasmaa) asserted the need for the old centre to be flanked by a new one inspired by Anglo-Saxon and Dutch architectural structuralism (in particular the designs of Van den Broek and Bakema). Once again, as in the project for the northern part of Tapiola, won by Pentti Ahola in 1958, the orthogonal grid organised the settlement.

The new centre was built in the 1970s gradually distancing itself not only from the garden city but also from the competition project, becoming a place of conflict and contradictions. In the late 1980s, on the site of the theatre indicated by Ervi, the Espoo City Cultural centre was built by Arto Sipinen.

The ideological support abundantly provided by Heikki von Hertzen, and the emphasis on biological functions in the urban design, contributed to the creation of a unique settlement situation. The forest is the space of a protective and welcoming nature, it is a mythical space and at the same time the implementation of the modern biopolitical project.

The grammar of Tapiola

When I love rock, when I love granite,
let it be permitted me.
It's my childhood' bedrock
that bears people, crystals squeezed
into the holes of crystals, multicoloured and jagged.
Out of the jags, the rock, the pine
a language is born and lives
with winter's longest words
snow's shortest: it is us,
it lives beneath the sky.
Helvi Juvonen, 1992, *Bedrock*, (or. 1958)

Tapiola represents an inversion of the traditional idea of urban space. The forest oscillates between an element of separation[59] and an element of freedom in the fact that it is fully accessible, for example. The forest is an interior in which places of living meet; the forest becomes a space of the home, a domestic and relational space.

The design methods used in Tapiola are somewhat different from those used in other exemplary places of reflection on the city. Meurman prepared an overall scheme covering the first part of Tapiola. The landscape architect Nils Orénto thoroughly surveyed the wooded areas, individual trees, remains of fortifications and rocky outcrops. Blomstedt, Ervi, Revell and Tavio supported the first sketches of the groups of buildings. Meurman revised the overall plan. Projects at different scales and dealing with different themes influenced each other.

The infrastructure work proceeded together with the construction of the buildings and gardens, making it possible to govern and utilise the land movements. The residential streets were only three metres wide and it was not deemed necessary to pave them. The previously cultivated areas form a

59. In Meurman's idea of decentralisation, cities must be separate from each other and so too the neighbourhood units and residential cells within them.

Fig. 23
Aarne Ervi, project for Tapiola city-centre, 1967 (Tuomi, 1992).

Fig. 24
Juutilainen, Mikkola, Kairamo, Pallasmaa, project for the extension of Tapiola city-centre, model A, 1967 (aa.vv. 1973).

continuous surface of parks and gardens that intersect the already wooded areas and the new masses planned by Orénto.[60]

The groups of houses are positioned independently from the design of the road network: this means that the building support is not the road but rather the ground with its specific characteristics. The settlement is guided by the lithological formation, tending to avoid the high cost of the foundations of roads and buildings in rocky terrain. The location of many groups of houses is decided directly on site, the design of the open space is contemporaneous with that of the buildings.

For these reasons, Tapiola is not the result of a pre-established plan, but rather a settlement strategy that is not represented in regular organisational geometries. The search for order takes place at an intermediate scale involving a few groups of buildings. At large scale it is entirely entrusted to the landscape, rocks and forest. If we were to superimpose a lithological map on that of the buildings, we would find correspondence between the unbuilt spaces and the rock strata. On the other hand, the idea of placing a city among fir and birch trees, resting on the granite layers and contour lines, continues to represent an alternative to the idea of a settlement that withdraws from environmentally valuable places and places itself in areas with less landscaping.

The grammar of Tapiola can only be read by carefully observing the relationship established between buildings and the ground. The tall buildings are placed at the top and often face the steepest side of the terrain, defining small clusters skirting the forest. The long multi-storey bars intersect the contour lines, never running parallel to them. The low houses, with patio or terrace, are arranged on the gentle slopes, completely immersed in the light birch forest, slightly offset following the slope. Between the forest and housing units there are gardens, courtyards and a landscape of plants which are often deliberately non-native, introducing differences in colour, transparency, grain and plant combinations unlikely to be found in nature.[61] The main streets run around granite roundabouts, and short, often cul-de-sac-like stretches lead off from them, ending in small parking areas and paved clearings overlooked by larger buildings. A dense network of pedestrian paths branches off from the clearings and parking areas, separated from the road network, which does not avoid height differences, almost seeming to mark them out by connecting the accommodation to the services of the forest city. Between

60. Orénto spoke about "shock plantings" to describe the new green masses introduced by the project. See Ria Ruokonen, *Landscape design in Tapiola*, in Vv.Aa., *Heroism and the everyday - Building Finland in the 1950s*, cit.

61. Most of Tapiola's gardens (i.e. the parts of the open space that are not forest, private gardens or large parks) were designed between 1956 and 1966 by Jussi Jännes, a Finnish landscape architect who studied with Carl Theodor Sørensen in Denmark, among others, and whose references include Roberto Burle Marx and the American Thomas Church. Jännes created the famous Kontionkettä Park that marked the entrance to Tapiola, now disrupted by the removal of the central roundabout.

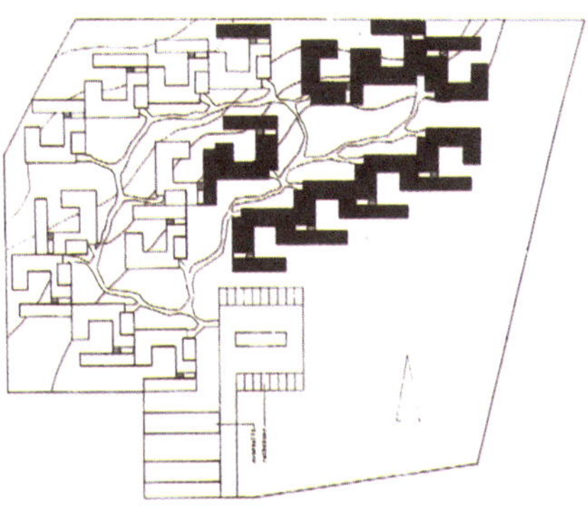

1:2000

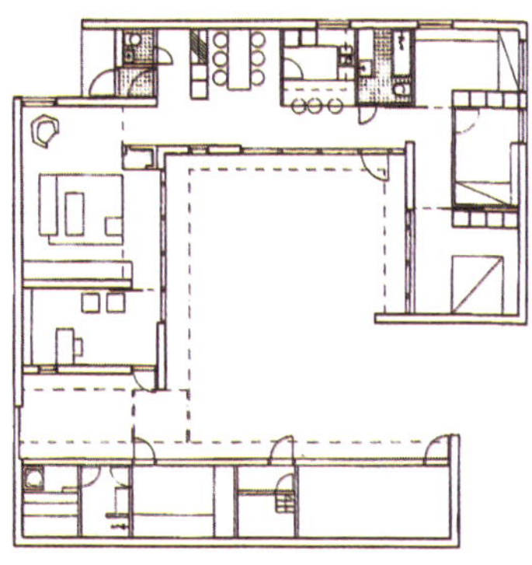

1:400

Figs. 25, 26, 27
Pentti Ahola, patio houses, 1962-1964 (Tuomi, 1992).

the tall buildings of Viljo Revell and the shopping centre, a path climbs up the smooth red granite walls amidst the fir and birch trees, leaving the visitor bewildered and fascinated by an almost surreal spatial experience.

The individual type

Without being a catalogue of architecture, Tapiola is a place where important research on ways of living was carried out. The great arrangement of housing types also seems to allude to an open and variable idea that supports different housing styles and family configurations. Despite later criticisms on the lack of clarity in its overall layout, this research became widespread and influential in European architecture. More than other forest cities, Tapiola is torn to shreds in architectural histories and typological manuals. While its overall plan is not easy to memorize, the individual niches that comprise it have had great influence throughout Europe as models that can be replicated in different situations.[62] Similarly, certain elements of Tapiola's architectural language have become widespread, also replicable elsewhere and in some cases conceived as belonging to a system of light prefabrication, a concept dear to Aalto and which clearly differentiates the Finnish experience, and Tapiola in particular, from the Swedish experience of heavy prefabrication, as used in Sven Markelius' Vällingby (1950–onwards).

The reproducibility and transmissibility of Tapiola's architecture is not accidental and is perhaps rooted in the commitment of most of the architects working on it to the reconstruction and dissemination of the standard house. Consistent with the research of the modern movement, the design research "combines the quest for [the] primordial cell of the dwelling, the pursuit of the general principles of housing and the project to create building types." (Saarikangas 1993:232). The long reflection developed by the architects of the Finnish Association of Architects' Reconstruction Office (founded in 1942, chaired by Aalto, directed by Viljo Revell and by Aarne Ervi for the part related to the Institute of Standardisation, i.e. by the future designers of Tapiola) revolves around some main operations and questions: breaking down the housing unit into its basic components and reassembling them by constructing sequences that are often different from traditional ones, or remodelling them by altering their dimensions; and defining an evolutionary path of the house, a growing house that over time must be able to expand and alter its distribution.

62. For example, Blomstedt's houses and the Sirens' wooden houses appear in the handbook of types of residential terraced housing, *Tipologie residenziali a schiera* by Cambi, Di Cristina, Steiner (Be-Ma Editrice, Milan, 1980), cited as one of the first examples of light prefabrication; Aarne Ervi's nucleus of in-line houses built in 1960 is published in *Tipologie residenziali in linea* by Cambi, Di Sivo, Steiner (Be-Ma Editrice, Milan, 1984).

These operations lead to the development of the modern housing unit in Finland and to the clear separation of functions: the large multipurpose space of the rural home becomes the functional space of the modern kitchen separate from the living room. The "chronic effort" of the housewife (addressed in the previous chapter on functional space, which became highly relevant in Finland in the 1950s) is dealt with by home economics experts who were members of the Household Work Efficiency Institute founded during the war, with proposals for the standardisation of bathrooms and kitchens, as well as collective storage, laundry and freezer spaces (Pantzar 2013:21). Home economics experts also suggested that housewives should reflect on unnecessary time wasted.

People sleep only in bedrooms, separated from the rest of the house to ensure privacy and isolation. Some of Aalto's writings emphasise the search for the primordial cell and the need for an additive approach: inherent in the concept and nature of living is the idea of permanence, and the heat source in the centre of the house can be imagined as the primordial and at the same time generative cell of the housing unit.[63]

In reducing the components of the habitable space to the limit, the differentiation between urban housing and rural housing is consciously lost: the search for the primordial cell is enough to demolish a clear distinction between country house and town house. The space of the housing unit starts from the inside and moves towards the outside, as in the functionalist approach; it is placed within a new model that moves away from the opposition of town and country and defines neither town nor country.

While in standard houses the exterior seems to be linked to certain stylistic features of the rural housing unit, in the architecture of Tapiola, designed for the most part by the same designers, the architectural language is modern and uses certain materials taken above all else from tradition. The Sirens' wooden houses and the minimalist language of Pentti Ahola's patio houses (1962-1964) built in the forest do not choose which of the two contexts they belong to (research into constant, long-term elements tends to overshadow contingent differences such as location) or, rather, they imply a different context.

The implicit context of the standard house and the Tapiola experiments is the mythical context of nature. While in similar suburban situations nature is reduced to its mediated allusion by the garden of the isolated house, in Tapiola reality is more closely anchored to myth. There is less detachment, the myth is pressing. The name of the town, Tapiola, replaces the pre-existing Swedish place name, Hagalund, and means "the home of Tapio", the Finnish

63. Saarikangas also cited some of Aalto's writings published in *Arkkitehti* in 1941 (Saarikangas 1993:265).

god of forests. Nature is a symbol and concept of freedom, which also knows how to preserve. Nature is insistence on permanence and mutation. Consciously emerging from the opposition, or distinction, between town and countryside leads to a new problem, that of the characters of a new excipient, a new surface of continuity: neither country, nor town. This excipient, in Tapiola, is the forest, and Tapiola is an exemplary reflection on a habitable space that is neither city nor country. The project's response is the space that has been created in Tapiola. This space does not arise from the hybridisation of features of the countryside and the city, but is instead unprecedented in the history of settlements. Its characteristics—distances, heights, density, openness, closure, porosity, transparency—are unique, as well as the spatial experiences they allow.

Against space

...This society isn't quite advanced enough yet, he says
our leader
that gets buttermilk up his nose every time he
drinks buttermilk for breakfast
Unemployment, environmental problems
a balance-of-trade deficit, inflation
a shortage of kindergartens
flagrant alcohol-abuse
tax-fraud almost a necessary condition of life
...
doesn't he see
he's a cultured man
that an advanced society is a contradictio in adjecto...
Pentti Saarikoski, *The obscure dances*, 1992 (or. 1983)

Tapiola is therefore not an urban space, and on this point the criticisms of subsequent years take on the burden of clarifying what an urban space is, as opposed to what Tapiola was in the 1950s. The space proposed by the projects of the 1970s and 1980s is a denser, more ordered, more functionally articulated space. Greater density is sought in the new centre of Tapiola; order is reconstructed by inserting fragments of the orthogonal grid; greater functional articulation, in addition to the centre, is achieved by incorporating some areas for production (in recent years a science park has been set up next to Tapiola, also immersed in the forest).

The designed space for vegetation is equally subject to criticism. The dozens and dozens of small gardens and parks designed by Jussi Jännes, created by C.-J. Gottberg and strongly supported by von Herzen, have been criticised for the use of non-native species and for the confusion and contrast they bring to an otherwise homogeneous and restful landscape. Jännes has been accused of the "heretical use of vegetation" (Roukonen, 1994).

The experimentalism seen in Tapiola and therefore its uniqueness too are seen as indicators of its elitism. As an isolated project, Tapiola is judged as separate from the rest of society and a sign of the detachment between architectural theories and society itself. Its scattered structure is considered devoid of stimuli for collective and individual life. Opposition to Tapiola gave rise to the 1967 seminar: *What does Tapiola teach us?* in which criticism was directed at not only the built experience, but also how it is conveyed and disseminated, the slogans, and the search for legitimacy in the use of non-transparent theories, such as biological ones. Timo Tuomi wrote that these criticisms tell us as much about Tapiola as they do about the 1960s and the problems and issues of that period (Tuomi 1992). Vällingby, a Swedish new town, and Tapiola are seen as opposing models, not only of cities, but of society. The debate does not seem to grasp, as we do today and beyond the ideology that inspired it, the novelty of this act of spatial imagination that is the forest town. The new projects carried out there today aim to bring Tapiola in line with the contemporary urban condition "with a sympathetic approach to its [Tapiola's] traditional values"[64]; "The goal is to create a vibrant and pleasant urban centre within this leafy neighbourhood". The ongoing projects imagine its regeneration with new underground car parks and a focus on public transport, with a new metro line and a renovated bus station, new commerce and cultural offerings, and the densification of its city centre (adding 2,000 new inhabitants). In the official policies, "The regeneration of Tapiola will transform the city into a more functional and versatile commercial and urban hub combining the best of both worlds: a traditional city centre with modern shopping facilities."[65] All references to the forest city have disappeared and Tapiola has been normalised.

A philosophy of space-nature

Heavily criticised by Le Corbusier as false nature and an expression of the anxiety provoked by endless urbanisation, and by Jane Jacobs for its superficially pacifying role, the model of the garden city has been implemented in different parts of the world: in the denser French version of the *Butte Rouge* near Paris, or in the Finnish forest city, and even in the garden suburbs that marked elitist urbanisation in China, Russia, Latin America with gated communities isolated in greenery or hidden in the forest, connected to a motorway interchange and patrolled by guards. Le Corbusier's criticisms

64. https://www.tapiolankeskus.fi/en/Welcome-to-Tapiola (consulted 5 January 2020).
65. Idem.

seem less relevant today, while others assume greater weight: forgetting the social and political project underlying this model, the difficulty of integrating jobs and a mixed fabric of functions to escape economic and social dependence, elitism.

There remains the question of biopolitical space, which cannot only be traced back to the governance of bodies, their disciplining and protection, but also, in the example of Tapiola, the influence of a different idea of nature, an active nature that involves its inhabitants in a relationship that is at once intimate and collective. In the former case (the governance of bodies), Tapiola can be placed alongside *Menschenökonomie* (human economy) theory and the conviction that space can play a supporting, optimising role in the enhancement of a population for economic purposes. The Austrian sociologist and philosopher Rudolf Goldscheid developed a treatise on social biology at the beginning of the twentieth century that aimed to guide "the management of the conditions of the (re)production of human life" (Lemke 2011:107), an "organic capital" encompassing work and life. Distancing themselves from purely Darwinist and social hygiene visions, Goldscheid, a supporter of the Social Democratic Party and Heikki von Hertzen of the Finnish Population and Family Welfare Federation pointed to the improvement of living conditions through the design of space, with Tapiola being the prototype of the welfare state (Pantzar 2013:15). Alongside education, health, and security, the redefinition of urban space contributes to the process of a "rational cultivation of life" (Lemke:108) in opposition to forms of capitalism that are incapable of satisfying the full range of human needs and that favour comprehensive planning: "restocking of the entirety of the nation's human material" (Goldscheid 1911:577 cited in Lemke 2011:108). The formation of capital, through investments in industry and quality of life, and to benefit the country's economic equilibrium, characterised the post-war period in Finland, and likewise in the rest of Europe. After concerns about population *quantity* (the 1930s crisis), the theme radically changed to a concern about the *quality* of human capital (Pantzar 2013:29).

In the latter case (the agency of nature), at once intimate and collective, the active role of the ground, vegetation, and open space brought to the fore the concept of co-evolution and a different idea of "nature-space" that embraced the philosophy of evolution, co-evolution and life cycles (of which we continue to experience some steps today, wondering how far we can push it). In this sense, space-nature imposes a specific way of thinking about the transformation of the city, of which nature, and therefore different plant, animal and human forms are structuring and active elements. In both approaches, the space of Tapiola, its grammar and the concepts that unify it are not an inert background, but a space that acts in a biopolitical sense.

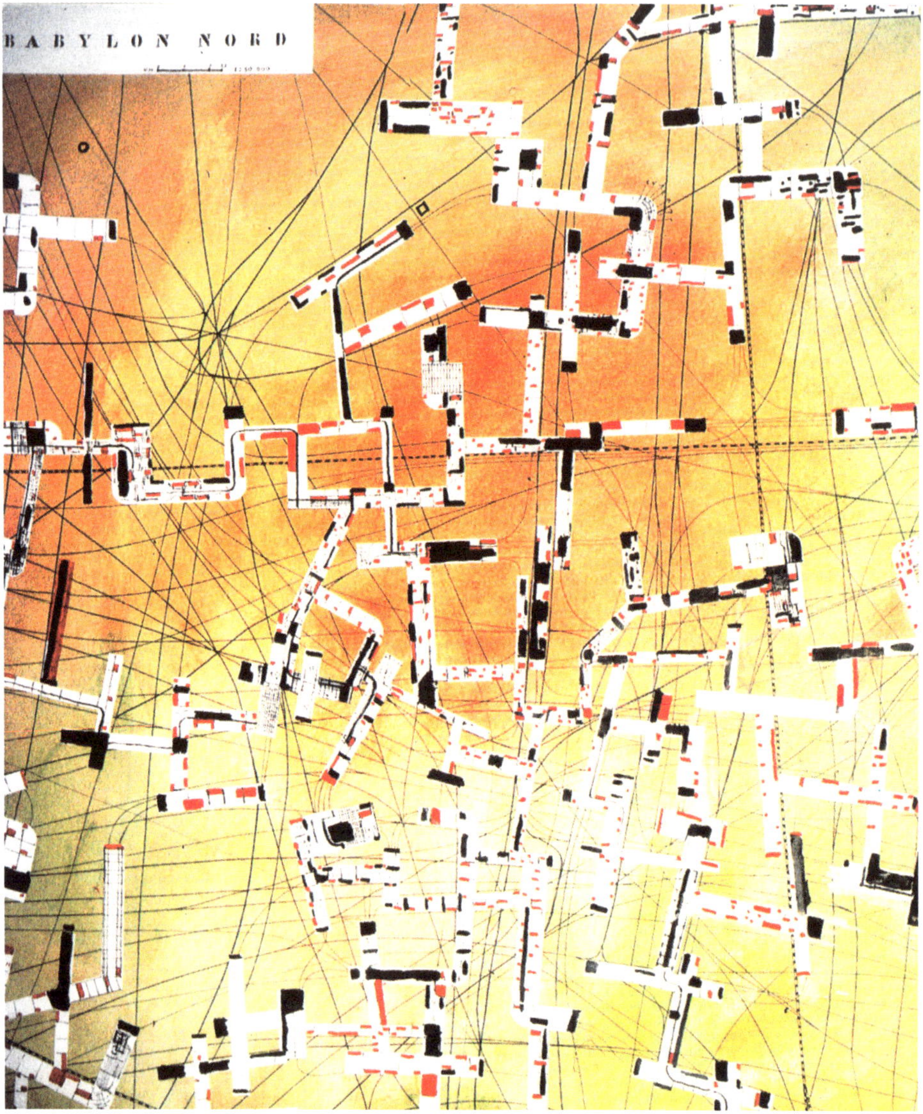

Fig. 28
Constant Nieuwenhuys, New Babylon North, paper, pencil, and watercolor, 1958, 100 x 106 cm (Wigley, 1998).

1.4 SOCIAL SPACE

The decades following WWII saw growing criticism of elitist pilot experiences, such as those of Tapiola and the pacifying use of "nature" developed by the garden city, criticism of the organic nature of the northern modern neighbourhoods (Piccinato, Quilici, Tafuri 1962), and a rejection of the dogmatic modernity of the CIAMs, which led to their dissolution in 1959. There was no longer interest in the capacity of space to order/reorder, to govern a life disrupted by war; instead interest was in the capacity for space to support infinite decisions and initiatives within spatial structures referable to permanent elements and patterns rooted in the collective memory. The hypothesis that paths and mental structures can be reflected in physical structures drove Alison and Peter Smithson's patterns of association: the pattern of "life on the street", a physical and mental structure, for example, is considered a stable and permanent invariant in the construction of a space that is afforded a social and supporting role (Söderqvist, 2011).

It is the recovery of memory as a conceptual repository of relational spaces and atemporal and universal associations to which Kevin Lynch's *The Image of the City* (1960) refers, relying on the hypothesis of the existence of a spontaneous collective consciousness and feeding a reading using the signs of urban space. Leaving aside eras, cultures and differences, the city is made up of meaningful structures capable of communicating and encouraging mutual exchange. *Structure* is a crucial term in the development of a social space, a spatial metaphor that does not cease to exist, like many others of the same kind, and of which Georges Matoré notes, in his book on contemporary space, its fixity and at the same time its scarce evolutionary nature. Vocabulary relating to spatiality is not easily renewed (Matoré 1976:XIII).

To talk about the third idea of space, the social space that stimulates relationships between people and practices of living, I will use two important experiences: New Babylon and Toulouse-Le Mirail. Two stories that run along often parallel paths: in time, since they cover the 1960s and part of the 1970s together; in space, since they draw on common references and participate in the criticism and renewal of the debate on the modern city. Many of the themes running through them have immediate similarities.

In recent years, something important and still not fully understood has created a profound divide between the two experiences and how they are judged. In recent years, New Babylon has been re-read, re-studied, re-published and appreciated. Toulouse-Le Mirail, like other similar examples, has been rejected, partly demolished and is considered by many to be a controversial, if not entirely negative, reference.

Toulouse-Le Mirail, conceived for 100,000 inhabitants, is currently a collection of neighbourhoods with around 23,000 inhabitants. New Babylon is a collection of models, drawings, canvases, sketches and texts.

The space of New Babylon

Although it is not a real city, New Babylon (1956-1974), like Tapiola, has exerted great influence on the architecture and urbanism of past decades. Mark Wigley defined New Babylon as a place of convergence for many of the ideas, images, and theories that spanned the 1950s and 60s (Wigley 1998). Segments of situationism, fragments of architectural structuralism, pieces of avant-garde art from constructivism to the sculptures of Kiesler and Naum Gabo, structural details in which Wachsman and Friedman are mixed—all are the sources that drive the lengthy work of imagining and constructing a city.

The hypothesis of a city and not a utopia, New Babylon (even in terms of its plural and heterogeneous references) is what a city could be like. Constant confided in an interview that the city will be produced, because it is the direction we are going in anyway (Lootsma 1999).[66]

The themes that New Babylon addresses are and remain topical.

Milieu

In the early 1950s, artists were often found among architects and in their cultural circles and associations. Immediately after the war, the exponents of the modern movement reproached themselves for their inability to represent and provide society with symbols, unlike the architectural works of the neoclassical regime that had been able to interpret the climate of the time, albeit in a reactionary way (Lootsma 1999). In the CIAM devoted to the *Heart of the City*, in 1951, Giedion and others placed great hopes in joint work between architects and artists to overcome criticism of the four points on which the functional machine governed by the Athens Charter rested: living, working, moving around, recreation. In the meantime, criticism of the International Style, Functionalism and the massive interventions that were taking place all over Europe took on radical overtones in some intellectual groups such as the Situationists and within the CIAM. The positions put forward by Team X led to the end of CIAM's congresses in Otterlo in 1959.

66. Lootsma cites passages from an interview with Constant by the young Koolhaas, editor of *Den Haags* in the 1960s (Lootsma, 1999). I have always been struck by the assonance between Wright's idea of the inevitability of Broadacre City and Constant's similar belief about NB. Both would then, and at least in the authors' intentions, constitute a description of the existing city rather than a criticism of it.

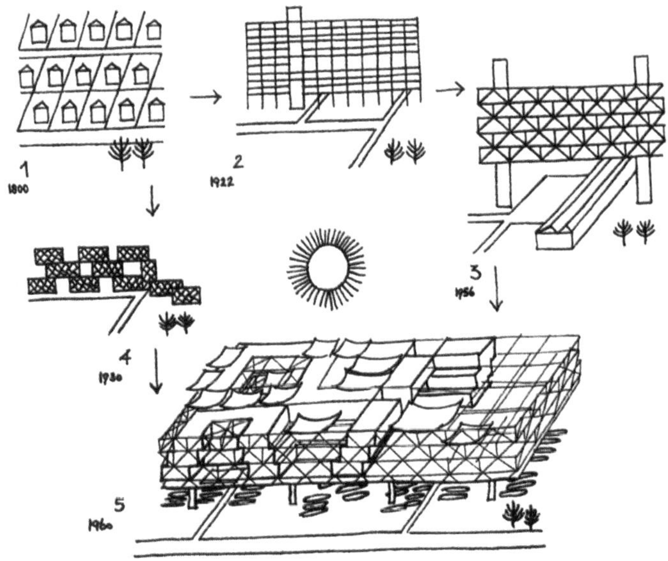

Fig. 29
Yona Friedman, "Stages in the Development of Housing Forms," 1958. (Friedman & Orazi, 2015).

Constant spent time with both the Dutch exponents of Team X, in particular Aldo van Eyck, after having frequented the Dutch CIAM group *De8*, and the Situationists, in particular Guy Debord, proponent of "unitary urbanism", who was, at least initially, enthusiastic about the reflection on the city Constant had proposed.

Social space vs individual space

In the creation of New Babylon, Constant focused on the notion of social space. In his criticisms, which echo those of the Situationists and Team X, the city of the modern movement lacked a reflection on the potential of individuals and their relationships. New Babylon is thus a reflection on the infrastructural condition that allows the free play of social interaction, encounter, exchange; it is the idea of a space that, by defining *ambiences*, generates social interaction and individual free expression.

When, in 1962, Constant joined the *Groupe de l'Architecture Mobile* (*Geam*) founded by Yona Friedman in 1957, a mild controversy developed between the two, highlighting differences that were made less conflictual by a technological aesthetic that was in other ways not so far apart. Constant reproached Friedman for the lack of a critical reflection on society in the construction of the Mobile City and pointed to the new use of social space (defined in terms of ecology) as the central theme of the future city. Friedman argued for the impossibility of influencing the development of the city in a cultural and social sense, and the risk that may arise from "forcing people into a collective creativity", instead

Fig. 30
Konrad Wachsmann, a spatial reticular structural system with tetrahedral forms, 1955. (Wigley, 1998).

of allowing it to happen organically, as for instance by accentuating freedom of movement (Wigley 1998). Friedman's criticism was the criticism that many used against the numerous experiments and attempts to construct a social space between the 1960s and 70s. This criticism was essentially correct and, along with other criticism, of which there was much in this period and in periods that followed, it definitively demolished the idea of the architect and urban planner as a demiurge, and of urban planning and architecture as practices capable of determining human behaviour.

This criticism, however, overshadowed the lengthy research on the *social space* conducted by sociologists and scholars of human geography that preceded Constant and before the rigidity and naivety that followed. Constant always referred to this research in the creation of New Babylon.

In 1952, sociologist Paul-Henry Chombart de Lauwe published *Paris et l'aggomération parisienne* (Chombart de Lauwe 1952), a seminal piece of research that did not receive much attention in France, but went on to have great international resonance. The fundamental concept that opens the research conducted on Paris is that of *social space.*[67] The multiplication of spaces (economic, legal, demographic, cultural, religious...) could not be

67. "Dans quel espace se situent les populations, les structures, les groupes et les personnes sur les quels portent les recherches? Quelles sont ses limites et ses divisions? Quels sont les rapports entre les structures inscrites dans cet espace et les représentations collectives et individuelles? Nous parlons à ce sujet d'un espace social et non seulement d'un espace géographique, d'un espace économique, d'un espace démographique... », Chombart de Lauwe 1965:22.

avoided, spaces overlap and intersect forming a total social phenomenon, wrote Chombart, echoing Marcel Mauss. The relationship between them and social life can be grasped by superimposing their different representations and observing the points of overlap: "*...le dessin qu'ils forment sur le sol corresponds à la structure encore très grossière d'un espace par rapport auquel, du point de vue de la vie sociale, tous les autres vont s'ordonner. C'est un premier élément de ce que nous appelons un espace social.*" (Chombart de Lauwe 1952). Social space is not only defined by the superposition of different distributions, but it is a space in motion "*qui se deplace sur le sol dans le temps*" and which, to be studied, needs to be observed over time. This is the second element that identifies social space, to which a third is added: collective representations and their power to construct social spaces.

A place of overlap, mobile in time and central to the imagination of its inhabitants, New Babylon is put forward as the creation of this particular space.

Chombart's ideas, with their emphasis on the role of mental representations and imaginaries borrowed from Maurice Halbwachs and his *The Collective Memory*, published posthumously in 1950,[68] received much attention from architects and urban planners for the reasons I mentioned above. Modern architects and urban planners emerging from the collapse and ambiguities of the war felt they had not been able to interpret society, nor had they been able to represent myths, desires, symbols and collective imaginaries. The focus on basic needs as destroyed Europe was being reconstructed made the recovery of these dimensions even more difficult and the criticism, even within CIAM, increasingly cutting.

Chombart and his idea of *psychogeography*, mental geography, also greatly influenced the Situationists with whom Constant travelled a stretch of his intellectual journey (it was Guy Debord who suggested the name of the city to Constant).[69] The attempt to represent social space, according to Chombart, allowed the inhabitant of the Parisian agglomeration, for instance, to "become aware": *se situer* (in italics in Chombart's text) in a concrete space.[70]

Those years saw the emergence of the neighbourhood crisis, of the city project that developed in large homogeneous units, "disciplined space" (Lomi, Masé 1979: XXVII) that does not manage to represent and be the theatre of a real urban experience. The modern neighbourhood started to be judged as the "metaphorical image of the assembly line" (Tafuri 1980). The modern urban planning crisis was transmitted to the urban materials developed during

68. Spatial structures, according to Chombart, are only in part determined by material conditions and techniques, collective representations play an equally important role and this is why an ethnography of the big city is needed (see: Halbwachs 1950).

69. *New Babylon*: from the book of Revelations, to Rome as a new Babylon, to Dickens who describes London as a new Babylon.

70. The practice of drifting allows us to read and become aware of the fragmentation of space (Chombart de Lauwe 1952 :27-28).

industrial modernity: the neighbourhood seems to be the representation of the Taylorist division of labour, as well as the creation of functional separation.

It was precisely between the end of the 1950s and the mid-1960s that in Italy the attempt to "understand and construct the form of the city" (Lomi, Masé 1979: XXVII) started to produce studies on urban elements and the relationship between typology and morphology. One turns to the city of the past because it is stratified and because it is a collective work, in continuous movement: "...the city rejects monolithic proposals, absolute truths, totalising values...the city claims its right to grow, to complete itself, to continue its writing..." (Lomi, Masé 1979: XXVII).

While in Italian culture the stratified and complex city (and therefore in particular the ancient centre) is once again seen as the place concerned with the formation and evolution of social space (from Muratori to Rossi, Aymonino, Polesello...), a different line of research is that of New Babylon, centred around the same question. This second path moves away from the close analysis of the material conditions in which urban transformation takes place and looks at the construction of radical scenarios. What would happen if technological development were to free us from the necessity of work? What would happen if the city were no longer a space of work, but a space of play? How would the territory change if there were no residential areas, introducing a break between the inside and the outside and the disintegration of urban relationships? What would happen if we considered the city in terms of individual and individualised environments, and social spaces, instead of functional zones? What would happen if the process of artificializing the world reached saturation? New Babylon represents an exercise conducted as an experiment, a laboratory test for these questions.

The issues Constant proposed were informed by debates already spreading through European culture between the mid-1950s and early 1970s. New Babylon recorded its changes and innovations and also, with disarming and tragic lucidity, represented its crisis. New Babylon was therefore an exploration, in the form of a city project, of ongoing trends (mainly changes linked to technological development, the emergence of the theme of leisure) the relevance of which is documented by their presence in the debates of that time.

Play (leisure) and structuralism

Let us take for example the great theme of *loisir/leisure*: free time, time of freedom, time lost, a time of transition between one activity and another. Georges Candilis, in his 1972 text *Planning and Design for Leisure*, traced the concept's history: in 1870, the word *leisure* entered the *Littré* dictionary defined as a "state in which one is allowed to do what one wants"); Marx defined it as a space for human development (growth); in 1890, it was embodied in the eight-hour workday; in 1906 in France, leisure was the introduction of a weekly rest period; in 1936, it was the introduction of the right to paid holidays by Léon Blum's Popular Front government (which also set the minimum wage, granted trade union rights, established the 40-hour week and founded the *Sous Sécretariat d'Etat aux loisirs et aux sports*). The introduction of the 35-hour week in France in more recent years seems to have definitively marked the transition to a society no longer based on work. *The Geography of Recreation and Leisure*, also from 1972, discusses the transformation of work and leisure time (Cosgrove, Jackson 1972) and, as in *Planning and Design for Leisure*, questioned their spatial expression.

According to Candilis, the Athens Charter is totally devoid of the concept of *loisir,* and to Le Corbusier's three *établissements humains* we must add "the organised site for the *loisir* of the masses", an unprecedented need for society. The extent of this change is epochal: "The acceptance of the primordial importance of *loisir* in everyday life, its permanent and generalised presence, must revolutionise the conception of tomorrow's *habitat.*"[71]

The weight of *loisir* in contemporary civilization can be attributed to three aspects: *loisir temps, loisir activité* and *loisir état*. It is the notion of *loisir état* that "*réclame une nouvelle attitude spirituelle et sociale, une nouvelle manière de penser et de vivre...une culture nouvelle*." (Candilis 1972:9).

Johan Huizinga's *Homo Ludens*, which appeared in German in 1939 in Amsterdam (Huizinga 1997), had a great influence on Constant's work and in the Dutch debate. The author observed play as an activity that precedes cultural activity and establishes its foundations. Play is a free activity detached from ordinary life that carves out its own space and time. New Babylon is imagined as the great playground of a society free from work that expresses its creative energy in designing and continually recreating its own space.

Placing play, i.e. an activity with set rules of behaviour, at the centre of the new space almost necessarily implies an emphasis on the infrastructure of play, its architecture. The structure intended to allow free play in New Babylon is heavy, entirely artificial, a new nature that opposes and detaches itself from the ground. This "heaviness" appeared in many other representations of the future city during this time, as in the work of groups like Archigram and Archizoom, which tended to highlight the role of technology.[72] Recently these themes have reappeared fully transformed, in representations by Andrea Branzi for example, in the muffled and lighter ways that derive from the encounter/clash with ecological themes.[73]

71. Candilis 1972:140. "*Le monde serait-il entré dans la civilisation des loisirs*?" wrote Joffre Dumazedier, cited by Candilis, p.7

72. See for example Reyner Banham and the role of technology (Banham 1966).

73. This is the case of *Agronica*, in which the main elements of the *No-Stop City* can still be recognised, and in particular the large plane-support.

New Babylon is intended as an invention of large *environmental structures*, an open plane "in which the construction stages represent significant intermediate configurations" (Carini, Farina, 1979: XXXIII). While, as I will mention later, the rediscovery of Constant in the 1990s focused on his production of *environments* and his development of an urban language,[74] in the 1960s, while New Babylon was being created, the interest in his work, shared by Constant himself and the structuralist architects, centred around themes linked to the idea of *spatial possibility* and architecture as a device that allows the user's design contribution by defining a spatial framework on a territorial scale.

The architecture of the Centraal Beheer, Herman Hertzberger's well-known office building built between 1967 and 1972, is designed as a structure that houses the subsequent interventions of those who use it. It is conceived as a settlement rather than a building, defined by multi-purpose units that can accommodate different functional programmes over time. In 1990, on the eve of a major renovation of the building, Hertzberger recorded the end of the creative period that had characterised the 1970s: "The heyday of personal expressiveness in the 1970s has given way to neatness and orderliness. It seems as if the urge to make a personal statement has faded, and that people are more inclined to conform, nowadays." (Hertzberger 1991:24).

Thinking about the game of chess, according to Hertzberger, is the simplest way to approach the concept of structure: based on a few simple rules, infinite configurations can develop that evolve from the experience of the players themselves who intervene by introducing new rules that enrich the game.

Rules do not restrict the individual players' expressive possibilities, but rather constitute a system analogous to the concept of generative grammar developed by Noam Chomsky in the late 1950s.[75] In most cases, generative grammar is able to generate an infinite number of strings (finite sequences of symbols) from a finite set of rules.

74. See for example the exhibition dedicated to New Babylon curated by Mark Wigley in 1998-1999 at the Kunstmuseum in The Hague; the exhibition "Another City for Another Life: Constant's New Babylon" at the Drawing Center in New York (Nov-Dec 1999); or *Documenta XI* in Kassel (2001), which exhibited some models of New Babylon.

75. Hertzberger 1991:93, *Structure and interpretation*. In this text, Hertzberger briefly outlines the theoretical basis of architectural structuralism, referring to the concepts and positions of Claude Lévi-Strauss, Ferdinand de Saussure and Noam Chomsky, deploring the trivialisation that has occurred.

The grammar of New Babylon: supports and ambiences

The grammar of New Babylon is therefore a set of rules that structure the construction of space by its inhabitants, just as language is structured by grammatical and syntactic rules (which govern the position of words within a sentence) and the form of each (the morphology of the word that accounts for its formation, and its different meanings and roles). According to Chomsky, there is a universal grammar, addressed by the theory of generative grammar, which attributes to the innate faculty of language the ability to use its basic principles. These are timeless and general principles that, in the case of New Babylon, concern the free unfolding of practices of living, deconstruction and reconstruction, a collective game, starting with the basic elements that compose its space.

Technology plays an essential role in defining the grammar of the space of New Babylon. Among the various trends taking place in the world of prefabrication, New Babylon belongs to the line of research put forward by Nicolas John Habraken (Habraken 1972). Among the systems tested in the 1960s, the one proposed by SAR (Foundation for Architects Research, of which Habraken was director between 1965 and 1975) proposed "the distinction between a 'support' frame understood as a real artificial ground and the 'detachable' units (the other systems constituting the general building system)." Unlike other research that tends towards maximum flexibility and openness, SAR defined some aggregation rules (the rules and margins) that "make it possible for the meaningful participation" of the users in the project (Nuti 1979: XL).

In New Babylon there are no "houses" in the sense of specific residential building types, but individual living situations that adhere to the needs and desires of each person that can be constructed, with their continuous alteration and abandonment in order to move on to other, different, artificial environments.

Artistic research into the perception of space always makes use of artificial conditions: in New Babylon, the city is a place of artificiality, investigated using the means of art. Continuing his criticism of the modern movement's city, which does not offer an adequate range of spatial experiences and social relations, Constant continued his research on the perception of space and its diversity. In addition to criticism of the voids and distances of the Le Corbusian city, there was also criticism in the 1960s and beyond of the first and second generation of English New Towns: both approaches, although very different, were interpreted as spaces that disperse, where the democratic objective of ensuring the same conditions for everyone, including the degree of appropriation of space, produces situations that are judged as excessively homogeneous, repetitive and alienating.

Constant produced a series of highly differentiated environments in his many models, albeit contained within the "heavy" structure I referred to above.

Figs. 31, 32
Constant Nieuwenhuys, New Babylon, large yellow sector, 1967, metal, plexiglass, and oil paint on canvas. (Wigley, 1998).

The different types of lighting (which we can see in old photographs) help to alter the perception of them and multiply their spatial qualities. The study of light, colours, the degree of transparency or opacity of the different materials, the possibilities of juxtaposing different materials, whether reused or highly sophisticated, was perhaps Constant's most lofty and original contribution to the reflection on the city and architecture.[76] In the New Babylon models the development of a new heterogeneous urban and architectural language of reuse and recycling can be seen, which is not detached from the environment but is a substantial part of it, constructing and inventing it. The theme of the environment, dear to all Anglo-Saxon thinking in the 1950s and 1960s, was one that Constant transcended and transformed into art.

From Buckminster Fuller, who argued for the possibility of environmental control and the disappearance of the concept of the house (1965), to Reyner Banham and his *unhouse* (1965) and the text *The Architecture of the Well-Tempered Environment* (1969) and *Megastructure: Urban Futures of the Recent Past* (1976), to Cedric Price's Fun Palace started in 1961, there are many common themes (Whiteley 2002).

The Fun Palace was conceived by Price and Joan Littlewood, founder of the Theatre Workshop at the Theatre Royal in Stratford, London, as a place for creative improvisation, active participation, and collective play; the scaffolding architecture was to allow for hanging stages, while the walls and floors were to be mobile, dissolving the building into "...a facility, a responsive environment" (Whiteley 2002:212). Cedric Price's designs can be imagined as part of New Babylon. The architect, according to Price, distributes opportunities and constructs experiential spaces (Whiteley 2002:214). The theme of environmental control by the user, who can invent new, as yet unnamed, activities, and the reference to Huizinga in the need to eliminate the artificial division between leisure time and work, recur in this case too.[77]

An important part of New Babylon's image relates to its detachment from the ground, the concept of a global environment and "vertical zoning":

76. As evocative as they are, drawings and collages of New Babylon also contain formal references to works by others, for example the Smithsons, but the great impact of the rediscovery of New Babylon in that period derives rather from the suggestion made by Constant's models. My hypothesis is that many aspects of Rem Koolhaas' architectural and urban language stem from a careful observation of the New Babylon models. It is not only the use of the same materials in the models of OMA and in New Babylon; it is the choice of materials and the criteria of their juxtaposition in the built architecture that reinforce this interpretation. On the other hand, from the 1990s onwards there was a very strong revival of interest in the urban architecture themes of the 1960s: Koolhaas in his project for the new Almere centre (published in *Archis*, 11, 1999) spoke about the construction of environments, the use of techniques of assemblage, alienation, and compaction of experiences.

77. Cedric Price, *Fun Palace*, 1965 (now in *Cedric Price: Works II*, Architectural Association, London, 1984.) Banham's *Los Angeles: The Architecture of Four Ecologies* (1971) is dedicated to Cedric Price. Around the same time, Banham co-wrote with Price, Peter Hall and Paul Barker the essay "Non-Plan: An Experiment in Freedom" published in *New Society* on March 20, 1969.

Fig. 33
Constant Nieuwenhuys, New Babylon, detail of a sector. Model made of metal, plexiglass, and wood. (Wigley, 1998)

some of the images by the Russian Khidekel are reminiscent not only of New Babylon, but in general of the explorations conducted by Friedman and others. The concept of the aero-city (Khan-Magomedov 1987:281), developed in some 1920s projects, is the result of spatial layering: underneath the buildings lie nature, canals, and the incisions of road tunnels that sometimes re-emerge.

The space of Toulouse-Le Mirail

Toulouse-Le Mirail, in Toulouse, by Candilis, Josic and Woods, is a particular type of city organised by a linear relational space detached from the ground. Its design rediscovers the urban element of the street, a "universal" mental pattern banned by Le Corbusier, and the life that takes place there. "*Dalle*, street deck" or "street in the air" (the term used by the Smithsons), the central linear space of Toulouse-Le Mirail, four metres above the ground, organises the services of the new city. One of the last meetings of Team X took place in Toulouse-Le Mirail in 1971.[78]

The new city grew out of the debate on the *Métropoles d'équilibre*, which at the end of the 1950s addressed the problem of the enormous and unbalanced attractiveness of Paris to the detriment of the rest of the country. The need to decentralise activities and services led to a new national policy and the selection of a few large cities as possible rebalancing centres, to be reinforced through large-scale investments and projects. In Toulouse, a city experiencing strong demographic growth due to a rural exodus and the arrival of repatriated populations from North Africa, Le Mirail, a vast agricultural area with large estates, sparsely inhabited and with important heritage and landscape elements, was chosen for the construction of a new city of 100,000 inhabitants. It was to house metropolitan facilities and create a new urban centrality of the same weight as the existing centre.

The proposition by Georges Candilis, Alex Josic and Shadrach Woods, winners of the competition carried out in several stages in 1961, enhanced the existing parks and lakes (Gruet, Papillault 2008), developed a dense habitat and accounted for Candilis' positions with respect to the dramatic housing crisis of the post-war period. In his book *Bâtir la vie*, Candilis mentions his disagreement with Abbé Pierre who, in that period's climate of urgency, defended the cause of housing for the poorest. According to Candilis, Abbé Pierre would have created poor housing and a "poor man's ghetto", convinced as he was that not creating poor housing for the poor would simply mean

78. This meeting (9-12 April 1971) took place at a critical moment in the construction of Le Mirail. After ten years and the construction of housing for around 20,000 inhabitants, Candilis resigned and left the coordination of the project, following the replacement of Mayor Bazerque and his administration, to a conservative team that blocked its implementation. The issues addressed at the meeting concerned the contradiction of operating in a centralised welfare state, the limits of standardised building production systems and the difficulty of repetition in architecture and the city. See Max Risselada: http://www.team10online.org/team10/meetings/1971-toulouse.htm

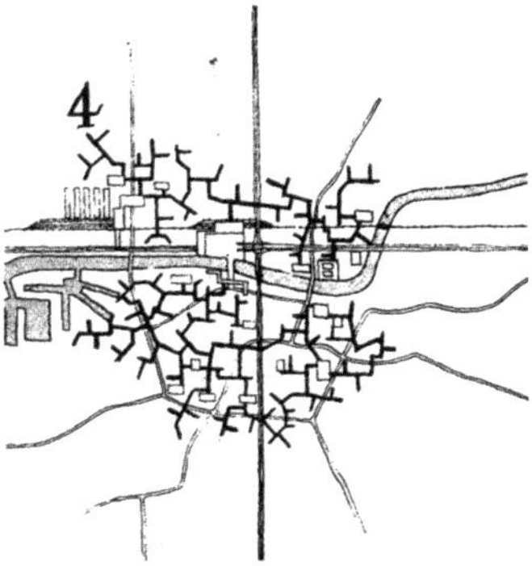

Fig. 37
Alison and Peter Smithson, The City, diagram, 1952. (Smithson Family Archive).

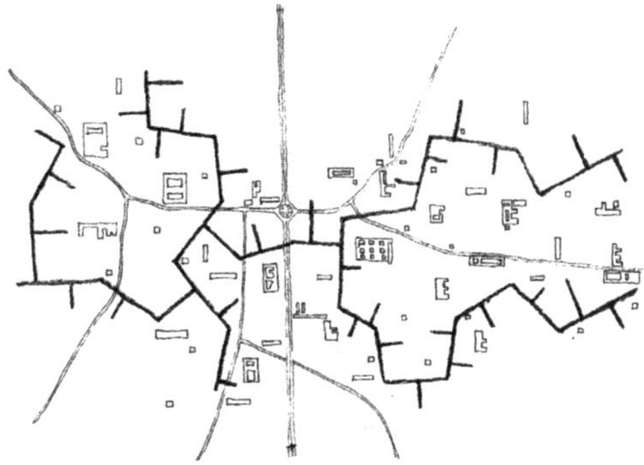

Fig. 38
Alison and Peter Smithson's diagram of the Golden Lane as the Basis for the City Fabric, 1953. (Smithson Family Archive).

not creating housing for the weakest classes. The deep divergence between Candilis and Abbé Pierre concerned temporary housing: "*l'alibi, le camouflage du médiocre permanent*", said Candilis (Candilis 1977). Hence the commitments of Candilis, Josic and Woods to participate in the competitions launched by the French government under the name of Opération Million in 1955, following the appeal launched by Abbé Pierre one year earlier, and the creation of buildings and neighbourhoods like the HLM Emmaüs of the Cité Pierre-Montillet in Blanc Mesnil (1956) in collaboration with Jean Prouvé who designed the façade panels or *immeuble type* in Gagny. These experiences saw Candilis, Josic and Woods develop their idea of standardisation, replacing the concept of spatial composition with that of the organisation of space "*d'une cellule autour d'une gaine centrale technique*",[79] an idea of assemblable, flexible units around the fixed infrastructural element.

From 1958 onwards, the French state launched a vast urban concentration operation by financing the Z.U.P. (*Zones à urbaniser en priorité*), genuine "state procedures" (Gruet, Papillault 2008:27) that followed and attempted to improve on the experience of the Grands Ensembles by moving away from the monofunctionality of the neighbourhoods and enriching them with services to be built alongside housing. This was the context in which the Toulouse competition was carried out, and Candilis, Josic and Woods developed an urban structure idea and a new language for it.[80] *Construction continuity, street,*

79. Alexis Josic in a 1993 interview reproduced in Gruet, Papillault 2008:26.
80. Alexis Josic in the 1993 interview reproduced in Gruet, Papillault 2008:27.

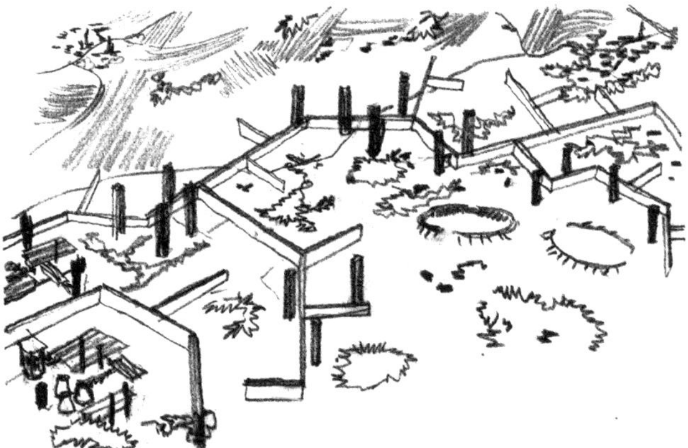

Fig. 39
Alison and Peter Smithson, study for the Golden Lane Deck Complex multiplication, 1952. (Smithson Family Archive).

structures, and *system* are the terms Josic used to signal the new approach,[81] opposed to the formalist simplification of towers and bars. The keywords were *articulate*, *bind*, and *unite*: the street of the ancient city, with its trade and life, the conceptual reservoir.

As in New Babylon, the reference to the Smithsons' "First Cluster City" diagram (1952) is evident; it introduces a specific aggregation model, requiring integration of the parts and their integration with what was already there. It is also interesting to note that, more or less in the same period, Le Corbusier (with whom Candilis and Woods had worked overseeing the Unité d'Habitation site in Marseille) had begun the Chandigarh project, with the review of the street and the proposal of the seven 'V's. Initially invited by Le Corbusier to be his representative on site, Candilis declined the offer, despite his great admiration for the Swiss architect (Gruet, Papillault 2008:37).

Criticism of the *mass plan*, the centrality of human ecology and the interplay of social relations, the idea of a "whole" space and "universal society" (Candilis, Josic, Woods 1962)—these were the themes the group considered in response to the Le Mirail competition for the creation not of a neighbourhood, but of a second and new centre of Toulouse, complementary to the existing one, on the other side of the Garonne.

81. Alexis Josic in the 1993 interview reproduced in Gruet, Papillault 2008:34.

Fig. 40
Candilis, Josic and Woods, Toulouse le Mirail, urban context plan, 1961. (Candilis, Josic, Woods, 1975).

Alex Josic referred to the starting point of the routes: "We were systematically looking for a Y-triangulation at 60° for better visibility than right-angle intersections. (...) The whole image of the project was made up of bifurcations and ramifications that perfectly complemented the site."[82] In the first round of the competition, the project aroused great interest: it was new, different, special. In the second round, the questions became more specific, the project stood out for its economy of streets, even though the "architecte conseil", Dufau, questioned the centrality of the *dalle* and its status: is it part of the road network or does it belong to the buildings? (Gruet, Papillault 2008:61) The Y-shape superimposed on the centre of Toulouse relied on the large number of triangular squares in the old city centre, revealing a supposed Toulouse root of the project. But, reported a collaborator of the Candilis studio, "*C'était une fumisterie parce que il n'y a rien de toulousain dans le Mirail.*"[83]

The choice of Candilis, Josic and Woods' project was strongly supported by Mayor Louis Bazerque and the Ministry of Reconstruction; the presentation of the project, in a video containing Candilis' narrative (from the reading of the territorial morphology to the project description) accompanied by Josic's drawing, in parallel, was a resounding success.[84] Candilis spoke about road networks, green spaces and water using terms such as *permanent framework*.[85] Josic's diagrams were enthralling for their distance from the traditional language of architecture and urban planning. In the video, parts of the drawing are erased to show that the space should not be taken up with parking areas so as to restore the centrality and dignity to the new city's squares and plazas.[86] The subtraction of the areas needed for parking spaces is the subtraction of humans and the territory from the "*esclavage de la voiture*" that was relegated to the interior space of the *dalle*.

The term *ambiances* recurs in Candilis' discourse, as in Constant's descriptions, along with the possibility of choosing density, full of urban activity, or the quiet atmosphere of the natural environment also mediated

82. "*On cherchait systématiquement une trangulation à 60° pour une meilleure visibilité quel es croisements à angle droit. (...) Toute l'image de l'ensemble du projet était constituée de bifurcationis et ramifications qui s'intégraient parfaitement au site*", Alexis Josic in a 1993 interview reproduced in Gruet, Papillault 2008:55.

83. Jean-Marie Lefèvre, Agence Candilis, Josic, Woods in a 1993 interview reproduced in Gruet, Papillault 2008:82

84. In 1956 Henri-Georges Cluzot produced the film *Le Mystère Picasso*, in which Picasso created twenty drawings and paintings. Using the same procedure, drawing or painting on glass, Josic asked the science filmmaker Mario Marret, who had followed the project, to create a film.

85. See the video: Toulouse le Mirail 1962 réalisation : Mario Marret construction de la ville nouvelle Toulouse le Mirail, commentée par l'architecte urbaniste Georges Candilis - Video Dailymotion (accessed July 2023).

86. The heuristic value of cancellation and subtraction were at that time the artistic subject matter of the emerging visual poetry and conceptual art movements; in 1953 Robert Rauschenberg framed a blank sheet of paper entitled "Erased de Kooning Drawing." In 1964 Emilio Isgrò made his first deletions in encyclopaedias.

Fig. 41
Candilis, Josic, and Wood, Toulouse le Mirail, scheme of La rue, 1961 (Candilis, Josic, Woods 1975).

Fig. 42
Candilis, Josic and Woods, Toulouse le Mirail, the “dalle”. Photo Paola Viganò.

by a transition to the low-density fabrics of patio houses between the city and the country. Situation, atmosphere, context—the term *ambiance* could easily be superimposed on them, but Georges Matoré's vocabulary of spatiality proposes a deeper reading: accepting Minkowski's reflections, ambiance "*indique que des rapports affectifs sont noués avec le milieu, des relations à la nature surtout tactile...*" (Matoré 1976:128). Matoré quotes Minkowski who recalled how ambiance is not "*chose faite*": "*elle se fait au contact de l'homme comme celui-ci se fait au sien. L'ambiance, primitivement, est un océan mouvant. Elle est le devenir.*"[87]

The urban structure, the result of the accumulation of ideas, sketches and diagrams, is an "unexpected" structure. While it was primarily Alex Josic who oversaw the Le Mirail competition, the idea of a linear structure was explored, at the same time, by Shadrach Woods who worked, in parallel, on the Caen competition (1961) and who in 1960 published the famous article "Stem" (Woods 1960). In opposition to the *plan masse*, the project uses an evolutionary device which adapts to the growth of part of the city and organises the *prolongements* and the serving elements of the dwelling (taking up Louis Kahn's distinction between served and servant). In his book *Bâtir la vie*, Candilis recalled that the *rue-centre-séjour collectif* was the project's starting point, a linear structure along which services, activities and residences are located, a car-free space, a sort of valley, a *tracé*, an element of permanence and guarantor of the possibility of continuous adaptation of what it organises. The hypothesis of continuity was strongly supported by the group: linear continuity crosses the buildings and is linked to vertical circulation (which will then, for cost reasons, be reduced and fragmented by the reduction of lifts). The proximity between the idea of linear space as a device of social as well as spatial organisation, and the widespread use of the axis/armature as distinctive terms of the vocabulary of spatiality compiled in the same years by Georges Matoré is striking. Here, the axis is "*l'armature solide et stable qui permet à une portion contigue de l'espace de s'articuler, d'osciller, d'opérer une rotation, etc.*" and "*L'axe... devient un tracé vital, un concentré d'existence*", a "*parcours vécu*" (Matoré 1976:104). "*De tels trajets fortements magnetisés*" are found in mythical thinking and relate our body to the axis of the cosmos. The axis/*rue* is also the central urban element in Chombart de Lauwe's sociological analysis: "*On pourrait dire que la vie de la rue donne la mesure de la vie du quartier*" (Chombart de Lauwe 1952:67). Commerce and equipment are structural components of it. In Le Mirail, more than eighty commercial cells, in addition to social services, drove the social life of the suspended space. The project used social relationships to design the space; despite this, the combinatorial play and extreme rationalisation of the elements mark an unbridgeable gap between the spatial variety of cities of the past and the possibilities for variation in the new city.

87. Matoré 1976:128 cited Eugène Minkowski, 1934 (III), *L'Evolution psychologique*.

Fig. 43
Candilis, Josic and Woods, Toulouse le Mirail, the "kindergarten". Photo Paola Viganò.

Fig. 44
Candilis, Josic and Woods, Toulouse le Mirail, social centre, 1960. (Candilis, Josic, Woods, 1975).

Structure is certainly the other important term in the design discourse and grammar of Le Mirail. It is a multi-dimensional figure, which belongs to a complex geometry involved in creating relationships between heterogeneous, but integral elements that can change while the structure continues to exist (Matoré 1976:144). The structure is understood as the expression of a vision of reality based on relationships and not on essences, of interdependence, interaction, a return to the continuous, while being aware of the existence of discontinuities. "Witnesses and authors" of a process of reconstruction that paradoxically relies on discontinuity in an attempt to rediscover "*le sens de la totalité et l'unicité individuelle*" (Matoré 1976:151), we are downstream of the criticism that from the end of the nineteenth century attacked the concept of the "continuous" and Bergson's philosophy with which it had reached its apex; and we are also downstream of the affirmation of the break as a procedure that characterises modernity. The "whole space" is the biopolitical space sought by Candilis, Josic and Woods.

Indeed, Team X carefully reconsidered the idea of a break with the existing context (Avermaete 2004:248). Starting with the different positions emerging in the CIAM in Otterlo (1959), Candilis, Josic and Woods stood out for their original convictions that considered the material forms of the past and the practices of the inhabitants in the space as permanent elements that need to be taken up, re-read, renewed, and repaired (Woods 1975:107). The project relates to structures underlying the material articulation and urban spatial practices. The element that accommodates them and makes them possible is the street/*tracé*. The concept of stem described by Shadrach Woods fosters the slightly earlier reflections of Gutkind (*The expanding environment*, 1953), an important social geographer in contact with Team X (Avermaete 2004:255).

The transition to the construction of the new Toulouse-Le Mirail city is complex: from the procedures of land expropriation for public utility, the lack of state support (probably related to the presence, during the construction of Le Mirail, of the Minister of Reconstruction, a political opponent of Mayor Bazerque and a Toulousian), to the complexity of managing the imagined spaces (the *dalle*, the *coursives* with public walkways, the overlap between private car parks and public *dalle*). The beginning of the construction of 3,000 social housing units (HLM) coloured the image of the new project with "*misérabilisme*" (Candilis 1977).[88] The cell of the large collective buildings of Le Mirail was developed with its "fixed", "variable" and "mobile" elements (Marfaing 2009:153), a

88. The episode was experienced as a defeat by both Candilis and Bazerque (Marfaing 2009:146). The construction of the Bellefontaine portion, the only one entirely handled by Candilis, Josic and Woods, was completed in 1972, after repeated attempts to stick to the costs and regulations governing social housing. It was only after the third tender and numerous sacrifices (reduction of surfaces, ground floor *pilotis*, mobile and glazed parts...) that the building site could start operating (Marfaing 2009:153-160).

50-centimetre difference in height between the sleeping and living areas, and a double living loggia. Unlike the urban space, the housing units of Bellefontaine, the first part of the project to be created, have always been highly appreciated (Gruet, Papillault 2008:75). The housing cells translate the full experience of Candilis, Josic and Woods, which they fine-tuned in the projects they did in North Africa and in the Opération Million. The characteristics of their work are traverse housing units, generous outdoor spaces, half levels that transform the interior spatiality, and flexible walls. The difference in height within the housing unit was not only intended to separate the sleeping area from the living area, it was the creation of an intermediate space, a threshold that could be used in different ways by both sides.

Interviews with the first inhabitants described the experience of pioneers learning to use a non-traditional space (Gruet, Papillault 2008:146) devised not so much to create communities, but to allow individuals the greatest freedom in their quest for collectivity in a complete environment (Candilis, Josic, Woods 1975). The large structure of the suspended street represents its conceptual centre, and its evolution was to be ensured by the inhabitants themselves. The *dalle* was initially used by families who would meet along its route in the evenings. The population was in essence made up of civil servants, teachers, engineers, etc. who would come down from their apartments and engage with their neighbours, as well as children who would find a space free of cars and who could move around the city unaccompanied.

The idea of continuity is embodied in the arborescent pattern of the Le Mirail diagrams, a set of open spaces such as the *dalle*, or covered, the *coursives* that cross buildings on all floors and attempt to restore the continuity of a living space. Shadrach Woods described them as a flexible, open and generating system (Woods 1962).

What is striking, when going over the rich bibliography and filmography of Toulouse-Le Mirail, is the contrasting positions, whether of inhabitants or bureaucrats, officials, politicians or professional experts, on space. Le Mirail is at the same time a flexible space and so rigid that only demolition could have allowed it to evolve; a space rich in landscapes, a lake, large trees, greenery, and at the same time hard, mineral, separated from nature, a single reinforced concrete floor; a meeting place, a social space of appropriation and isolation, and at the same time detachment, a social desert; a space designed to give freedom and autonomy to children and a place of risk for everyone. With the passing of the decades, the positions became more polarized, the population changed and became more and more fragile and the difficulties of daily life in Le Mirail increased dramatically, until the beginning of 2001 when the Grand Projet de Ville procedure (again at national level) started a demolition campaign. At the same time, the explosion of an ammonium nitrate silo belonging to the AZF industry, located in one of the areas set aside for industrial activities in Toulouse-Le Mirail and which claimed some thirty lives, once again placed the spotlight on Le Mirail's economic and moral misery. The demolition campaign was a new shock for the inhabitants, many of whom continued to emphasise the great quality of the housing, arguing, moreover, that "*Ce n'est pas comme cela que l'on règle le problème de la discrimination sociale*" (Gruet, Papillault 2008:368). The *dalle*, where demolition had begun, a social space par excellence, is missed as a convivial place, which allowed people to get to school without having to use a car.

In 1992, Candilis was invited by a local television station to go to Le Mirail. Despite knowing full well the tension this would generate, he walked through its spaces, entered its flats, and had conversations with people. Once again, direct attacks were followed by appreciation for the neighbourhood and its apartments.[89] Candilis reflected on this return to Le Mirail in an interview the following year in which he acknowledged Peter Smithson's role as the theorist of Team X, and defined Josic (who was disappointed by the Le Mirail affair and abandoned it long before Candilis) as an artist in an atrocious world that left them no right to exist (Gruet, Papillault 2008). The announced demolition of the commercial *dalle* with no more customers brought his reflection back to a level of political and critical realism: those who can pay avoid contact with the other; the other does not spend enough to bring a shopping centre to life.

A philosophy of the social space

In the 1960s, the crisis of the modern movement's city project, reconstruction, the Grands Ensembles, and the first post-war New Towns overlapped with a much broader crisis affecting the whole of Western culture, which dragged on into the following decade. Constant interrupted the long construction of New Babylon models and at the start of the 1970s produced a series of paintings in which the conflict exploded in its space. The space of play seems to be ruined in unplanned revolts, or perhaps what is represented in Constant's paintings is just the extreme play of an affluent and bored society. The titles of the three paintings are emblematic: *Entrance to the Labyrinth* (1972), *The Revolt* (1972) and *Terrain vague III* (1973). Those words anticipate the themes that, after the ideological discouragement, the disappointments of many and the closure of architecture in a limited ivory tower, would see architecture and urbanism, slowly and cautiously, address the city and its space as they underwent profound and epochal transformation.

Between the early 1960s and the mid-1970s—and during this period the inertia and time necessary to actually complete a city project must be

89. Vent Sud - 27.11.1992 - 06:13 – vidéo. https://www.ina.fr/ina-eclaire-actu/video/rbc03004501/l-architecte-candilis-retrouve-le-mirail

Fig. 45
Constant Nieuwenhuys, Labyrinth Entrance, 1972, oil on canvas (Wigley, 1998).

Fig. 46
Constant Nieuwenhuys, The Revolt, 1972, oil on canvas (Wigley, 1998).

Fig. 47
Constant Nieuwenhuys, Terrain Vague [iii], 1973, oil on canvas (Wigley, 1998).

considered—Toulouse-Le Mirail (1961), Cumbernauld (designated as a New Town in 1955) and Milton Keynes (designated as a New Town in 1967) were built. Also built at this time was the Metastadt system (1969), a three-dimensional steel grid from which flexible spaces could be hung (Bergdoll, Christensen 2008), and Les Marelles in Boussy-Saint-Antoine, an example of the Réalisations EXpérimentales (REX) of the French Construction Plan (1971-1975). The latter consisted of open structures whose flexibility was due to the "Meccano" type procedure that gave inhabitants the possibility of building a customised flat.[90]

Many other new settlements introduced elements that were highly critical not only of the city of the modern movement, but of modern society as a whole, and this legitimised questions about the radical nature of this criticism: did the spatial concept proposed by structuralism contain the idea of a social and economic alternative to bourgeois society? Or did it propose cautious reformism similar to what we find in the stones of the nineteenth-century city or the city of the 1920s advocated by CIAM? From a biopolitical viewpoint, the space challenged the disciplinary character of modern space in definitive ways, opening up play as a social and productive activity (an alternative production of space), enabling free individual expression and the construction of relational spaces.

The enabling space, or infrastructure space, acts on many levels. It increases our capacities for movement and appropriation by soliciting and influencing our social behaviour, thanks to its flexibility, modularity, and allowing inhabitants to participate in its construction. It is an expression of a "philosophy of enabling" (Royston Landau, AA) rooted in Benthamian utilitarianism and developed by Cedric Price in his proposal for the Villette Park competition in 1982.[91] But the biopolitical space is also the site of a social experiment: the behaviour of the inhabitants is observed. The objectives of the report "Les Marelles. Habitat adaptable : les premiers acquéreurs" were to observe, following an experimental method, "le comportement des futurs usagers et le processus de commercialisation qui devait comporter une assistance architecturale et psycho-sociologique aux futurs acquéreurs des logements, d'analyser d'autre part leurs réactions en fonction de leur situation familiale, socio-professionnelle et financière, dans cette situation de participation à la conception de leur logement"[92].

90. Les Marelles was a project with 116 housing units conceived by architects Georges Maurios and Bernard Kohn. See: Christophe Perrocheau, edited by, 2012, *«Rendre possible». Du Plan construction au Puca : 40 ans de réalisations expérimentales*, Ministère de l'Écologie, du Développement durable et de l'Énergie Ministère de l'Égalité des Territoires et du Logement Direction générale de l'aménagement, du logement et de la nature Plan urbanisme construction architecture.

91. I mentioned it in: *I territori dell'urbanistica*...cit.

92. Michel Herrou, Georges Maurios, Claude Beauvir, Pierre Feral, Jean-Luc Le Roy, Brigitte Paszt, 1975, "Les Marelles. Habitat adaptable : les premiers acquéreurs", UPN – Université Paris Nanterre.

Fig. 48
Pierre Buraglio, Chassis, 1974-1975, wood, paint, nylon thread. (Arnal and others, 1998).

If we analyse Toulouse-Le Mirail as a partially created New Babylon, observing the projects and transformations that have altered it in recent decades, and the distance between those projects and what was actually realised, then we will find that it is necessary to address the multiplicity of layers that compose the urban and architectural discourse. It is not a question of an ideological reading of the project, but of pointing out the need for the joint presence of different levels—to look at both, for instance, Aldo Rossi,[93] who on several occasions reiterated the naivety of considering the boulevard as being "of the right" and the working-class neighbourhood being "of the left"; and Manfredo Tafuri, who recognised, in the impossible separation between ideology and architecture, the limit of architectural discourse (Tafuri 1980b).

Autonomy and limitation of the field seem to me to be indispensable elements for dealing with the space of the structuralist city in its biopolitical dimension. Like Tapiola, Toulouse-Le Mirail is both an everyday space and a mythical space, an ideological space (*No barracks for our kids*; *Sous le pavé, la plage*) and a space that has contained and can contain different and non-converging ideologies.

As always, time, a fundamental dimension in the construction of the city and architecture, shook up the flat schematism of oppositions and allows

93. Aldo Rossi, in the highly politicised debates of the 1970s, was sufficiently detached that he could insist on the urban project being autonomous from the specific political and ideological conditions in which it was implemented. See for example the *Notebooks* produced for the creation of the detailed plan of the historic centre of Pesaro by the architecture group in the mid-1970s.

unexpected situations to arise, each of which forms its own space, unforeseen and yet contained in the previous space.[94]

Attention to relationships between the environment and behaviour, and the attempt to make mental patterns adhere to concrete spaces (almost without cultural and epochal mediation) as stable and universal values, contain a biopolitical reflection that is still little analysed because quickly expelled. In Toulouse-Le Mirail and New Babylon, unlike Le Corbusier's Ville Radieuse (the reformism that prepares the revolution), it is revolt that emerges, the suspension of time as Furio Jesi wrote, preparation for the day after tomorrow and not for tomorrow, perhaps because tomorrow cannot be altered, the "exasperation of the bourgeoisie" (Jesi 2000:100). It is the losing revolt that stems from the enormous expectations launched at the future[95] and that the emphasis on infrastructure (on the structure collectively built to benefit individuals and their social relations) represents; the idea of an internal logic, of an underlying formal structure that should have withstood the impact of the irruption of diversity, of individual differences. Perhaps forgetting that structure, as catastrophe theorist René Thom wrote, is not a given *a priori*, but directly derives from the conflict between two or more forces that generate and maintain it precisely through conflict.

94. For example, a revolution such as the Lutheran one can take place in a Gothic church built within the precise ideology and ritual construction of the Catholic cult, and this does not mean the abandonment of that architectural space, but rather a rearrangement of the relative positions of those who practise it. The minister does not take the central position but instead places himself at the central edge of the nave with the faithful arranged around him; the entire group is no longer inserted in the main central perspective and its east-west orientation. The hierarchical idea has disappeared: the step on which the minister stands does not serve to separate him from the faithful but only to make him more visible.

95. The crisis of that period was also a crisis of urbanism, a kind of breakdown that was all the more devastating due to the perhaps excessive role it played at the time. "The position of the urban planner in the contemporary cultural framework, a framework that allows for intervention in the not only physical, but also social and economic structure of the environment, and therefore attributes a sphere of responsibility to the planner to an extent never before experienced, evidently requires the support of a general theory, understood in the deepest sense of the term, and therefore referring to certain "first principles" that necessarily go well beyond the scientific domain of the discipline." Scimemi 1968.

The last of the three spaces takes us to the threshold and well beyond the crisis of modern space, to the rediscovery of the existing city, a conceptual reservoir, a rapprochement mediated by the concepts that inspire it but do not directly affect it. The three spaces, in addition to possessing their own well-defined characteristics, propose, as we have seen, different interpretations of the relationship between space, life and power: in transparent ways in theoretical experiences, such as New Babylon, an extreme effort of the imagination, and in more ambiguous and contradictory ways in the projects that were accomplished, such as Le Mirail. Different ideas of freedom and of living together, three different aesthetics. Together, the three spaces highlight the changing themes, words and metaphors relating to space and life and their complex relationship with *weltanschauung*, the air of time, visions of the world. From the prevalence of defined spatial metaphors it is possible to give rise to a "contemporary space" (Matoré 1976) and at the same time grasp the inertia of these metaphors, their limited number and their repetitiveness and inadequacy.

The three spaces contain paths that are only partially interrupted, and this was one of the reasons that prompted me to retrace them, allowing a biopolitical reading to emerge at times that would not obscure the others, but one that we should not lose sight of. I think it has become clear how much the proposed projects' themes and the conceptual metaphors used continue to return as unresolved problems, as aspirations that persist, and as images that motivate our actions—because our relationship with space is marked by great continuities that concern our being in space, our position, or because of an inertia that touches our ideas about the relationship between space and life. The projects I will introduce in the third part stem from a long examination of the themes raised by the three spaces.

Functional space, space nature and social space are then primarily a collective capital of which it is interesting to understand the distribution and qualities, whether explicit or latent. This is what justifies their revisitation, reuse and reconceptualisation, not only by studying their legacies (in many cases now considered part of our architectural, urban and cultural heritage), but by continuing to question the permanence of some of the ideas that accompanied them. Spatial capital is added to other forms of capital (social, environmental, cultural...).

Functional space, space nature and social space are projects that stem from a fundamental conviction: space enables and defines living conditions and is open to (or denies) emancipation possibilities. It is an essential instrument of redistribution: opportunity, justice, horizontality.

This conviction has marked the entire history of modern architecture and urbanism and cannot be evaded, above all at a time of transition and adaptation, such as the present day. Space is a support.

Finally, functional space, space nature and social space go beyond mere support or an enabling extension; they are agent spaces, and not passive, capable of acting and reacting, beyond the discussions affecting them, about life, bodies, emotions and relationships, including those of power. Space is made up of subjects, it is not only resource, capital, support, object: space is agent.

This epistemological and ontological shift enables us to treat the ecological and socio-economic transition for what it is: "the complex metamorphosis from one type of society to another" (Morin 2020), which I will address in the second part of this book, the theme of biopolitical space, the hypothesis of an affirmative biopolitics and a new project.

2. SPACE AND THE BIOPOLITICAL PROJECT

2.1 Urbanism and the new Biopolitical Project
2.2 Biopolitical Spaces: Capital, Support, Agent
2.3 Three Fields

Fig. 49
Studio05-10 Secchi-Viganò,Theaterplein,
Antwerp. Photo Tom Cortoos, 2014.

2.1 URBANISM AND THE NEW BIOPOLITICAL PROJECT

Introduction

The purpose of this second part is to link the first and third parts of the book. In a functional diagram it would be represented as a connecting element and, at the same time, a filtering surface that opens up certain paths of communication and exchange between the two parts, beginning and end. At the start of this book I spoke about concrete spaces—the concepts that they interpreted or proposed through their creation, the features of their landscapes and their grammar, their atmospheres and environments, the antecedents that prepared them, their influence and fortune, longevity or failure. And I highlighted the main biopolitical aspects of such spaces. The second part focuses on the potential role of space in shaping an epochal transition, as capital and collective patrimony, a more or less welcoming and open support capable of acting, adapting, and reworking the relations of individuals and populations with and in this same space.

I do not intend here to examine the relationship between architecture and power during the long construction of the city, but to instead start with three explicitly biopolitical variations of the role of space and then place them within an "affirmative biopolitics" (Esposito 2004) of the urban and territorial project.

In the first part I attempted to read the symbolic, ideological, value-based and utopian content that some space projects contain, without delimiting it in unambiguous ways. The physical space of the city can be reinterpreted outside and beyond the ideology that generated it or the hopes that gave rise to it. It is malleable and rigid, heavy and light, both support and capital, binding and adherent, and open to our movements. A number of themes emerged from this reading which require further in-depth study and contextualisation in an era of profound change, the present-day. Thinking about space is a bit like thinking about ourselves, and in this book space is not a metaphorical entity.

The second part of this book reflects on the re-emergence of proximity between the project of space (including its political and governmental weight) and life, on the consequences of their renewed closeness, and on possible openings and aporias. In two sections (Biopolitical Spaces: Capital Space, Support, Agent and Three Fields) I aim to address the hypothesis of ecological and social transition as a new biopolitical project. While the ordering of the built environment, the spatial organisation of resources and their exploitation, together with the medicalisation of space, were the main fields of Foucauldian biopolitics and the modern city (Foucault 2004), we now need to redefine the project's engagement in the broader terms of living together, extended to human and non-human agents. However, we are perhaps no longer in a position to do this as it has been weakened over time and due to our persistent marginality. The ecological transition will in any case and inevitably be a new biopolitical project.

Space and life: Evidence of a return

In recent decades the frequency of terms and metaphors referring to life has greatly increased, to the point that it seems impossible to avoid their presence and not question the meaning of this return after the biological and organic metaphors of the past. Beyond ecological and health crises (our new awareness of planetary limits), this semantic thickening highlights the complex relationship between life, space and power; and its fundamental and inevitable presence in contemporary thinking, not only in modern urban planning and architecture.

It is therefore, and in the first place, a question of observing the recurrence of words, expressions and locutions that connect the city project to the question of life. Language,[1] the expression of the spirit of the time, reveals, through the homogeneity of images, buildings and figures, the prevalence of concerns, impositions, prejudices and expectations (Klemperer 1996:34). If this language speaks in our place, paraphrasing Klemperer who borrowed Schiller's couplet,[2] then today we never stop talking about space, life and power.

The return of the theme of life in the reflection and design of the city and the territory does not follow the old biological organicism that marked the modern adventure, but deals with the ecological, socio-demographic and economic transition; the quality of life, the reduction of the risks to which a population is subjected and its safety; urban metabolism (a metaphor that is sometimes misunderstood and taken literally) which speaks of energy and material flows; adaptation to climate change and the integration of new lifestyles as a metamorphosis of space; the start and end of life cycles (Viganò 2012a);3

1. Victor Klemperer, LTI-Notizbuch eines Philologen. This text, written during the Second World War and considered a "réfléxion pionnière sur le langage totalitaire" (Sonia Combe, Préface à l'édition francaise, Klemperer 1996:13), contains a ruthless analysis of language and forces us to consider its structuring capacity of thought: "Le nazisme s'insinua dans la chair et le sang du grand nombre à travers des expressions isolées, des tournures, des forms syntaxiques qui s'imposaient à des millions d'exemplaires...", Klemperer 1996:40.

2. La "langue cultivée qui poétise et pense à ta place", Klemperer 1996:40.

3. Observing the city and the territory as a repository of life cycles, an alternation of rhythms, is the starting point for a theory of the city as a renewable resource. The strategy of reusing, reconditioning and recycling the city, by parts, episodes or as a whole lies at the heart of this theory. The hypothesis is completed by the conviction that the process of growth, decline, and the start of new life cycles can be understood by reading the space, anchored in different situations.

and biophilic urban design (Wilson 1984; Kr má ová, 2009), including biotic relationships in the city, nature-based solutions and co-evolution (Alberti 2016). All these and many other topics consider the confusing use of organic and biological metaphors and analogies from the past, as well as space and real life.

Architecture and urbanism are certainly concerned with life, but beyond the profound conviction of the need to practice and discuss the themes mentioned above, the frequency with which it is mentioned in contemporary discourses and projects cannot help but question it. Interest in these themes has in fact varied greatly over time: before the emergence of this new wave of concern for life, architecture and the design of the city focused on language issues that marked, for example, the postmodern season, from Venturi's gentle manifesto in Complexity and Contradiction in Architecture (Venturi 1966), to the structuralist and Freudian reading of invisible walls in Chicago in Mario Gandelsonas's The Urban Text (Gandelsonas 1991), along with the fortune of other constructive metaphors of thought such as that of the city as text, from Aldo Rossi to André Corboz. It is, therefore, a novelty, albeit not absolute, anticipated by the blossoming of concern for life at a planetary scale, marked by the Limits to Growth study and the oil crisis in the early 1970s, and by more recent feminist and decolonial literature. The importance and consequences of this return are only now, I believe, beginning to be felt.

2.2 BIOPOLITICAL SPACES: CAPITAL, SUPPORT, AGENT

In his last essay dedicated to the tradition of European urban planning, Bernardo Secchi focuses on the Foucauldian hypothesis of biopolitics and places the entire course of modern urbanism within it. Also taking up Andrea Cavalletti's work on the biopolitical city (Cavalletti 2005), Secchi recognises the European tradition as being part of "a broader biopolitical action" and committed, in terms of the construction and transformation of inhabited space, to keeping alive, protecting, educating, and emancipating a population. Modern urbanism, the regulatory space of society (Rabinow 1989:12), is defined in relation to this commitment.

The twentieth-century city is the imagined space for a new society, for a "new man", and the three narratives that structure its evolution (Secchi 2005) also identify its different fears and anxieties. The third narrative, which focuses on the physical dimensions of well-being, the joint work of doctors, architects, biologists and the new individual and collective dimension of space, is the one that raises the deepest questions today. By raising the complex relationship between life, space and power, which is always opaque and full of contradictions, I aim to determine its possible openings, starting with the relating and mediating role of a capital, supporting, and agent space.

In 2009, Edward Soja published a seminal article in the first issue of the journal Justice spatiale/Spatial Justice dedicated to spatial justice (Soja 2009). That same year, Secchi and I developed a vision of Greater Paris as a "ville poreuse" and discussed this with Soja himself. At this time, too, La città dei ricchi e la città dei poveri was being written (Secchi 2013).

Soja spoke about "intentional spatialisation which aims to bring to the interpretive surface the fundamental spatiality of human life which embraces everything but is frequently buried or placed in the background."[4] This intrinsic spatiality requires critical imagination that includes space in any attempt to understand the social condition, because "what is described as social is always at the same time intrinsically spatial" (Soja 1989:8). Here Soja acknowledges his debt to two figures, Henri Lefebvre and Michel Foucault, and the as-yet-unexplored value of their joint presence in Paris in the 1960s. It is by starting with these two authors that a conceptualisation ("radicalement nouvelle de

4. "...intentional spatialization that aims to bring to the interpretative surface the fundamental and all-embracing, but frequently buried or backgrounded spatiality of human life." (Soja 2000: preface xiv), "spatializing critical thinking".

 l'espace et de la spatialité ainsi que d'un concept de justice spécifiquement ancré dans le spatial et l'urbain" (Soja 2009)) is possible.

Returning to speak about space in relation to the profound crisis of the urban and of urbanization already represents a stance on the role that this could play in building new relationships with life and power. A place for the reproduction of social relations (Lefebvre 1972), space is political and shaping space is a social action.[5] While for Roger Friedland and Deirdre Boden "space and time ... were understood as a medium through which to rethink the organization and meaning of modernity"[6] (Friedland, Boden 1994:1), space/time and life today can be the medium through which to form and organize thoughts about the project of transition and coexistence.

Capital space

The words spatial capital do not simply reduce the qualities of space to their economic value. The meaning of these words is not to make space more real through its transformation into a monetizable entity, its commodification. Rather, it is a question of considering the idea of capital space as an endowment of collective resources, unequally distributed, useful for producing new goods and contributing to the emancipation of all.

The definition of spatial capital as a set of accumulated resources that allow the actor "de tirer avantage, en fonction de sa stratégie, de l'usage de la dimension spatiale de la société" (Lévy and Lussault, 2003) extends the definition of capital proposed by Bourdieu to space.[7] Space practices are not homogeneous and a greater or lesser possibility of movement, of passage between one geographical scale and another, is linked to the possibility or impossibility of increasing one's own spatial capital, which does not end in the fluidity of geographical space but is also a function of the social networks and the milieux frequented. In the definition of spatial capital, Lévy and Lussault focus on the human agent: the agent has potential based on the ability to imagine strategies that allow one to extract advantages from the intrinsic "spatiality" of socicty. Similarly, in the "Lessico del XXI secolo" of the Treccani Encyclopaedia,[8] "spatial capital" corresponds to "the set of potentialities of an individual in relating to space" and does not concern the potential inscribed in the space itself and in its characteristics.

5. Space is appropriately modified and adapted by different social groups according to their ethics, aesthetics, and ideology. See also Ilaria Agostini's comment on the Italian edition of Espace et politique: http://www.casadellacultura.it/857/spiragli-di-utopia-lefebvre-e-lo-spazio-rurale

6. "Space and time have...become a medium through which to rethink the organization and meaning of modernity".

7. As is known, Bourdieu proposed resuming the concept of capital to study the circulation of assets in the social space and added "cultural capital" and "social capital" to "economic capital" (Bourdieu 1986).

8. Treccani, Lessico del XXI Secolo (2012) Spatial capital.

I would like to attempt to overturn this point of view and move from the agent who uses space to the agent space, remaining close to its material consistency, its willingness to be used, its malleability to change. Close to its inertia and strength, regardless of the intentions and goals of the interpreter/agent.

It could be argued that without the interpreter, space is dumb and insubstantial. At the same time, natural space and built space follow their own logics, have rationalities that are the product of multiple and heterogeneous intentions and, even when in conflict, are always deeply inscribed in the characteristics of a place, a geography, a climate, and in a process that associates accumulation and sedimentation by developing new material entities, spatial materials bestowed with properties that are not just the sum of the properties of each layer. Human agents have always had to negotiate to get their intentions implemented into and with this space. This is why I invert the viewpoint: the problem is not only that of space as an "endowment", a resource for producing new goods and their unequal distribution among the members of a society—a theme that crosses utilitarian thought and that of neoclassical economic thought—but of the city and the territory as a collective capital that accumulates and designs over time. Bourdieu dedicates the beginning of his essay to accumulation when, speaking about capital, he described the process that generates it: "Capital is accumulated labor...".[9] The accumulation of work in the "body" of the territory (embodied) and its solidification in roads, canals, and rows of trees evokes the "great deposit of labours" of Carlo Cattaneo, or the descriptions of the Italian agricultural landscape by Emilio Sereni, as well as some little-known pages by Paul Valéry.[10] The work is not only that carried out by settled populations, it is work on the water systems, regulated or not, of the woods, the slopes, the processes that allow the regeneration or destruction of landscapes. The criticism of the "history of nations" developed by Paul Valéry, wrote Ludovic Pépion, "proposes another understanding of the historical world: not starting with spectacular historical figures, but with what is accumulated and transmitted" (Pépion 2022:151). In this regard, Valéry spoke about a "sovereignty" not directly linked to political power, but to territorial functionality, opposing real sovereignty with "les milliards d'heures de labeur spécialisé"[11] which have transformed space.

9. "Capital is accumulated labour (in its materialized form or its 'incorporated,' embodied form) which, when appropriated on a private, i.e., exclusive, basis by agents or groups of agents, enables them to appropriate social energy in the form of reified or living labor.", Bourdieu 1986.

10. I would like to thank Ludovic Pépion for touching on some pages by Valéry in his doctoral thesis Architecture ou destruction. La question de la durée dans le projet architectural et urbain à travers la modernité, PSL Université, Paris, 2022.

11. Paul Valéry, OEuvres..., Paris, Gallimard, coll. « Bibliothèque de la Pléiade », 1957, vol. II, p. 1137, cited by Pépion 2022:153.

The resulting capital cannot be valued solely in terms of economies and practices, unless we include natural dynamics within them and extend the value of spatial capital beyond the human element and its intentions. And not as an element alone, even though its unequal distribution continues to be, and increasingly so, a serious problem in all parts of the planet. Similar to Bourdieu's cultural capital, here it is interesting to consider the embodied state,[12] rather than the objectified or institutionalised state, as that which presupposes, for cultural capital, a process of "embodiment, incorporation."[13] In the case of space, what is needed is continuous, collective work, essential to maintain its value (understood in a broad sense and not only monetary, symbolic and cultural, but of ecological functioning, risk reduction, safeguarding and protection, maintaining habitability). Labour and the time devoted to it accumulate in the form of spatial capital, and its transformation into other forms of capital requires, in maintaining its value, the construction of duration,[14] labour time.[15] Capital space becomes "heritage."[16]

Support space

Not just endowment, physical space is support when it does not prevent or resist but enables. It is not so much the distinction that Habraken proposed in the early 1960s between support and infill, which I think is interesting to take up, nor the recalling of imagery of three-dimensional grids and inhabited cells explored in the first part of the book. It is rather a matter of delving into the "philosophy of enabling" of Royston Landau,[17] a lecturer at the Architectural Association and a figure who has not yet been fully appreciated. Speaking of space, the philosophy of "enabling" is the philosophy of making possible, which activates the subject and also activates beyond its intentions. And it gives power, approaching the concept of empowerment, in two ways. The first by making something capable, thanks to its characteristics, or more capable (this is the case, for example, of the space that minimises effort, which I discussed in chapter one). The second is by offering the means to do, to acquire abilities not initially possessed (in this case it is close to the idea of endowment).

12. In the case of cultural capital it is the disposition of mind and body "i.e., in the form of long-lasting dispositions of the mind and body", Bourdieu 1986.

13. An approach that translates into educational paths and long-term work on oneself, Bourdieu 1986.

14. Here the concept of longue durée is echoed (Braudel 1958).

15. "The labor-time accumulated in the form of capital and the labor-time needed to transform it from one type into another", Bourdieu 1986.

16. See the transition from the idea of capital to that of heritage in Caye 2020.

17. He was invited to edit the Architectural Digest issue "Thinking about architecture and planning" (1969) and direct the graduate studies programme at the Architectural Association, which he did from 1974 to 1993.

The starting point for this argument is Royston Landau's article about Cedric Price's "philosophy of enabling" (Landau 1985). Landau highlighted the ethical dimension of Price's architecture, which is rooted in deep concern for its effects and consequences on users and inhabitants. In the context of the themes addressed in this book, I could use other terms to describe the centrality of Cedric Price's concern: it implicitly denotes a full understanding of architectural design as a fundamental biopolitical action that translates, admittedly, into a space of given conditions, imposed discipline, and the limitation of possibilities. But Landau also highlighted the opposite aspect of this conditioning space: "But the obverse must certainly also apply, for architecture can be liberating, enhancing and supportive." The design of space is a device to liberate the potential found in everyone, a support for individual and collective freedom, which grows, enhances and increases the possibilities of emancipation of the subject and social relations. This supports and makes possible the constructing of a different society, starting with different spatial conditions. The connection established between Price's work and Benthamian Utilitarianism is just as important.

Agent space

Simultaneously, with its relevance in the social science debate, physical space (and its multiple roles) seems to dissolve and paradoxically disappear from the political and social agenda at the end of the second millennium. The world is "Le plus oublié, le plus meprisé, le plus delaissé" of the objects of philosophy and science (Serres 1980:100).[18] The problem of space extends to its nature as a "subject", an agent subject. Space is no longer a receptacle, or just a scene, but "une force active qui façonne notre expérience de la vie" (Soja 2009).

The conviction of the vitality of matter, of the non-passivity of things has fuelled a philosophical approach that has traversed Western thinking and emerges strongly today. It is a matter of defining its "vitality"—in our case the "vitality" of the space we can touch and walk upon, "things" and materials—beyond their ability to limit or enable our movements, a space capable of acting "as quasi agents or forces with trajectories, propensities, or tendencies of their own." (Bennett 2010, from the preface). The interrogation posed by Jane Bennett concerns the political impact of the emergence of a matter that shares much more with life than we usually understand; which can make a difference thanks to the logic of its movement/behaviour, as an entity capable of transforming other entities, beyond the idea of resource and commodity. Using the central lemma in Bruno Latour's thought, space is actant (Latour, 1996), space is agent beyond the sharp separation between

18. See also: Collina 2003.

life and matter. An anthropological symmetry conceives of human and non-human entities as capable of acting (Latour 1991). But these themes were already present in Foucauldian thought: with the notion of milieu developed in Territoire, Sécurité, Population, Thomas Lemke recalled that Foucault connected a multiplicity of living beings to a set of material elements that act on them, reciprocally influencing each other: "Here, Foucault quite clearly accepts the idea that agency is not exclusively a property of humans."[19]

The spatial turn opens up to the material turn, which allows us to criticise the combination of nature and artefact as a mere resource of a technological progress marked by economic exploitation and a conventional understanding of the living. From these reflections and deep ecology, I will develop the hypothesis of the "territory subject" at the end of part three.

19. "The idea of a 'government of things' takes a more concrete form when Foucault analyses the concept of the milieu [2007, 20-23; 77-78). Lemke cites the English translation of Sécurité, Territoire, Population]. He argues that the milieu defines an "intersection between a multiplicity of living individuals working and coexisting with each other in a set of material elements that act on them and on which they act in turn" (Ibid, 22). Here, Foucault quite clearly accepts the idea that agency is not exclusively a property of humans" (Lemke 2016; Foucault 2007, Security, Territory, Population: Lectures at the Collège de France, 1977-78).

2.3 THREE FIELDS

The hypothesis of transition as a new biopolitical project places my reflection within a broader conceptual framework. I use this hypothesis as a theory-building device to clarify the new centrality of life in all new research on the future of urban space at different scales and in its different forms; to measure the distance between us and the modern and postmodern biopolitical project;[20] and to reconsider the role of space in the process of improving the quality of life and the construction of a better world. Space understood not only as a coercive tool, but a reserve of possibilities for subjects to emancipate themselves.

In the agent, capital and support space, three distinct fields of thought can be recognised, along with the relationships they weave between them reciprocally.

The first field: the emergence of what Foucault described in terms of bio-power, a power with the intention, typically modern, to maintain and make life productive (this power is not conceived as the right to give death or to let live, as in the age of sovereignty, but to keep alive).[21]

The second field: the thought of deep ecology that recognizes living and non-living bodies as subjects and considers their interactions as interactions between peers. In this field "...the ecological crisis is a crisis of modern systems of thought." (Escobar 2008:8).

The third: the field of the emancipation of the subject and the thought related to it. While the main forms of modern biopower can be distinguished in a discipline imposed on the individual body and in the forms of control and regulation of the population (Foucault 1976), this field gives rise to the

20. In this regard, we need only refer to Hardt and Negri's research on the new type of (post-modern) capitalism: the differences between economy and politics and between production and reproduction are loosening, and so too are the folds of empire. Biopolitics locks the individual into an exploitative and utilitarian system but allows new political subjects to grow. (Hardt, Negri 2000; Hardt, Negri 2004).

21. This is how Foucault started his course Securité, Territoire, Population at the Collège de France, 1977 78 (11 January 1978): "Cette année, je voudrais commencer l'étude de quelque chose que j'avais appelé comme ça, un petit peu en l'air, le bio-pouvoir, c'est-à-dire cette série de phénomènes qui me parait assez importante, à savoir l'ensemble des mécanismes par lesquels ce qui, dans l'espèce humaine, constitue ses traits biologiques fondamentaux va pouvoir entrer à l'intérieur d'une politique, d'une stratégie politique, d'une stratégie générale de pouvoir, autrement dit comment la société, les sociétés occidentales modernes, à partir du XVIII siècle, ont repris en compte le fait biologique fondamental que l'être humain constitue une espèce humaine. C'est en gros ça que j'appelle, que j'ai appelé, comme ça, le bio-pouvoir" (Foucault, 2004:3). See also Foucault 1997:216.

paradox of a rationalising modernisation that not only disciplines bodies, and orders and exploits populations and resources, but also introduces new possibilities of expression for the subject, increases its level of awareness and the ability to act to improve the living environment.

First field

As is known, Foucault described the construction, development and limits of biopower, the intentions of which, in the modern era, are to keep a population alive, useful and disciplined. Security mechanisms and disciplinary devices are both part of biopolitics. Foucault clarified this in the last lecture of his course at the Collège de France, 'Il faut défendre la société' on 17 March 1976. But while discipline is exercised over the very bodies of individuals, taking charge of the health, safety, and lives of populations is achieved through a series of regulatory and control mechanisms (Foucault 1997:183). Organisation of the space is part of this project; it is biopolitical because it is explicitly intended to keep human and productive capital alive.

For Foucault, technologies and security devices are a counterpart and essential condition of liberal government: spontaneous forms of self-regulation can be maintained by protecting a population from the risks it may run due to its very nature. In the lecture given on 17 March, Foucault spoke about security devices and milieu (Foucault 1997): while sovereignty capitalises a territory and discipline "architecture un espace et se pose comme problème essentiel une distribution hiérarchique et fonctionnelle des éléments", security plans a milieu that is regulated "dans un cadre multivalent et transformable".[22] The third form of power linked to security has now taken on a fundamental and overarching role that partly justifies the omnipresence of life in the debate on the future of the city: in the form of making it safe from risks and dangers perceived as increasingly present, and from changes that we know we do not know how to manage. This is the crisis of absolute security, of the ability to protect a population that brings to the fore the concept of resilience, its paradoxes and its necessity. In this sense, the terms Foucault used also have the advantage of rediscovering the political sense of daily action because, if politics deals with life, then everything is political (Keck 2008).

The return to themes concerning the relationship between life, space and power has, it has already been noted, many similarities with the Weltanschauung that characterised the late nineteenth century, strongly

22. "alors que la souveraineté capitalise un territoire, posant le problème majeur du siège du gouvemement, alors que la discipline architecture un espace et se pose comme problème essentiel une distribution hiérarchique et fonctionnelle des éléments, la sécurité va essayer d'aménager un milieu en fonction d'événements ou de séries d'événements ou d'éléments possibles, séries qu'il va falloir régulariser dans un cadre multivalent et transformable." (Foucault 2004:22).

 influenced by Darwinian theories (Abrahamsson 2013), Ratzel's biogeography[23] and the Lebensphilosophie (philosophy of life) that emerged in the second half of that century (Schopenhauer, Nietzsche, Bergson).[24] Abrahamsson referred to these authors when addressing the contribution of the Swedish geographer Rudolf Kjellén, known for having introduced the term geopolitics in 1899, within a taxonomy of state politics in which the term biopolitics also appears. For Kjellén, the relationship between state and soil represents the fundamental dimension of the organic state theory, but the entire taxonomy unites the set of physical, anthropological, economic and biological dimensions of the state conceived as a large organism. Roberto Esposito identified Kjellén's Staten som lifsform as the transition from a constitutional structure to an organic, biopolitical one (Esposito, 2004:6-7). However, according to a more recent reading (Gunneflo 2015), Kjellén's contribution can also be read as a stance on the need to cover ever larger intervention areas with state policies, including "the guarding, refining and securing of the population stock" (Gunneflo 2015:25). This not only brings Kjellén's contribution closer to Foucault's work but also anticipates the formation of biopolitical thinking that finds its distinctive expression in the social democratic welfare state of those countries and in the forms of social engineering that characterised it from the 1930s (Gunneflo 2015). The proposal for a strong intervention by the modern state, beyond maintaining the legal order, concerns the material well-being of its constituent population, understood not as a legal subject, but as an aggregate of biological life, for which education and culture are to be provided. This is an overall political project that does not seem to be too far from the process described by Foucault in Securité, Territoire, Population as "governmentalisation of the state" (Gunneflo 2015:38; Foucault 2004).

The previous readings bring us back to the start of this second part, the commitment that modern architecture and urbanism have been made to the design of space and its planning. "Governing by design" indicates the emblematic title chosen by the historians' collective Aggregate (Aggregate 2012) to define the role of architectural and city design in relation to the "gardening-breeding-surgical" ambitions of state biopolitics (Baumann 1991:32); and of the role design, manipulation, management, and engineering had in ordering space and society, as Baumann wrote (Baumann 1991:7). It is not the monumental symbolism of architecture that is of interest to the

23. Ratzel used the concept of Lebensraum "as a concept that gathers together the biological, geographical and anthropological conditions of a given environment", but to this basis we should add the problem of the growth of a population as a spatial problem for which dealing with life means dealing with the space necessary for it to move around (Abrahamsson 2013).

24. The lebenphilosophie sees life "as a fundamental category and normative criterion of the healthy, the good, and the true." The concept of life, the prevalence of instinct, intuition and experience (Erlebnis) oppose the strong tendencies of "rationalization, civilization, mechanization, and technologization" (Lemke 2011:9).

research of a collective of historians like Aggregate, but the tangible ways in which designed space controls everyday and basic aspects of our lives: "How are we fashioned as citizens by our homes, cities and heritage?" (Aggregate 2012: vii). The theme is that of an architecture and a space that governs at different scales, acting as a mediation between bodies, individuals, populations and different forms of power.[25]

Second field

Biopolitics and the environmental question have already had their shared moments. In the 1960s and 1970s, in parallel with the ecological crisis reported by Limits to Growth, use of the term was revived to indicate the urgency of maintaining living conditions on the planet; the evolution of biotechnology has re-proposed the biopolitical theme in relation to the survival of humanity, with the emergence of a Technocentric Biopolitics (Lemke, 2011:26). The protection of the natural foundations of life against the risk of their manipulation has brought bioethical issues to the fore.

Awareness of the degradation of the environment in which we live and the loss of biodiversity form the basis for the perspective of deep ecology (Naess 1973), which introduces a paradigm shift in the design of space, a disruptive perspective from which abstractions cannot be made, once it has been understood. Even if the process of our alteration of ecosystems cannot be completely stopped, we must question the nature and extent of these interferences to achieve a less destructive and lighter presence: the nature and extent of these interferences are the issue at hand (Naess 2008:113).[26]

Deep ecology deals with fundamental aspects by developing "deep arguments" starting with "ultimate philosophical premises" and based on maximising the achievement potential of individual beings (Naess 2008:108). Life, in its various forms, has an intrinsic value and this value does not depend on the usefulness of the non-human world for human ends. The move away from anthropocentric thinking and consideration of the biosphere as an interconnected whole integrates, among other things, the rationalities of the natural world, its reasons, logic and dynamics (Dryzek 1987). In a new biopolitical project, mankind's problems, expectations and reasons are part of the same world, but they are no longer at its centre. Resource rarefaction and climate change, population growth and ageing, the obsolescence of the infrastructures of modern cities and the territory—these become biopolitical issues to be dealt with by cooperating with the natural system, allying with

25. Frédéric Keck orients himself within the complexity and diffusion of these terms, reconstructing their "contexts of use" in different cultures: "un usage réflexif en France, un usage critique en Italie, un usage analytique en Angleterre et aux États-Unis" (Keck 2008:296), perhaps forgetting the Nordic biopolitics instead taken up by Esposito (2004) and Gunneflo.

26. "At issue are the nature and extent of such interference."

and not against it: "Come high water, there is an accession of new books", wrote Aldo Leopold commenting on the piles of timber carried by the flood, each of which conveys a tale of the farms and farmers located upstream in the valley (Leopold 1966:27 [1949]). Every flood is a new library: "The land yields a cultural harvest..." (Leopold 1966: xix [1949]).

In the heavily transformed regions of our anthropocentric planet there is a glaring hiatus between the vision of deep ecology and the actual reality of things, between the ecological crisis and its contradictory relationships with economic processes. And the scandal, according to Naess, is not to start with the "emergence of work to be done" in order to produce jobs (Naess 2008:101) in an era of crises like the one we are currently experiencing. The hypothesis of the transition as a new biopolitical project is therefore based not only on a new social pact, but on a different ecological pact, beyond "sustainability" and in the direction of real "ecological development".

The cultural-ecological bases for the idea of nature add further layers of difficulty to this already complex pact. The problem is the decolonisation of nature itself: imagining forms of conservation other than those inspired by modern rationality (Escobar, 2008). The problem is also to understand the technonature (Escobar 1999) which is produced as new nature together with the technological and cultural stratifications that have transformed cities and territories into conglomerates difficult to deconstruct, into histories whose beginnings have been lost, into fragments of meaning juxtaposed with each other. "Life itself becomes a hybrid of the biophysical and the technosocial. It becomes impossible to decide where biology ends and technology begins", writes Escobar (2008). The increasing complexity of reality transcends the idea of nature: "technonatures" formed in a hybrid environment, complex subjects, "living things" (Bennet 2010) with which the design of space is concerned. Modern science and even more so our designs are often incapable of describing and understanding this process and its complexity: it is not enough to employ interdisciplinarity. Making an epistemological break is an action intrinsically linked to the formation of a new "environmental knowledge" in which nature, culture and technology produce and are the product of original and complex environmental rationalities (Leff 1998).

The project at territorial scale is particularly interested in the different rationalities that have, over time, designed functional processes to create new forms of nature (second nature and beyond). The effort of understanding and reading is an inevitable tribute to their complexity at different scales.

The intersection between soils, water, biodiversity and modern technological spaces accounts for these new natures and raises the important issues of urban political ecology. "The history of cities can be read as a history of water", writes Matthew Gandy (Gandy 2003:22) and the hydraulic infrastructure—extended to its biopolitical dimension (between ecology, epidemiology, town planning and urbanisation)—is among the main agents in the production of space (Gandy 2014). The set of flows, the "multiple metabolisms of water" mentioned by Eric Swyngedouw, are structured and organized through relationships of power, domination and subordination, emancipation and repression: "The circulation of water produces a physical geography and a material landscape, but also a symbolic and cultural landscape of power" (Swyngedouw, 1996).

The concept of technonature is not, however, unambiguous, and it lends itself to conflicting assessments of the role of technology: "Does technonature necessarily represent a new level in the domination of nature? Or does it open new, more ecological regimes?" (Escobar 2008:144). This depends on the evaluation of new technologies as part of "techno-bio-cultural assemblages" and their social and ecological character between utopia and dystopia. The political nature of these assemblages has structured the contribution of political ecology, a fundamental approach that aims to penetrate contemporary socio-environmental phenomena (Hache 2012) and makes their socio and biopolitical components intelligible.

The project as a tool for critical description and original conceptualisation (Viganò 2010) finds strong reasons for its existence and legitimacy in these controversial and conflictual contexts.

Third field

The emancipation[27] of the subject develops in parallel to the modern biopolitical project, in a strange, often conflicting and ambiguous set of individual and social intentions, governmental practices and singular initiatives that rely on the support provided by these same practices. While biopolitics deals with the human being as a set of biological characteristics, and the notion of population aggregates them into a measurable and abstract whole for which norms and standards can be defined, actual living beings and the singularity of individual experience are not distant, and separation is only fictitious and instrumental (Lemke 2011:59). Bodies and individuals belonging to a population governed by practices of "correction, exclusion, normalisation, disciplining, therapeutics, and optimisation" are nonetheless real bodies and individuals, moving and transforming along with their space.

The conflicting dimensions of freedom and subjectivation on the one hand, and discipline and control on the other, act and interact in space. Foucault addressed the rigidity of the machinery of individuation and control in Surveiller et Punir (Foucault 1975), a set of mechanisms that at the same time constructs conditions of freedom for the same individual categorised

27. Emancipation, in the broadest sense of the term, refers to all actions that allow a person or a group of people to achieve a state of autonomy by ending dependence (subjection) on some authority or power

and included in the control system of medical, school, military records, and so on. Giorgio Agamben emphasised the two faces of biopolitics that describe the spaces, freedoms, and rights conquered by individuals and, at the same time, the mechanisms of organisation of the state that include, with increasing intrusiveness, the life of each person within a constituted order (Agamben 1995). Power over life also concerns "the positive, polemical and affirmative dimension of political subjectification, the struggle and quarrel for equality in which the meaning of a political life consists." (Cutro 2005, about Rancière 2000). The modern city is the result of this complex biopolitical actions that cannot be reduced to just one of the two dimensions of freedom and subjectivation, but is the product of their fertile, although conflicting, interaction.

The Habermas/Foucault issue does not question the powerful Foucauldian reading of space, formed by bodies that give it form and at the same time are conditioned by it, but frees it from the risk of it being only a mirror, the mere mirroring of power, according to the criticism put forward by Baudrillard (Baudrillard 2007:30). Habermas describes modernity as the rationalisation and colonisation of the life-world (Habermas 1986).28 Foucault illuminates its governmentality and organisation through the institutional mechanisms of a new order. For Foucault, truth is an instrument and not an end of knowledge. Both truth and knowledge are traversed by currents of power: power over bodies that are rendered docile, power over making them secure and their normalisation. For Habermas, the truth is an end, the end of knowledge that rationalises a world of possible emancipation. Rationality and truth are the regulating ideas of our living experience.

In this relationship, the "homme-machine" described by Foucault in the chapter on the docile corps achieves a "majoration d'utilité", such as the one Laban imagined to be linked to a better conceived alternation of exertion and relaxation, unlike other and earlier forms of discipline and restraint exerted on the body. Obedient and useful bodies are organised in the closed, segregated or open cellular space (Foucault 1975), a functional space increasingly specialised to divide what might be dangerous if left close by: "La discipline est une anatomie politique du détail" wrote Foucault (Foucault 1975:164). Architecture becomes "opérateur pour la transformation des individus...Les pierres peuvent rendre docile et connaissable" (Foucault 1975:202) and is a great instrument of normalization. Correlation between body and gesture involves the space in which they are found, their measure and their rhythm. Emancipation, again paradoxically, grows and develops forms of resistance to disciplinary devices and security, to a governmentality that by placing life at the centre and as its object naturalises power and its

28. Habermas responded to Foucault's text "Qu'est-ce que les Lumières?" (Foucault 1994a).

 reference to "apparently self-evident and universal normative claims of biological life" (Lemke 2011:51).

The emancipatory aspect of rationalisation29 and, as far as we are concerned here, the emancipatory role of the rationalised space/territory are issues I would like to cover. My purpose, as I have already mentioned, is not only to better understand the distance between us and the modern biopolitical project, but to reconsider the role of space in the process of improving the quality of a life in transition.

In short, it is a matter of letting other sides of biopolitical centrality emerge. The biopolitical project is not exclusively an instrument of coercion, but a reserve of possibilities for the emancipation of the subject, or rather the subjects that the inclusive and incomplete nature of the Enlightenment emancipation project has gradually accommodated within it (Pelluchon 2020:75-80) from minorities, to living entities, to matter. The ecological transition is the starting point for rethinking this emancipation project: inside open assemblages explore original collaborative survival (Tsing Lowenhaupt 2015, "Arts of Noticing"), linking spatial, social and environmental justice.

The expansion to the territory, soil, water and animals of the subject status must not hide its rigidity in terms of the separation it implies between one subject and another, both bearers of rights. In any case, modern individualisation strongly underestimates the relational dimension of our existence (Pelluchon, 2020:87), oversimplifying the meaning of the entire process of constructing the subject. For this reason, taking up, prolonging and extending the idea of emancipation through the design of space remains a priority, also in defining the political meaning of an ecological transition. Interdependence and corporeality have always been the focus of the reflection on the design of space, where distances and proximities, densities and sequences speak of friction, pleasure, comfort and conflict between spaces, bodies and populations, of porosity and the lack thereof.

The three fields addressed in the previous pages should be seen as interacting with each other and should not be conceived separately. Indeed, they allow us to continue in the direction of the autonomy and emancipation of the subject (the self-determination of the individual moral agent traditionally understood as a subject), but they highlight the relational dimension that surrounds and nurtures each subject and its exchanges with the other, and therefore the responsibility for the vulnerability of each entity, human and non-human; and finally they affirm the centrality of a biopolitical reflection

29. Underestimated by Foucault and highlighted by Habermas in his criticism of Foucault's analysis of power, as indicated by Michael Kelly in his reconstruction of the discussion between the two authors (Kelly 1994).

in order to differently orientate the action of transforming space in an era of transition from one socio-eco-economic model to another.

I will discuss these three fields, albeit not in linear or deductive ways, in the third part of this book, where some of the projects I have developed in recent years will be used as a testbed for the hypothesis of the transition as a new biopolitical project—its concrete meaning in order to critically test its usefulness, potential and limits.

3. THE BIOPOLITICAL GARDEN PROJECTS

Fig. 50
The Biopolitical Garden, XVII Biennale, 2021.
Photo: StudioPaolaViganò. Paola Viganò with:
Studio021paolaviganò (Alessio Tamiazzo,
Simona Bodria, Qinyi Zhang, Laura dalla
Pietà, Bertrand Plevinski, Mathilde Meurice),
Tommaso Pietropolli – Lab U/HRC, EPFL

3.1 SPACE, LIFE AND THE PROJECT

The projects discussed in the third and final part of this book offer a set of reflections on unequivocally biopolitical issues. They do not claim to illuminate all the dark sides of the problem, but to restore, even if only in fragments, the salient points of an approach that has found the reasons for its formulation and expression in the folds of reality.

The themes belong to a project practice. In some cases they concern long-term crises that are not resolved, in others they test the first steps of an adaptation project in the absence of planetary agreements on climate change; some of them are at an initial and research stage, while others have been taking place for years now in actual contexts and also express their full ambiguity, together with the richness of the experiment of which the protocol can be analysed and the result observed and criticised.

As a whole, the stories told here highlight topics that not only raise biopolitical issues analytically, but also aim to contain arguments and proposals for the design of the transition space. The biopolitical viewpoint changes the design of space, just as the emergence of the question of life, the concept of population, and its administration and regulation (Lemke 2011:4), along with the redefinition of normality and abnormality, distorted it when modern urbanism was formed. The transformation of the modern city has shown the historically situated interpretation of these concerns. Beyond the trove of organicist and vitalist metaphors, these same concerns remain firmly, and with increasing evidence, at the core of contemporary politics and design. But it is their profound reformulation that we need to be able to discuss in order to design.

In the projects that follow, these themes construct relationships of some depth and interest, proposing a "visionary pragmatism" (Coles 2016) that does not lose its connection with utopian thinking and counter-project cultures. At the same time, the projects are the outcome of negotiations that are essential for including different planes of reality; they are conversations that include countless players confronted with the radical transformation of their habitat.

"Towards an Urbanism of the Living Soil", "Prototypes of the Transition", "Designing a Horizontal Metropolis", "Utopia for Our Time"—these four episodes that make up the third part of this book incorporate and nurture many of these reflections: on the hypothesis of the transition as a new biopolitical project,

Fig. 51
Zac de la Corrouze, Maisons dans le Bois Sector.
Photo: StudioPaolaViganò

on living together in a new horizon of coexistence, and the rarefaction of resources. They explore some of the extraordinary challenges concerning the future of the city and of the territory.

The third part concludes by taking up salient points of the epistemological, ontological and ethical shift I would like to account for: the first point is the critique of the categories of territory as object and territory as resource; the second, the critique of the strong structures of modernity; the third, the relationship to be reconstructed between the forms of the economy (new development trajectories) and the forms of space; the fourth, the need for eco-socio-spatial prototypes; and finally, the fifth point, the relationship between new nature and the production of space.

Insights, stances and knowledge accumulated through design experimentation outline the fragments of a new discourse on space, life and design.

Fig. 52
Zac de la Courrouze, Rennes and Saint-Jacques-de-la-Lande: Masterplan, 2021. Living the city, inhabiting the park. Studio 03-014 Secchi-Viganò, Studio015-024PaolaViganò (ongoing). Bernardo Secchi, Paola Viganò, Simona Bodria, Alessia Calò, Andrea Carlesso, Dao Ming Chang, Irene Cogliano, Giovanna Comana, Marine Durand, Stefania Dussin, Tommaso Fait, Carla Greco, Stella Armeli Iapichino, Griet Lambrechts, Adrien Lefèvre, Carlo Neidhart, Christian Nitti, Alvise Pagnacco, Tommaso Pietropolli, Larisa Rudko, Ani Tafilica, Alessio Tamiazzo, Uberto degli Uberti, Silvia Urbano, Kasumi Yoshida.

3.2 TOWARDS AN URBANISM OF THE LIVING SOIL

Climate change is planetary engineering without design. These facts of the Anthropocene are scientific, but its shape and meaning are questions for politics, a politics that does not yet exist.
J. Purdy, After-Nature, 2015

The soil has to do with urban design and urban planning, starting with its being the "ecstatic skin" of the planet (Logan 1995).[30] This skin is formed and degenerates, it deteriorates and is reconstructed, and is the outcome of the incessant work of living and non living beings. Leonardo seems to have written, "We know more about the movement of celestial bodies than about the soil underfoot", reproduced in a well-known text on soil (Montgomery 2007). Reading the soil in terms of its different components requires an adequate gaze, methods of representation and finally a project.

Bernardo Secchi posed many of the questions linked to soil in the mid-1980s, starting by highlighting the "space between things" (Secchi 1986; Bianchettin Del Grano 2015). In his thinking, soil and the "space between things" are strategic themes; they are so important for contemporary design that they justify and inspire new narratives, representations dedicated to them, oriented descriptions, and non-obvious conceptualisations[31] that give full depth to ecological reflection.

Rennes: Living in the city, inhabiting a park

A new gaze

The traditional way in which architects and urban planners have dealt with and observed soil has been primarily that of its consumption: the city and its growth are a threat to be stopped by borders that are almost always disregarded. The return of this viewpoint, e.g. in the European No Net Land Take on the 2050 horizon, now bases criticism of land waste on a deeper understanding of the relationship between "ecstatic skin" and the city. With its heterogeneity and variability, urban soil requires new reading efforts, together

30. The text partly takes up and revises my "Suolo. Note per una ricerca sulla città contemporanea." (Viganò 2016b).

31. Among the contributions to these themes I have been able to make in recent years, see Viganò 2014a and the issue of Oase 110, The Project of the Soil, 2022, edited together with David Peleman, Martina Barcelloni Corte, Elsbeth Ronner.

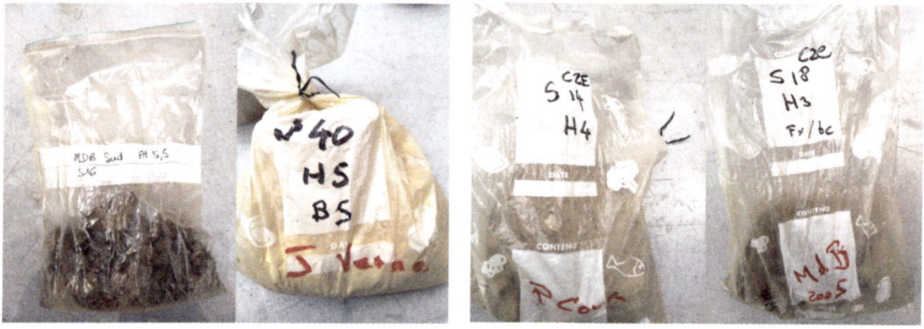

Fig. 53
Above: Soil samples of La Courrouze. Photo: StudioPaolaViganò

Fig. 54
Below: Soil coring, La Courrouze. Photo: Pierre Bazin.

with pedologists, biologists, geographers, hydraulic engineers, biodiversity experts, etc., who establish transformation/regeneration hypotheses that differ from the past as they seek to reinforce and reveal the multiple functions of each of its fragments.

Anthropic, urban, and infrastructural soil are terms that share certain aspects: they concern fragments of unbuilt space that can no longer be read in terms of wrecks, waste spaces, lost soil or, worse, areas inevitably destined to be densified. The famous "compromised areas" that triggered Bernardo Secchi's gentle irony regarding the category of "compromise", so often used to define life paths— usually female and unorthodox—have acquired a productive, ecological and collective value, even in public opinion, that fully participates in a change of outlook and culture.

Soil

However, condemnation of its consumption cannot be the only outcome of an urbanistic reflection on the soil. The rhetorical line that proposes considering the impoverished, eroded and urbanised soil as a non-renewable resource incapable of regenerating itself, enriching itself and becoming productive again is not entirely convincing. The condemnation, often, does not grasp the possible project nor the conceptual shift that has already occurred—the soil has already become an integral part of the contemporary urban planning project. There is also a risk of overshadowing the long reflection that cuts across the modern city project, from the radical positions of a geographer like Kropotkin to the project of the open space of the functional city. In this important research (referred to in the first part of the book), nature reconstructed through the regeneration of soil once again becomes the support for new forms of life, as well as the (public) space of the city. Recent writings, such as those by William Bryant Logan, also affirm this point.

Kropotkin dedicated a part of his classic Fields, Factories, and Workshops to the concrete methods of regeneration and enrichment of the soil, as "in the hands of man there are no unfertile soils" (Kropotkin 1901:48). Although the text is very well known, it is worth remembering that the manipulation/construction of the soil is central to the formulation of the theses advocated by the great geographer: only the soil's transformation makes it possible to escape a geographical determinism that leads to the specialisation of the entire planet (in function, in Kropotkin's time of British imperialism, the great manufacturing of the world, or of industrial concentration in a few hubs that the rest of the world should foster due to its supposed vocation to be cultivated, or to supply raw materials). It is only within a hypothesis for the treatment of the soil's characteristics that in Fields, Factories, and Workshops the intellectual can also be a farmer and, vice versa, that the integration of agriculture and small-scale widespread industry can be imagined. Taking up

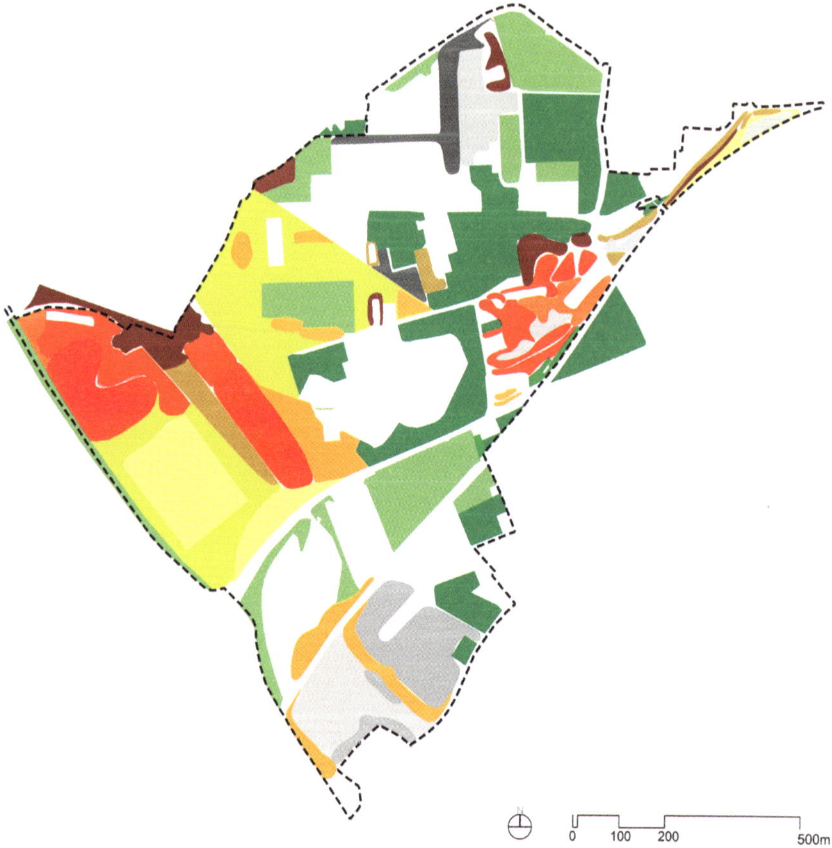

	Natural soil with little disturbance	Suolo naturale compattato. Aree ben drenate	Compacted natural soil	Stripped, stabilised or extremely compacted soil
Abandonment < 10 years	Moorland facies with broom and willow, with oak and other broadleaf trees	Facies of gorse heath and young birch forest	Willow and blackthorn scrubland facies	Broom heath
Abandonment from 10 to 30 years	Mixed forest of oaks (ash, linden, maple, hornbeam, etc.) with various deciduous shrubs.	Downy oak woods and a few oaks, heath substrate	Willow with aspen	Scattered gorse and birch heath (or willows at water points)
Abandonment from 30 to 60 years	Mixed ash-oak forest with a shrub and herbaceous layer rich in biodiversity	Oak woodland heath substrate	Willow grove with poplars and a few oaks	Broom heath and scattered clumps (or willows/poplars at water accumulation points)

Parts with different maintenance intensity
Horticultural exploitation Community gardens or orchards with very high maintenance and dense vegetation (mostly horticultural plants).
Careful 'park-like' maintenance, with undergrowth care, regular mowing of lawns, planting of non-native species, pruning and felling of dying trees
Agricultural maintenance (grassland or roadsides) with regular mowing, trimming or pruning. No planting or special maintenance

positions established in the mid-nineteenth century of "harmonised labour" and "integral education" (Kropotkin 1901: Preface iv), Kropotkin criticised the permanent division of labour in favour of enhancing the extreme variety found within individuals, territories and nations. On the other hand, Seebohm Rowntree's descriptions of Flanders (Rowntree 1910), of its agriculture which was so profitable that it was taken as an example of how to address poverty in England, tell of the long labour of peasants who enriched the infertile soils of the countryside with manure for centuries, altering their original conditions and making the soil productive.

Regenerating the city and its soil: Zac de la Courrouze

The soil project takes on depth and becomes even more relevant when the soil and city go through common regeneration processes, when the soil is to be reconstructed, an aspect we must highlight with the same perseverance with which we keep our attention focused on its consumption. With this attention a former industrial and military area undergoing transformation can become an opportunity to experiment with a common project on new nature and new urbanity, in difficult ecological conditions, on inert and polluted soils, reducing the input of fertile soil taken from other places, constructing an archetypal landscape rich in biodiversity. The Zac de la Courrouze project in Rennes, Brittany envisions the creation of a new part of the town on a layered and polluted military and industrial site of over 100 ha. The project began in 2003 as an experiment in the simultaneous regeneration of the city and its soil.

Zac de la Courrouze is a major urban project and explores the type of space to be imagined today to provide housing for some 12,000 inhabitants, jobs for at least 3,000 people, schools, shops, art galleries, important regional offices, space for alternative uses and strong accessibility for public transport, residents, visitors and users. The masterplan tool is too often a mere abstract canvas superimposed on diverse situations, with generic principles that avoid the fundamental question of "how to live together", what should be shared and why. La Courrouze is not a "new city" or even a neighbourhood, it is a part of the existing city: it is not far from the station, crossed by flows that are not only local, full of activities, and used by its inhabitants and those who choose to go for a run there or dine out with friends. Its design is based on the idea that a generous public space is what can connect heterogeneous languages (of architecture and society) and a variety of practices. In this project, the social and political objectives include prioritising affordable housing, but they do not include large metropolitan programmes: La Courrouze is an everyday place.

The project of a regenerated soil contains the hypothesis that has guided and still guides the implementation of the "Zac de la Courrouze"

Fig. 56
Left: Zac de la Courrouze, Sector Cleunay: Comparison 2004-2019

Fig. 57
Right: Bois Habité Sector: Comparison 2004-2018. Photos: StudioPaolaViganò.

project in Rennes:[32] that the unstoppable and unavoidable dispersion of social practices and architectural languages finds potential coherence in the public space project and therefore mainly in the soil project, whose legitimacy is built on precisely a project defined as such. The soil regeneration combines rainwater management and creates environments with different degrees of humidity; it designs a public space in which artificial topography and new nature form an articulated surface with a low degree of maintenance. Within it, certain parts ensure multifunctional and flexible spaces that reuse pre-existing sports surfaces.

The reading of the site was guided by an in-depth understanding of its complexity, between superficial soil pollution and subterranean groundwater pollution, where there was an exceptional plant heritage and industrial memory. The evolution of the project involved experimenting with the idea of the "landscape as infrastructure", clarifying the centrality of pre-existing vegetation and ecosystems as a structuring element of the new part of the city. The design hypothesis was transformed along with the growing knowledge of the characteristics of the soil (not only its polluted part) and its functional organisation was influenced as a result, leading to the redesign of certain parts within an overall ecosystemic vision. The result is archetypal landscapes where artifice recomposes areas of naturalness and measures the distance between environmental and human history.

The objective of a soil balance, between excavation and filling, the choice of water management in the public space, the link between the scarcity of fertile soil and the archetypes of the Breton landscape have created a varied canvas, not always inspired by maximum comfort, but one that enhances the different histories of soils and trees, within which building types, landscapes and public spaces create specific situations of living together. Bois Habité, Maisons dans le Bois, Dominos, the reuse of the industrial ateliers, the new bus station, the footbridge over the railway, the facilities spread throughout the inhabited and regenerated park—all this is the result of an inverted viewpoint. For this reason, the project received the "Nature en ville" award of the Palmarès Ecoquartier 2011 from the Ministry of Ecology in France. La Courrouze is now at an advanced stage of completion.

32. The project to recover a set of disused industrial and military areas for the construction of approximately 5,000 homes, public spaces, tertiary and commercial activities was the result of a competition announced by Rennes Métropole and coordinated by Territoires Rennes held in 2003. The team consisted of Studio Bernardo Secchi & Paola Viganò (now Studio Paola Viganò), Charles Dard, Orgeco (later replaced by AMCO, today ORA) and Pierre Bazin.

Fig. 58
La Courrouze's tryptiques : Bois Habité, Pole Courrouze, Maisons dans le Bois.
Photos ©Fabrizio Stipari

Following pages: Fig. 59
La Courrouze's tryptiques : Vallon Jules Verne, Grande Prairie, Pilate.
Photos ©Fabrizio Stipari

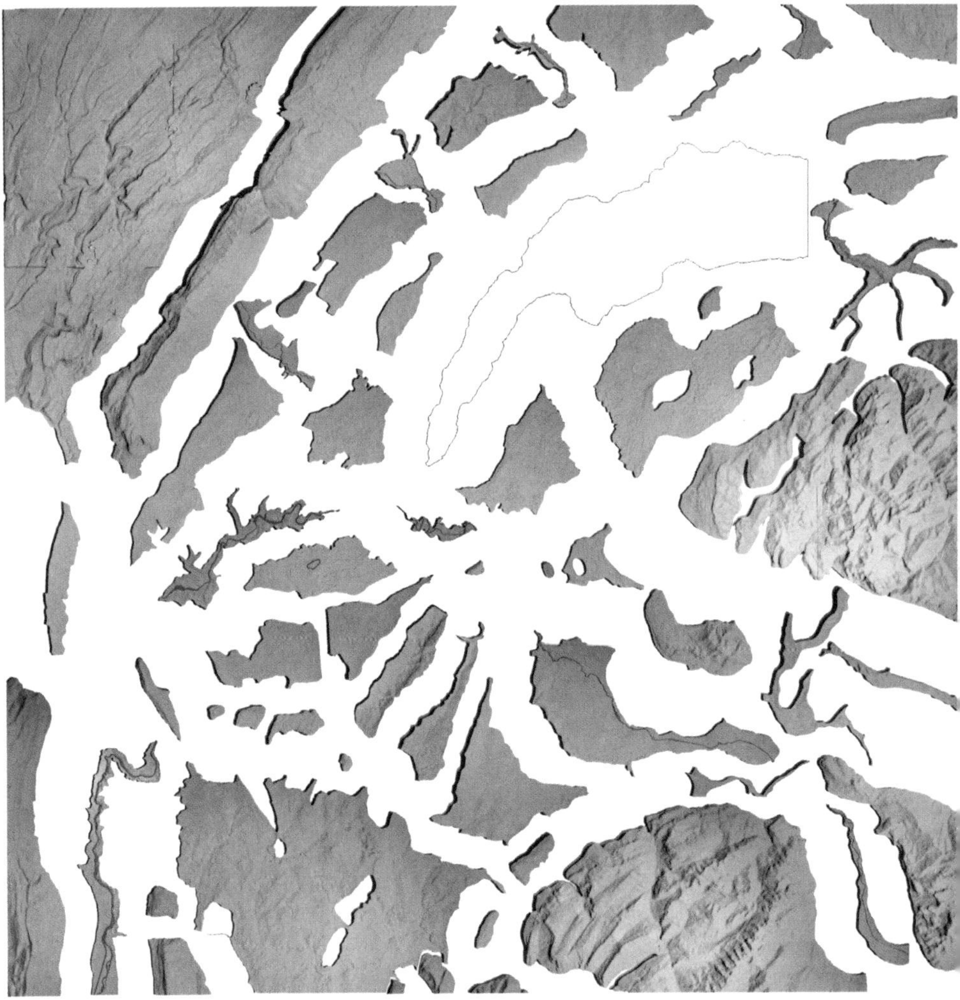

Fig. 60
Model of the Greater Geneva: the territorial subject. HRC/lab-U with students of the design studio Viganò 2018/2019, EPFL. Vision for the Greater Geneva: Living the City-Landscape of the 21st Century 2018-2021. Habitat research center, EPFL with the students of the design studios BA 5-6, MA 1-2, SAR-IA (In the context of the future plans for Grand Geneva - the Eco-Century Project®, Foundation Brouillard Architects, Geneva HRC/lab-U): Paola Viganò (HRC/lab-U Director), Vincent Kaufmann (HRC/lab-U-Laser), Alexandre Buttler (HRC/lab-U-Ecos), Luca Pattaroni (HRC/lab-U-Laser), Corentin Five (HRC/lab-U-SXL) with Roberto Sega (HRC/lab-U E.B., Coordinator of the team), Martina Barcelloni Corte (HRC/lab-U Executive Board Coordinator), Qinyi Zhang (HRC/lab-U E.B.), Tommaso Pietropolli (HRC/lab-U, Co-Coordinator of the Team) External Experts: Pascal Boivin (Intne-Hepia, Hes-So Genève), Olivier Crevoisier (University of Neuchâtel), Walter R. Stahel (Product-Life Institute), Jonathan Normand (B Lab Switzerland), Isabel Claus, Marie Velardi with: Fazaneh Bahrami (University of Groningen), Chiara Cavalieri (Catholic University of Leuven), Thomas Guillaume, Shin A. Koseki (HRC E.B.), Delphine Rime (University of Bern), Matthew Skjonsberg (HRC E.B.), Marine Durand (HRC/lab-U), Sylvie Nguyen (HRC/lab-U), Eloy Llevat Soy (Politecnico di Torino), Irène Desmarais. Client: Fondation Braillard Architectes, Geneva.

3.3 PROTOTYPES OF THE TRANSITION

The design of the Transition requires changes that we are not yet politically and economically able to implement and legislate: it is the short-sighted contemporary biopolitical project, implemented despite strong signals from the scientific world and from an increasingly significant part of society. This collective inability highlights the ineffectiveness of many of today's urban, social and economic transformations, their inadequacy in carrying out the transition, and the absence of radical choices. However, cities and territories are moving towards a review of practices, tools, and experiments in which the project—which has always been concerned with transforming existing conditions into preferable ones—finds itself in the position of having to explore, accepting the risk of being subjected to criticism and not immediately offering a proven solution to the problem posed. In such cases, proceeding by prototype is perhaps the only intellectually thorough way to embark on an unknown direction.

In urbanism, the prototype/experimentation space is mainly intended to inspire a collective debate supported by design explorations that give the future real colour, as if we could enter it and understand its qualities or, on the contrary, its shortcomings (especially those that are the undesirable outcome of a sum of good intentions). In the case of Greater Geneva, the "weak structure" of the territory is configured as an ecological, socio-political and economic opportunity, an experimental transition space representing the common interest. In Brest, the emphasis is on space and its potential role in social and environmental emancipation. A Finisterrae dominated by a history of destruction linked to World War II, a city fragmented by the presence of military areas extending over a large part of its geography can be thought of as a large "transition laboratory".

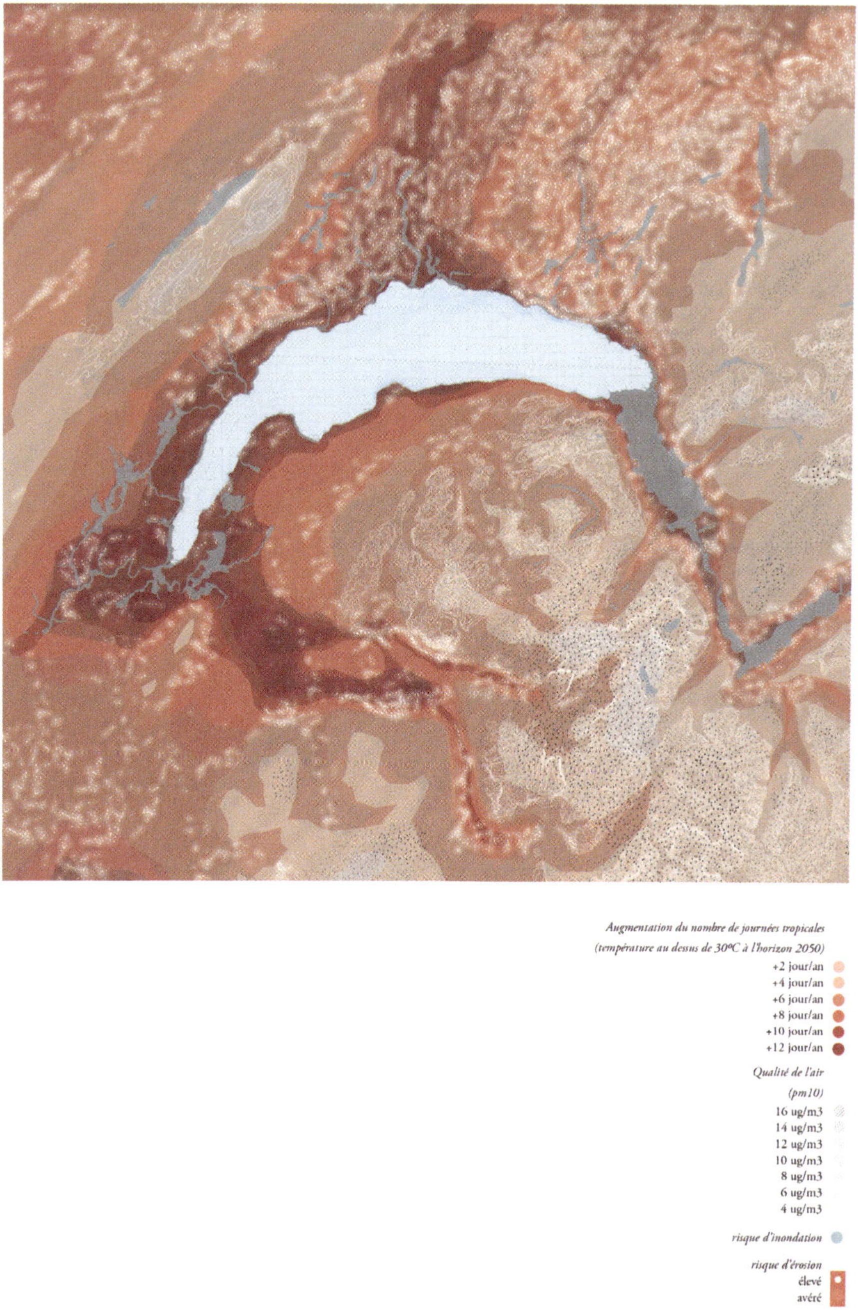

Fig. 61
Risks and climate change in the Alpine-Leman metropolis in 2050. Noélie Lecoanet, Master thesis EPFL 2020 (Prof. P. Viganò and T. Pietropolli).

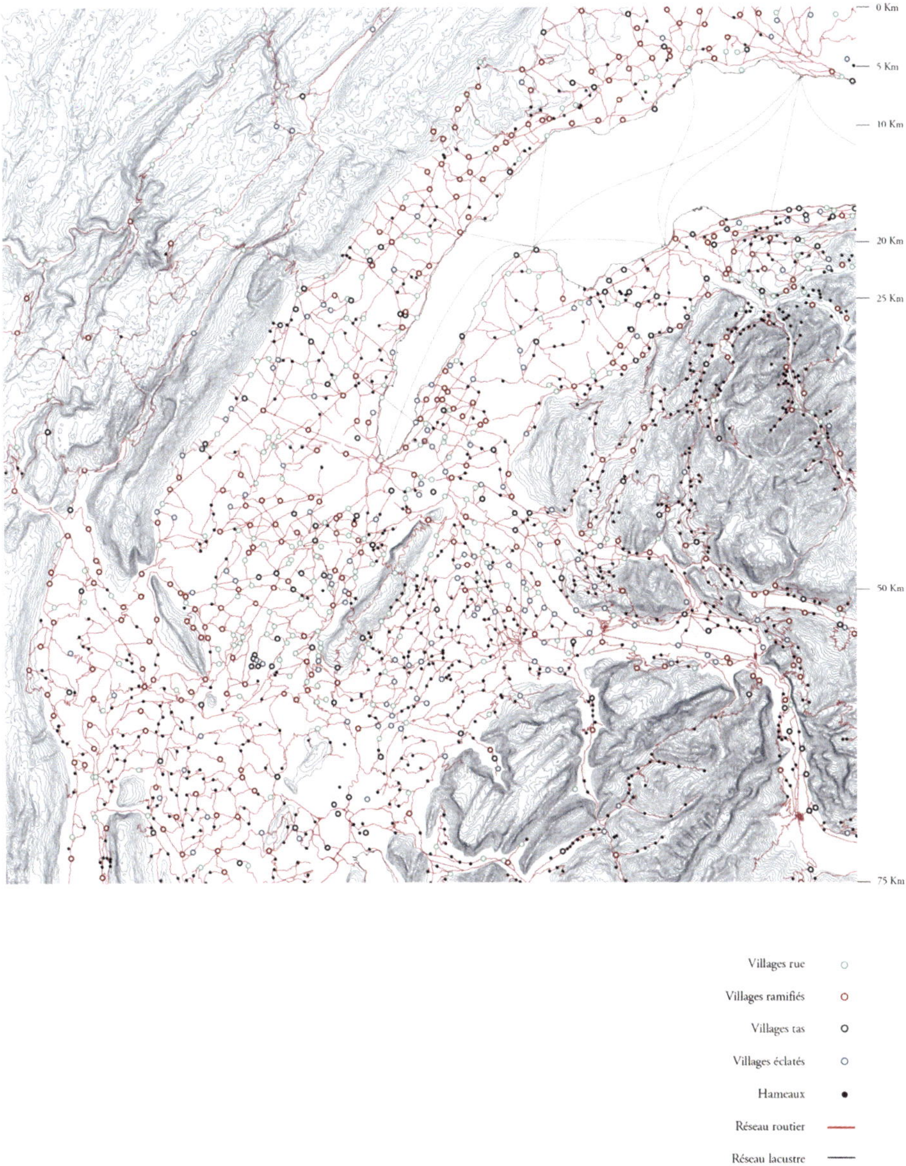

Fig. 62
A metropolis of villages, HRC/ lab-U, Epfl 2020.

Soil and Labour. Prototypes of weak structures in Greater Geneva

At the beginning of the twentieth century, soil and labour were the two great witnesses to the formation of a new urban condition capable of highlighting the ecological, economic and social stakes for the territory's future.[33] Likewise, they are now key factors in the interpretation of a metropolitan condition undergoing ecological, socio-demographic and economic transition in a context such as Greater Geneva. Placing soil and labour at the heart of the vision for the city-landscape of the twenty-first century was our first working hypothesis.

The second hypothesis, the transition as a new biopolitical project, considers the transition project as the possibility of a review, not only of the modern biopolitical project and all that remains implicit in space organization practices, but of the contemporary biopolitical project that has lost its ambition to achieve the universality of the right to a better life.

The two hypotheses were the focal point of the interdisciplinary project research on Greater Geneva carried out by the Habitat Research Centre (EPFL) as part of the initiative launched by the Braillard Foundation in 2018.[34] The focus on the soil has made it possible to traverse the complex issues of environmental crises (in particular on the transition to conservation agriculture), providing trajectories that nonetheless remain partial and unfinished if work, its spaces and its socio-ecological appropriateness, does not become part of it. Overcoming potentially destructive crises and imbalances requires deep reforms and the implementation of different financial models, spaces for "other" economies. "Soil and work" are therefore the lenses through which we have observed a polarised and unequal cross-border metropolis between Switzerland and France. In the proposed vision, soil is a crucial agent of the transition, and the space of work is a design opportunity to reflect on the dematerialisation/disappearance of manufacturing and the possible new rooting in the widespread settlement structure of Greater Geneva. We have placed space at the centre of our vision and in response to the issues raised: its role, its emancipation potential and its design.

Beyond the construction of a "Cross-border Atlas of transition", and having developed some scenarios on the two major themes of soil and labour, the

33. I refer to Rowntree 1910.

34. Habitat Research Center, DU SOL ET DU TRAVAIL. La transition, un nouveau projet biopolitique, HRC (Prof. Paola Viganò, LAB-U, Prof. Vincent Kaufmann, LASUR, MER. Luca Pattaroni, LASUR, Ass. Prof. Corentin Fivet, SXL; Dr. Martina Barcelloni Corte, Dr. Shin A. Koseki, Dr. Roberto Sega, Dr. Matthew Skjonsberg, Dr. Thomas Guillaume, Dr. Qinyi Zhang, Marine Durand, Tommaso Pietropolli, Eloy Llevat Soy, Irène Desmarais), with: Prof. Olivier Crevoisier (Université de Neuchâtel), Prof. Walter R. Stahel (Product-Life Institute), Prof. Pascal Boivin (inTNE-HEPIA, HES-SO Genève), Jonathan Normand (B Lab Switzerland), Isabel Claus, Ass. Prof. Farzaneh Bahrami (Université de Groningen), Ass. Prof. Chiara Cavalieri (Université Catholique de Louvain), Dr. Delphine Rime (Université de Bern), Marie Velardi.

 "eco-socio-spatial prototypes" go beyond the contemporary biopolitical project, transforming industrial platforms, dispersed districts such as turnery, transport infrastructures, and cultivated and urban soils into as many opportunities to mobilize the different parts of the territory, adapting them to climate change and new modes of coexistence. The "eco-socio-spatial prototypes" explore landscapes, economies and social practices through activities that create ecological and socio-economic value. In this vision, the inhabitants of Greater Geneva inhabit and cultivate a metropolis of villages, a city-landscape structured by a territorial public space, a "metropolitan infrastructure of socio-ecological continuity"[35] that connects them and represents the zero degree of its habitability: it is the federating figure of a dispersed, heterogeneous and contrasted metropolis. It is a set of spaces of socio-ecological continuity that rediscovers and enhances, connects and repairs the weak structure of the territory, reconsidering what has been destroyed, hidden, fragmented, and marginalised by the modern totalizing gaze. The metropolitan infrastructure of socio-ecological continuity is the most ambitious prototype.

The weak structure is multifunctional. It is a space for experimenting with ecosystem services and adapting to climate change. It is a tool for interpreting and enhancing natural and urban landscapes and their cultural characteristics. Alternative forms of mobility are developed within it and a territorial public space is created where it is possible to explore forms of urban intensification by allowing room for alternative, social and solidarity-based economies. The weak structure is a device for emancipation, which allows current development models to be re-discussed and critiqued. It is a "special surface", paraphrasing the surfaces publiques of the Bodmer-Braillard cantonal plan of the 1930s for the Canton of Geneva. In that case, too, it involved surfaces of continuity—a network of public spaces integrating villages, workspaces, plants and cultural heritage. It is a space for experimenting with the diverse and complex facets of ecological and social transition.

The weak structure is not a new topic for Geneva. From the Bodmer-Braillard grid to recent plans for the protection of biodiversity and landscapes, Greater Geneva has a history of promoting open spaces and endangered heritage. Our prototype seeks to go beyond the idea of protection proposed by Bodmer-Braillard in the mid-1930s and rather imagines the pioneering space of a new territorial organisation system that integrates open and built spaces, ecosystem services for regulation, support and production, alternative economic forms and active mobility.

35. See the research and project following the construction of the vision for Greater Geneva (Paola Viganò, Elena Cogato Lanza, with Tommaso Pietropolli dir., Marina Garlatti, Florence Bieth coord., Valentin Bourdon, Elena Calafati, Flore Guichot, Noélie Lecoanet, Mathilde Loiseau, Sylvie Nguyen, Marine Villaret, Canton of Geneva, 2021-2022).

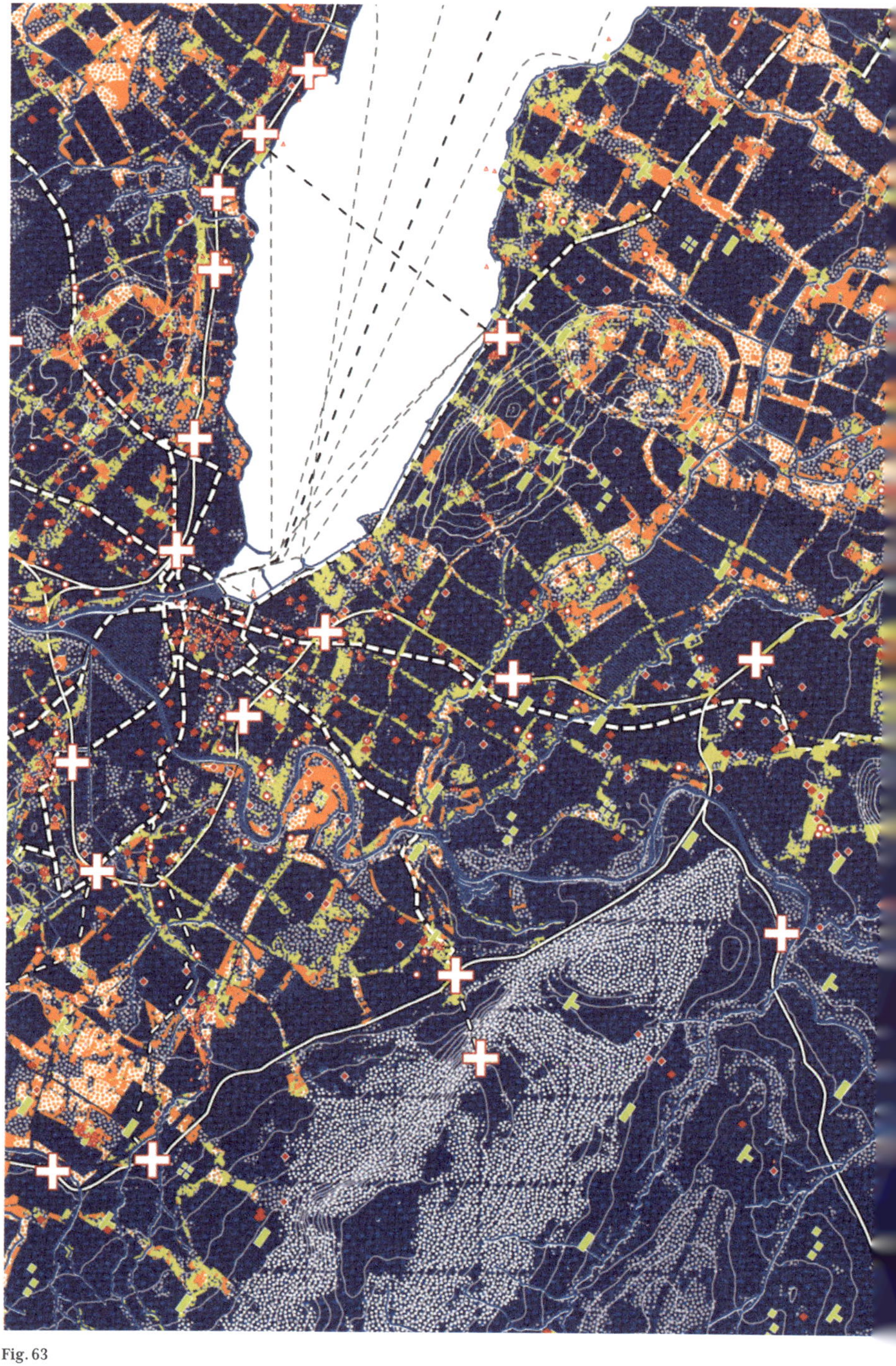

Fig. 63
The "carrying structure" of the transition: strong and weak structures. HRC/lab-U, EPFL 2020.

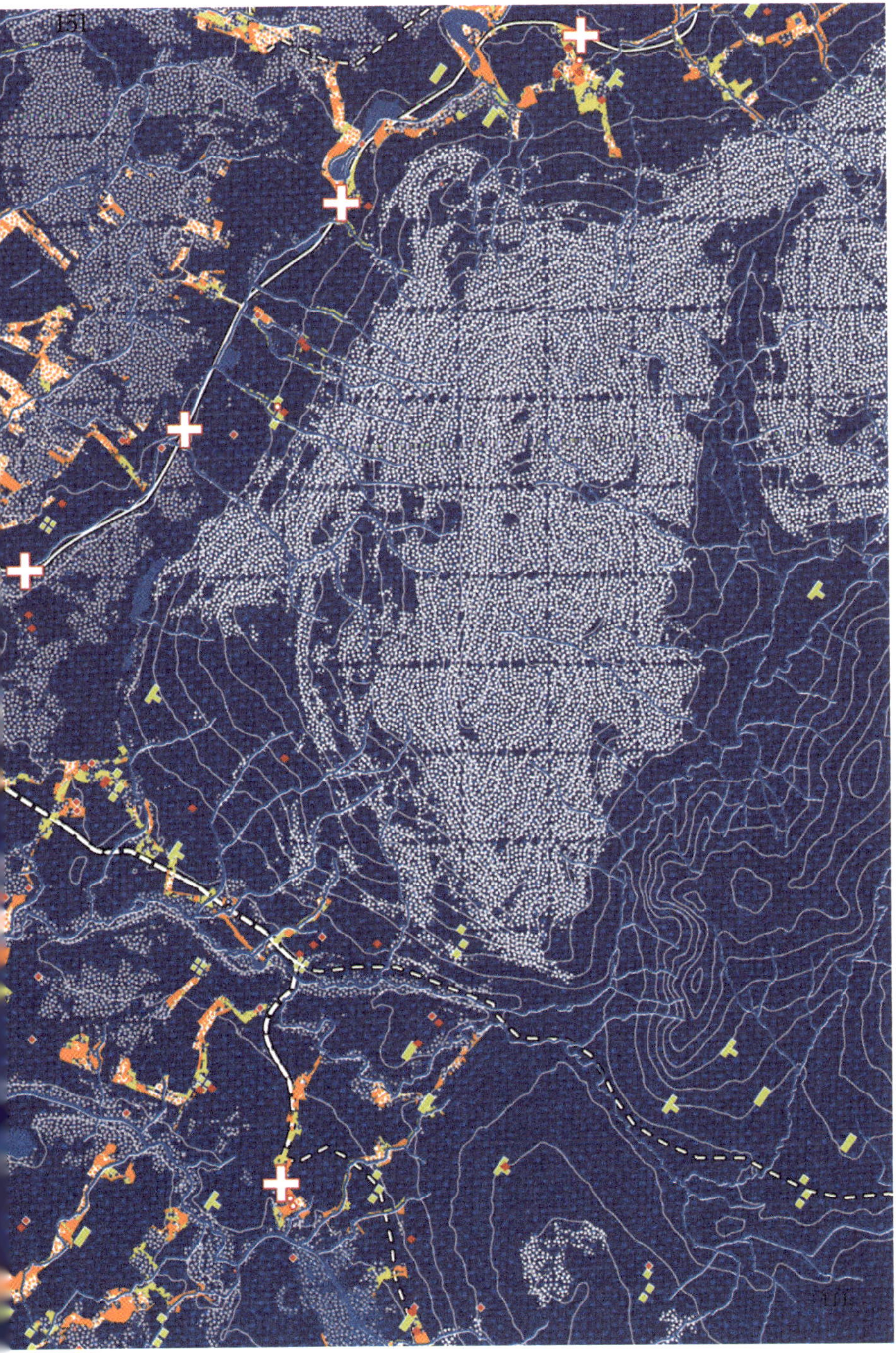

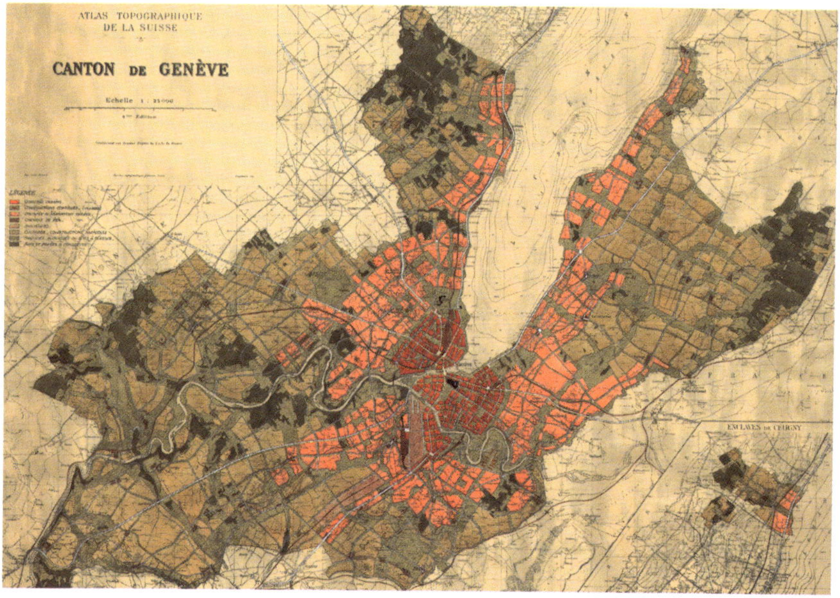

Fig. 64
Plan of the zones of the Genève canton, A. Bodmer, M. Braillard, 1936. © CRR IAUG (Centre for Research on Urban Renewal, Institute of Architecture of the University of Geneva).

We have some documents and interpretations of the Braillard grid. The two town planners imagined it on the scale of the Canton of Geneva: it is a network of public spaces covering about 30% of its surface area and is not limited to the urban part of the territory but affects the whole of it without changing its nature; it is a single structuring device for the urban organisation of the natural and agricultural space. Woods, villages to be protected, equipment, cultivated areas, urban and territorial parks such as the banks of the Rhone, paths and landscape viewpoints are part of it. It is a public space, equipped in several points and at the same time a tool for protecting and enhancing the characteristic elements of the Geneva landscape, which pays great attention to cultural landscapes, built and maintained by human activity, heritage sites made accessible to slow mobility. The grid's layout reflects the ancient Roman centuriation. Its lines are parallel to the contour lines where spectacular views of the lake open up and perpendicular to Lake Geneva, as are the incisions of the watercourses flowing down the slopes.

Conceived almost a century ago and unfinished,[36] except for a few limited exceptions, there are at least two reasons why it is not easy today to imagine its completion and continuation on the scale of Greater Geneva.

Firstly: it is not known what distinguished the perimeter areas from the rest of the territory, apart from legal status and the inclusion of certain natural and cultural landscapes. In general, Bodmer and Braillard did not describe or represent the grid in adequate detail. The borders between "surfaces publiques"[37] and the other components coincide in some cases with rows of trees and paths (Cogato Lanza 2003:227). Their diagram was produced (and this is its strength) on the basis of a photographic collection from a few decades earlier of the landscapes to be safeguarded.[38] The concern for preservation, the regional scale of the project and the relationship with the different forms of urbanisation rely on an aesthetic understanding of the landscape. The question of imagery and its icons is central to the legitimisation of the plan, but it is not fully explicit.

Secondly, not enough fragments were created to define an overall image, even at the original project scale: that of the Canton of Geneva alone. The traditional vocabulary of Olmsted's park system may be a pertinent reference, above all for the ecosystemic approach that pays great attention to the functions of the soil, water, vegetation and the continuity of paths,[39] but it is not sufficient to design the grid. The Braillard-Bodmer plan is a diagram that still holds fascination today, but it is a space without representation, without image and with no materiality.

Our intention was not to reread it with philological intentions—such operations have already been carried out in the past—but to decontextualise it, extracting it and placing it in the present time. Its radicality is contained in what made its accomplishment difficult. Representing its burning topicality is therefore decisive: it is a question of using drawings, different scales of

36. The Plan Directeur of Geneva of 1935 and the Plan directeur régional of 1936 (to which the grid belongs) are "one of the emblematic products of Red Geneva" by Léon Nicole (1933-1936) (Léveillé 1987). From 1933 to 1936 Braillard carried out his work at the Département des Travaux Public, elected by the Comité de direction del Partito Socialista et al Conseil d'Etat Chef du DTP (Vicari 1984). Together with Albert Bodmer, director of the Service d'Urbanisme, he designed some of the structure plans (Plan directeur des artères, 1934; Plan directeur de Genève, 1935, Plan directeur régional, 1936; or Plan des zones 1937), 1896-2001 Projets d'urbanisme pour Genève, Georg Editeur, Chene-Bourg, Département de l'aménagement, de l'équipement et du logement. Research directed by Alain Léveillé (IAUG).

37. In addition to the surfaces to be used for agriculture, the plan indicates the surfaces publiques ou sites à classer.

38. See Fatio 1899. Fatio uses the term parc to describe his vision for the Canton of Geneva. In the spirit of the time, it was un parc de villas that relied on the numerous transport infrastructures; for the heritage elements selected by the Plan des zones: Camille Martin, Sites et paysages genevois, 1919, text again accompanied by photographs by Fred Boissonnas.

39. The system is completed with a second, staggered grid of large networks with which the first establishes precise relationships. The continuity of the promenades was also evoked in Arnold Hoechel's article 'Allons nous promener. Pour la Cité moderne", La Suisse, 28 December, 1929.

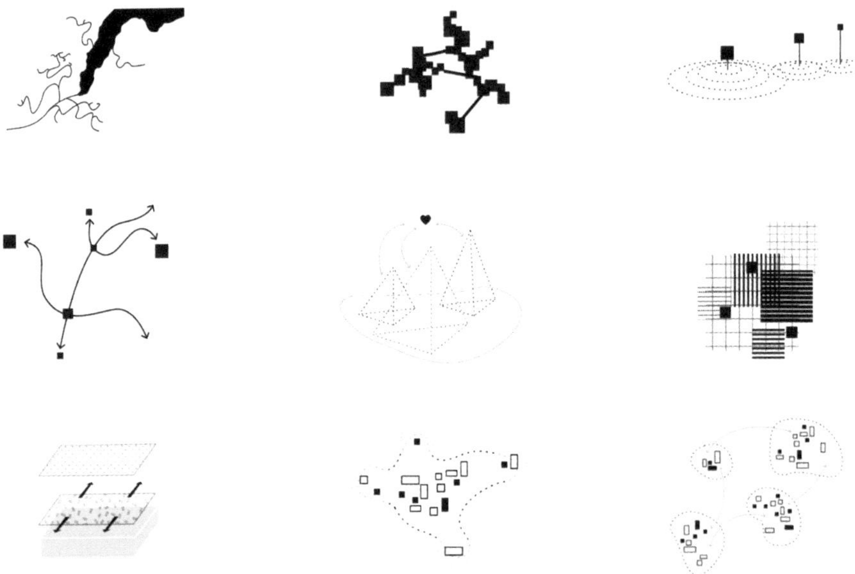

Fig. 65
A metropolitan infrastructure of socio-ecological continuity. Nine declinations. Mandate outside the building zone, HRC/lab-U (Paola Viganò, Elena Cogato Lanza, Tommaso Pietropolli, eds.). Client: OCAN (Office Cantonal de l'Agriculture et de la Nature), or (Office de l'Urbanisme) with Direction du Grand Genève.

models and diagrams capable of restoring the complexity and courage of the hypotheses contained in a plan from almost a century ago.

Starting with this inescapable reference, we followed three paths and made some moves. Firstly, it was necessary to take note of the strength of the diagram representing the grid as one, continuous, abstract and generalisable. While it is true that walking along some of its stretches shows it to be a sophisticated instrument of territorial reading,[40] the homogeneity of its representation, a smooth surface that does not deliver either the topographical richness or the variety of the territory, becomes an obstacle when it comes to filling it in with content. As a result, the first path was to represent the diagram differently, emphasising and giving value to the heterogeneity and the expression of differences. Works by contemporary artists like Jean Dubuffet, Yves Zurstrassen

40. Exercise carried out by Elena Cogato Lanza, who also uses contemporary landscape photography (Cogato Lanza 2003).

 and Sam Francis help to move away from the peremptory nature of the modern project without losing its demonstrative intent, which we instead want to keep intact. It is a matter of expressing the capacity of a "weak structure", water, woods and cultivated fields, as well as villages, schools, squares, work and care spaces, etc., to contribute to the construction of a federator project for Greater Geneva. Collages of various materials, freehand drawings, and models provide a new interpretation of the idea of continuity.

Alongside these representations, we carried out surveys to understand not only the structural aspect, but also the equally important "purely visual" aspect. The grid not only seeks to organise the territory but is also and above all a practical device for reading the landscape, for constructing sequences, and for aesthetic enjoyment. With some difficulty, since the grid has not been created, we followed its geography, made videos, sketched sequences and conceptually reinterpreted the kinematic flow of images. Other representations are based on those that are well rooted in the collective imagination of Geneva, such as the profile of the Alps sculpted against the purple and yellow sky with the thick black strokes of Ferdinand Hodler's paintings. The power of these representations can be read as an anticipation of the iconic power of the prototype of socio-ecological continuity once it has been achieved. Icon of the twenty-first century landscape city.

The second path questions the Bodmer-Braillard project starting with the performance and functionality it could offer if extended to the whole of Greater Geneva: to "design the transition" in a prototypical space of experimenting with its multiple dimensions. This path stems from an in-depth exploration of the initial ambitions of the Braillard grid that are still relevant today (among them all, the hybrid nature of the grid which crosses city and countryside without establishing borders, green belts or distinctions, pioneer of a new urban dimension). This space has a clear capacity to make the ecological system more robust—a privileged place for implementing climate change mitigation and adaptation strategies relating to water, air, soil and vegetation—by making space for watercourses squeezed into their channelled beds, reopening the covered ones and recreating the wetlands that characterised the Geneva basin, which have a high CO_2 absorption capacity. The soils of the continuity surfaces then become the prototypes of an agro-ecological regeneration project that can be extended to the entire territory, finding, as the scenarios demonstrate, the conditions for essential experimentation for the whole of Greater Geneva. The biodiversity spaces, already identified by the landscape protection plans, are integrated and strengthened by belonging to the prototype.

In addition to these functions is the space of active mobility in a territory that is still conceived as separated in two by the border and that continues to invest in large car-based infrastructures. Reviewing the space for the car

Fig. 66
Weak structures for the 21st-century metropolis. HRC/lab-U, with students P. Andelic, N. Lecoanet, Atelier Viganò, MA, EPFL, 2019.

Following pages: Figs.67-68
Above: Multifunctional section for the renaturalization projects along the Aire River in Bernex. HRC/lab-U with V. Bali, M. Bischof, A. Clarke, E. Kiosse, MAS-UTD 2021, EPFL
Below: Metabolic section of the Great Geneva: HRC/lab-U, EPFL, 2020.

allows us, as we have already demonstrated in previous research and projects (Viganò 2016; Viganò 2020), not only to regain parts of the soil, demineralize compact surfaces and reduce CO_2 emissions, but to rethink the city as a whole, starting with public space. The representations used in this second path clarify the systemic character of the prototype. They accumulate layers, each of which contains specific logics and rationalities. They reveal unprecedented geographies that develop internal and external synergies. In essence, it is a matter of imagining the infrastructure of socio-ecological metropolitan continuity as a space of experimentation encompassing ecosystemic services and social spaces, for the adaptation of the entire environment to climate change and not exclusively conceived in an anthropocentric way.

But the radicalism of the prototype becomes comprehensible if we add to the two previous paths a last hypothesis that has its roots in the status of the surface publique of the Bodmer-Braillard grid and in the conviction that the transition project cannot be achieved within the current socio-economic system. That is: the conditions for an adequate change of course do not exist as yet. However, criticism of the contemporary biopolitical project finds the very need for change to be an important testing and experimentation ground. But it requires the formulation of radical hypotheses. We therefore propose that the project of the infrastructure of continuity be configured as an experimental space, thanks to its surface publique and collective nature (we will see later the variations this term can take on), a space in which the common interest is represented. In Bodmer and Braillard's original project, the proposal of surfaces publiques is legitimised by the conviction of the importance of safeguarding the territory, a theme that runs through the modernity of the tabula rasa, the expression of a bad conscience that opposes generalised cultural and ecological destruction with the selection of a few places in which to entrust the task of memory and conservation of an undefined identity. The centrality of the theme of safeguarding the natural and cultural landscape in the 1936 plan des zones is still a priority today: it is a question of safeguarding, protecting, regenerating soils, work, landscapes. But while in the plan des zones and in the pages of La campagne genevoise d'après nature (Fatio 1899) the purpose of the inventory was to carve out the minimum plinth of permanence from the background of generalised modernisation, in our case the relationship between the infrastructure of continuity and the territory is of a completely different kind.

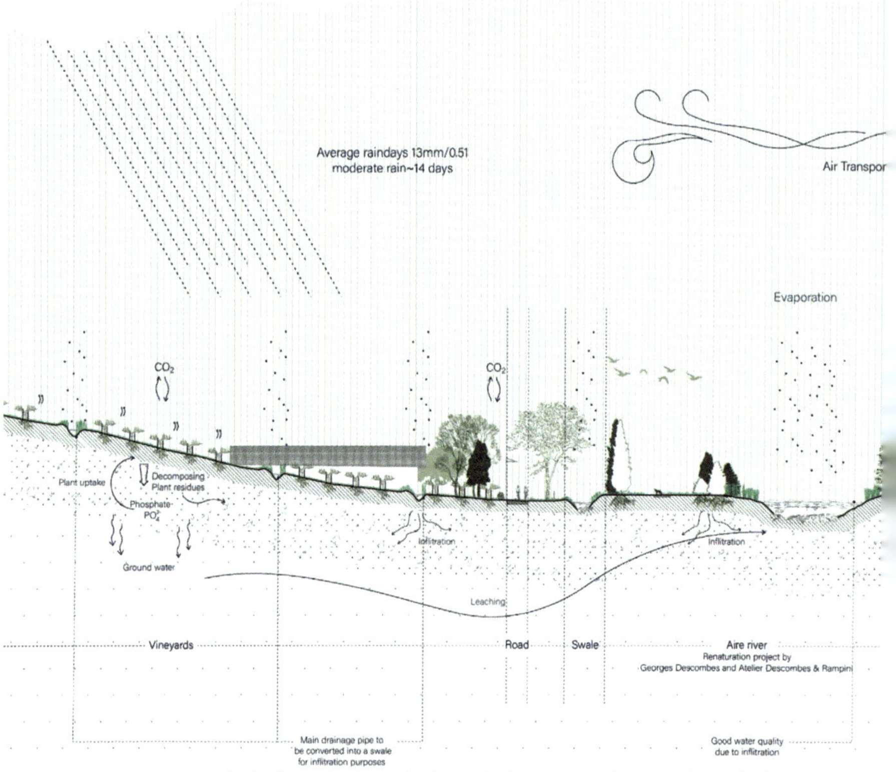
Average raindays 13mm/0.51
moderate rain~14 days
Air Transpor
Evaporation
CO_2
CO_2
Plant uptake
Decomposing
Plant residues
Phosphate
PO_4^{3-}
Ground water
Infiltration
Infiltration
Leaching
Vineyards
Road
Swale
Aire river
Renaturation project by
Georges Descombes and Atelier Descombes & Rampini
Main drainage pipe to
be converted into a swale
for infiltration purposes
Good water quality
due to infiltration

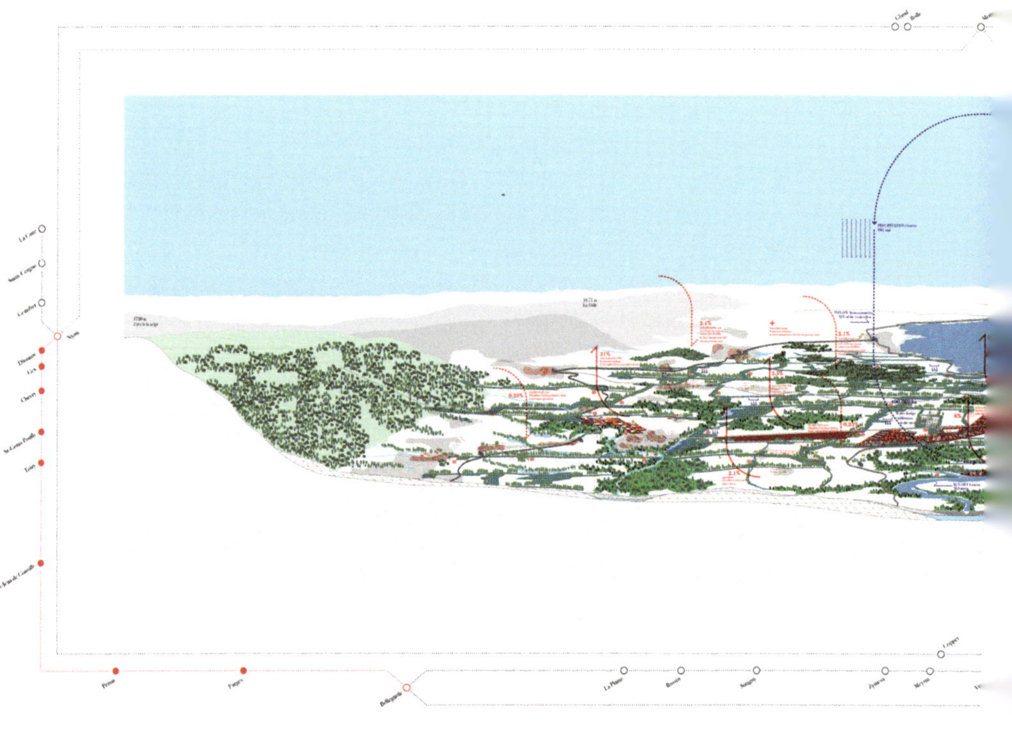

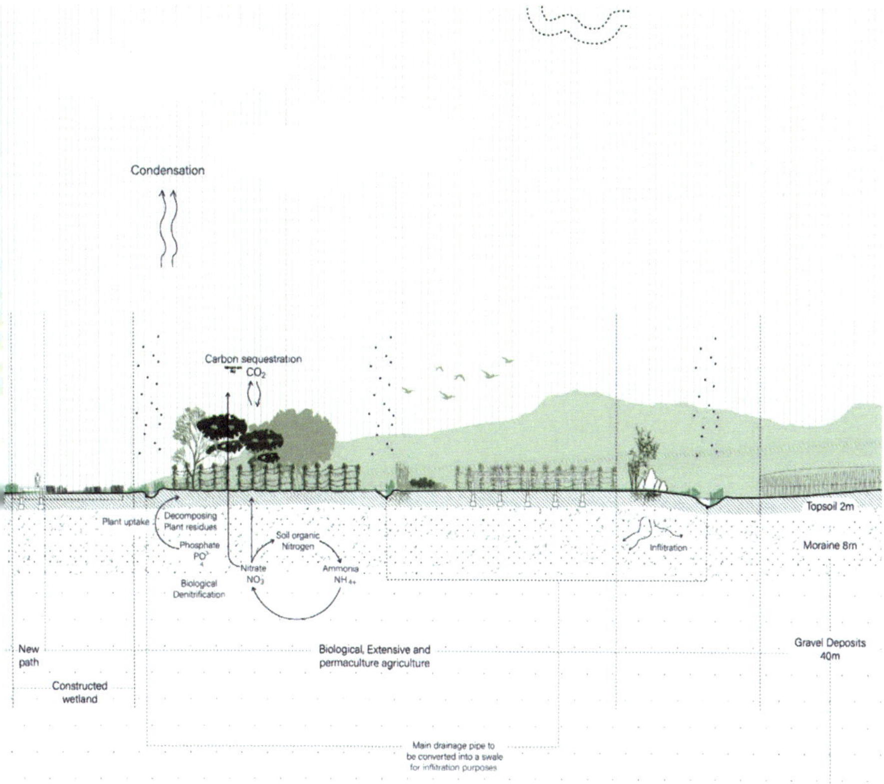
Condensation
Carbon sequestration
CO_2
Plant uptake
Decomposing
Plant residues
Phosphate
PO_4^{3-}
Soil organic
Nitrogen
Nitrate
NO_3
Ammonia
NH_{4+}
Biological
Denitrification
Infiltration
Topsoil 2m
Moraine 8m
New
path
Constructed
wetland
Biological, Extensive and
permaculture agriculture
Gravel Deposits
40m
Main drainage pipe to
be converted into a swale
for infiltration purposes

Fig. 69
Agropolitan development: Pays de Gex, St. Genis Pouilly, HRC/lab-U, with students G. Ravera, T. Nakamura, Atelier Viganò, Ma, Epfl, 2020.

Beyond the idea of safeguarding and heritage, the weak structure anticipates and experiments with a new and different project that could be extended to the whole territory. The question concerns how the territorial project can help to highlight the biopolitical nature of the transition, giving form to substantial action on the space of living together and the sharing of a common life (Viganò 2020).

This is not a scenario, but a proposal to create prototypes for coexistence, mitigation and adaptation, imagining the surfaces publiques not only, and not so much, as an entirely public space but rather as a "special zone" within which different forms and rules of design and management of the cultivated areas, public services, land maintenance, economy, living and so on can be tested. Special zones, free zones are used in cases of economic imbalance, when the current political-economic mechanisms are unable to provide appropriate responses to the seriousness of the problems.

The patrimonial space of the plan des zones[41] was a place of collective practices in which a common savoir faire was embodied. In the vision we propose, a radical reconstruction of practices, tools and positions can be imagined starting with the weak structure. The metropolitan infrastructure of socio-ecological continuity is the most ambitious prototype contained in the vision for the Greater Geneva "city-landscape of the 21st century".

41. Elena Cogato Lanza compares the two positions of Fatio and Camille Martin, reaching the conviction that the notion of heritage used is an expression of Fatio's positions (Cogato Lanza 2003:256; Fatio 1899).

Fig. 70
Brest 2040: City-Landscape Planning Guide, 2021. Studio018-023PaolaViganò (not ongoing anymore) Paola Viganò, Alessia Calò, Morvan Rabin, Pietro Manaresi, Mathilde Meurice, Bertrand Plewinski, Etienne Schillers, Laure Thierrée. With: Idea Consult, Egis, Scopic, Guam Conseil. Client: Brest Métropole.

Brest 2040: City Landscape in Transition

"Brest 2040, City Landscape in Transition" is the vision we have proposed for the heart of a metropolis of a Breton Finisterrae that has at its centre the Penfeld, an aber (estuary), a territorial incision bordered by cliffs that flows from north to south and crosses the centre. Brest is in the far west of Brittany and its centre was almost entirely destroyed at the end of the Second World War and then rebuilt following the plan of urban planner Jean-Baptiste Mathon. Without replicating the previous city, as was the case with the reconstruction of the centre of Saint-Malo, another city destroyed by the war, Mathon was inspired by the geometries of Vauban's plan from the eighteenth century. After building the city walls in 1694, Vauban designed a chessboard grid oriented north-west/south-east. Georges Milineau's plan in the 1920s was also based on this grid.

Far from the modern experiments being carried out in France at the time, Mathon's plan for the centre of Brest proposed a city with blocks that, in their size and the dry urban language, took in the hygienist thinking of the modern movement. But he built a neoclassical city.

The Plan Guide aims to accompany this part of the city through the transition to more fluidly connect the city and the great panoramas that open up on the estuary, to multiply the inland micro-landscapes in order to access the region's vegetational richness.

The Plan Guide is organised on two levels. The first level identifies three strategic spaces. The corniche brings the urban space closer to the Penfeld and encourages the collective appropriation of its surroundings by drawing a new continuity of public space (the surfaces in contact with water are still entirely dedicated to military areas). A metropolitan system of parks reconnects the wonderful secondary valleys and the hydraulic continuity to the Penfeld and the city centre (addressing hydraulic risk problems, public transport, heritage enhancement, urban regeneration and pollution). Finally, the metropolitan accessibility system (city-station-port), the endpoint of the national railway system, strengthens urban intensity and establishes relationships between the top of the cliff (city station) to the bottom (port). The strategic spaces enhance and structure Brest City Landscape.

Fig. 71
Above, left: The street as a catalyst for change: rue traverse (providing more space for water, vegetation, and pedestrians), 2020.

Fig. 72
Above, right: Inside the block; gardens, activities, collective services, 2020.

Fig. 73
Below: The belvedere station open to the harbour and "la rade", 2020

Fig. 74
Above: Brest 2040 City-landscape. The Corniche and the Metropolitan Facades: The city turns towards the great landscapes, 2020.

Fig. 75
Below: Renaturalisation of the Kerinou Vallon, 2020.

Fig. 76
Top to bottom and left to right: Finis Terrae City, City-Landscape, City of The Navy, Divided city, City of the Navy, Grey city, Sation-Harbour, 2020.

The second level of the Plan Guide concerns a broad and widespread regeneration project. It aims to transform the urban fabric of the reconstructed centre and Recouvrance[42] (buildings, public spaces and inner courtyards) in light of the ecological and social transition.[43]

The construction of the Plan Guide was accompanied by intense citizen participation. Some topics—the great images of Brest, the liberation of military areas, the quality of public space, and urban vitality—generated intense debates. Some occasions, such as the workshop involving several schools, in addition to the local geo-architecture school, were of great interest and extremely useful. Starting with the Plan Guide, we suggested thinking of the city centre as a "transition laboratory" and therefore as an opportunity to review the tools, policies and practices of city construction, urban aménagement. Its proposals, now being studied in depth and in the process of realisation, are also formidable opportunities to rethink the relationships between the different services of Brest Métropole and between the different policies (for example, with the guide to the creation of the public spaces of the transition, which we are currently drafting), moving away from sectorialisation and rethinking the urban project as a whole together with its Baukultur. Imagining a shift in the traditional relationships between design and collective construction, between temporality and duration, materiality and uses.

42. The undestroyed part of the Breton town, on the right bank of the Penfeld.

43. This complex set of actions invests public and private spaces (with action on energetic requalification, demineralisation of spaces, redevelopment of activities...) and has received important funding to start the regeneration of the centre reconstruit.

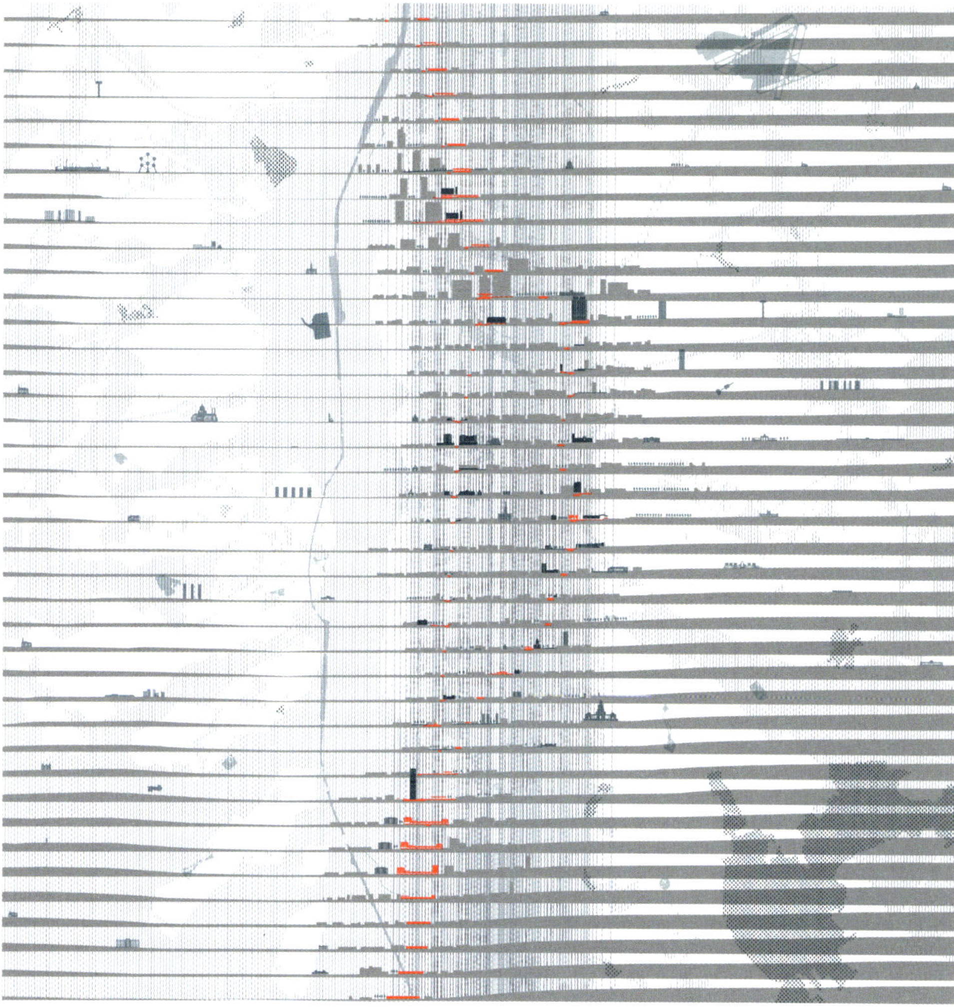

Fig. 78
Elaboration of a metropolitan vision for Brussels in 2040, Horizontal Metropolis, Tapestry (400 × 400 cm), 2013. Studio010-012 Secchi-Viganò Bernardo Secchi, Paola Viganò, Myron Devolder, Emmanuel Giannotti, Michele Girelli, Chunxiao Liang, Carlo Pisano, Ana Rafful, Veronica Saddi, Wim Wambecq, Qinyi Zhang

With: Creat- Centre for Studies in Spatial Planning, EGIS Mobility, TU München (Department of Building Climatology and Building Services) and IngenieurBüro Hausladen GmbH, Karbon', Idea Consult.
Client: Brussels-Capital Region.

3.4 DESIGN A HORIZONTAL METROPOLIS

The "Horizontal Metropolis", the vision we proposed together with Bernardo Secchi for "Brussels 2040" in 2010-12, was the basis for our interpretation of the diffuse territory of Brussels and, more generally, Belgium, and has inspired several research projects, exhibitions and publications that open up the definition of a new project for the city-territory. Two contrasting terms are juxtaposed: the traditional idea of the metropolis—the centre of a vast territory, hierarchically organised, dense, vertical, produced by polarisation—and horizontal, a diffuse, isotropic urban condition in which the boundaries between centre and periphery are lost. The two antinomian and paradoxical terms give rise to the Horizontal Metropolis that includes interconnected rural and urban landscapes, stratified territorial constructions where agricultural and non-agricultural activities, natural spaces, communication systems and transportation create original modes of coexistence. The figure of horizontality is radical and capable of challenging stable positions, static representations and established power relationships. This is why it often arouses disquiet and concern; it dissolves the centre and periphery and develops concrete spatial configurations to support and strengthen horizontal relationships. It challenges symbolic, economic and social hierarchies.

A number of themes emerge from the systematic design exploration we have carried out within this new form of dispersed metropolis; they question the situations and conditions of project implementation, the characteristics of its space, and the relationships between the subjects and players in the transformation. I have already commented on this topology in other texts. Here I will focus on just one of these themes: that of the inner peripheries.

Interior peripheries and development trajectories: the metropolitan condition is marked by holes and absences. A part of Belgium, especially in the Walloon region, is still suffering from the decline of the large steel industry and coal mining. The projects for the Val de Sambre, Herstal, La Louvière, and Charleroi outline more general considerations on development and transition.

Interior peripheries and public space: while the Horizontal Metropolis is a vast, largely fertile and productive populated area with a high quality of life, many of its problems are concentrated in the centre of denser urban areas. The "inner peripheries" require major redevelopment and

Fig. 79
Brussels 2040, hyper-realistic model, 2012.

regeneration investments. In the Peterbos district in Brussels (Anderlecht), the unprecedented reading of a late modern urban planning episode, located on a site of great beauty, developed a robust "ground project" that affected the open spaces and ground floors of the buildings. The design of the public space reveals its environmental and social complexity.

The different projects intersect a vision of socio-cultural and economic development, reactivating spaces and territorial energies at the same time.

Interior peripheries and development trajectories: Wallonia

The European mining corridor is a vast coal-rich geological complex stretching from east to west for over 400 km, from Nord-Pas-de-Calais (France) to the Ruhr (Germany) passing through the province of Hainaut (Belgium) and Limburg. This furrow was at the centre of European industrialisation in the nineteenth and twentieth centuries, linked to coal mining. The regions situated along the sillon underwent a similar evolution: in France, Belgium, Germany. Their reconversion has been slow and often contradictory.

The projects affecting this territory all share a threefold hypothesis: 1) they have gone from spaces left on the margins, polluted and exploited to becoming part of a larger park, at European scale, 2) they are the outcome of a dialogue between urban and territorial design and a plurality of development economies, including alternative economies, 3) they are places where the very condition of crisis can encourage ecological and social transition. They are the development plan for the Val de Sambre, the regeneration project for the former ACEC area in Herstal (Liège), the Blue Space of the Eurometropolis Lille-Tournai-Kortrijk (at the north-western limits of the coal belt and only partially in Wallonia), the vision for La Louvière 2050, and the masterplan for the South Gate of Charleroi. I will conclude with some notes on the strategic scheme for the Vesdre Valley, affected by heavy flooding in July 2021 and still under construction today.

Herstal: Green Life

Herstal and the ACEC site are located along the Meuse in Liège, at the crossroads of landscapes in the heart of Europe: large natural and fertile regions, the river and the European mining corridor. At the site, these landscapes are still fully recognisable: the proximity of a productive agricultural plateau stretching across the area through meadows and orchards in a rural atmosphere; the presence of the Meuse and the hillside sloping down towards the ACEC site; the industrial heritage with its monumental buildings and the various

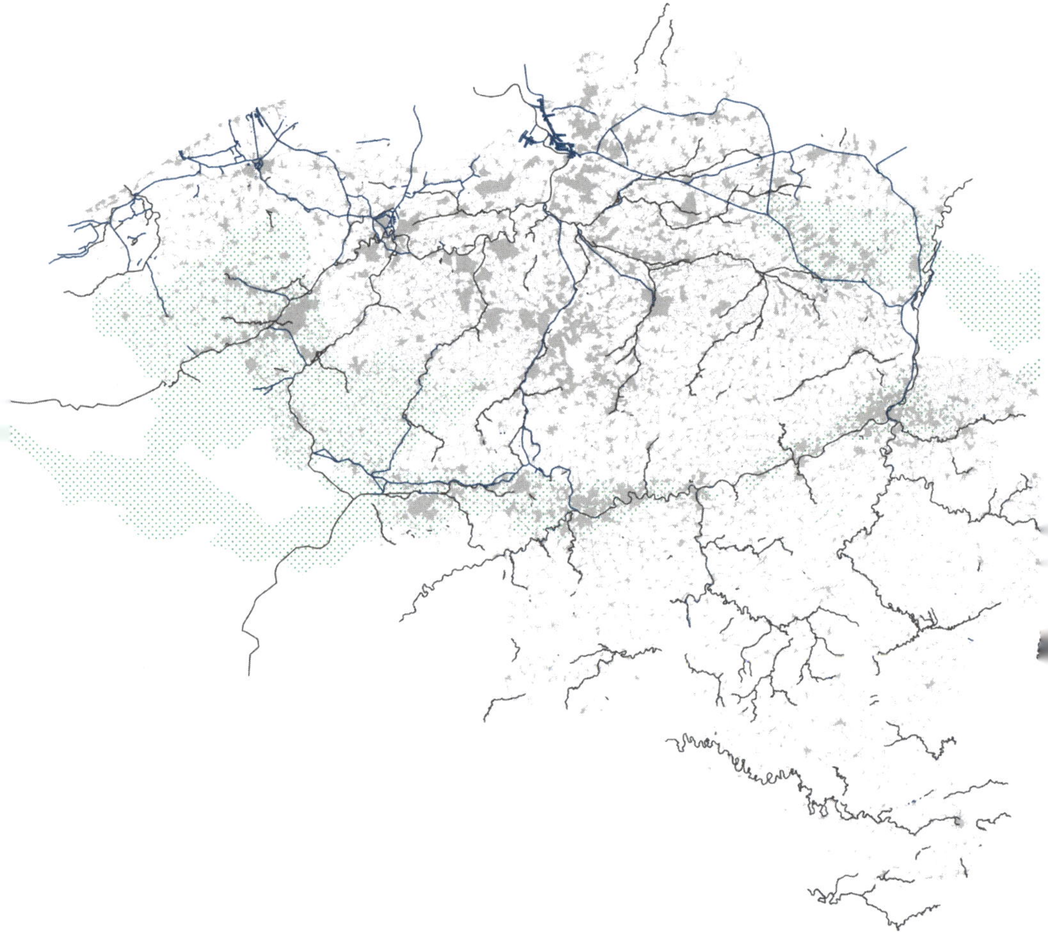

Fig. 80
Wallonia, from "black country" to park at the European scale, 2020. La Louvière 2050 city project. Studio018-020paolaviganò. Paola Viganò, Alessia Calò, Achille Pelletier, Klara Sladeckova.
With: Idea Consult, ICEDD.
Client: La Louvière Municipality

Following pages:
Fig. 81
Redevelopment of the ACEC site in Herstal in 2018. Herstal, Liège, site requalification of ACEC former industrial area. Green life. Studio017-018PaolaViganò Paola Viganò, Alessia Calò, Bertrand Plewinski, Morvan Rabin. With: Idea Consult, Sweco, Risk Benelux Sprl, Origin architecture & engineering. Client: Herstal Municipality, SPI

Fig. 82
Integrated Territorial Development Project of Sambreville and the Val de Sambre, 2018. Val de Sambre Development Plan. New life cycles. Studio017-018PaolaViganò. Paola Viganò, Alessia Calò, Bertrand Plewinski, Morvan Rabin, With: Idea consult. Client: Sambreville Municipalitiy.

traces of the infrastructure that served it (the water catchment points, for example, some of which are still active and usable).

In the past, the site hosted a flagship of the Walloon economy, the ACEC (Ateliers de Constructions Electriques de Charleroi). Today, the "Verdir" project, developed by the University of Liège, is dedicated (among other things) to the extraction of molecules for biotechnology. A new future for this site emerges around new agricultural practices and small and medium-sized enterprises. As a place of research, as well as of work, Green Life is a space for living and sociability. The large industrial warehouses located in the heart of the site become the meeting point of these different components (activities, housing, equipment, leisure). A path located on a former industrial railway line connects the site to Herstal station, crossing the town. The project uses this exceptional landscape to generate a new image, focusing on innovation and a new mix of residential properties and small and medium production.

Val de Sambre: Experiencing a landscape in transition

The Val de Sambre is shaped by the chemical and glass industry and by the landscape of the Basse Sambre located between the two natural regions of Condroz and Hesbaye. The industrial era has left a landscape littered with wasteland and a population with a shortage of skills. The decline has created substantial pockets of poverty. To collectively rework its economic and social fabrics, the Val de Sambre is launching new life cycles with a project that reflects the qualities of its population and enhances its spatial capital, its great landscapes, and its environmental and social capital.

If this is a shared ambition, then there may be many opportunities and resources: the exceptional landscape along the main valley of the Sambre and the secondary valley, the metropolisation dynamics stretching from Brussels to Walloon Brabant, the proximity of universities (Gembloux Agro-Bio Tech is just a few kilometres away), the pre-existence of numerous infrastructures, the high quality of the Hesbaye soils, the presence of numerous economic businesses, and the promotion and development of a recycling sector that can complement scientific research.

The vision does not provide a fixed image for the future of Sambreville and Jemeppe-sur-Sambre, but it intertwines three figures that represent its powerful geography (the Park), its industrial past (large areas to be de-polluted, regenerated and a solid infrastructural base: the "machine"), the widespread way in which the territory and agriculture have been built up over a long period of time (the "City of 50,000 inhabitants"), a specific way of thinking of a scattered urban system as a city, even if anchored to a long-term settlement dispersion. The three images, also evoked in other situations in the region, reveal potential and complementarity, fuelling strategies on a small and large scale.

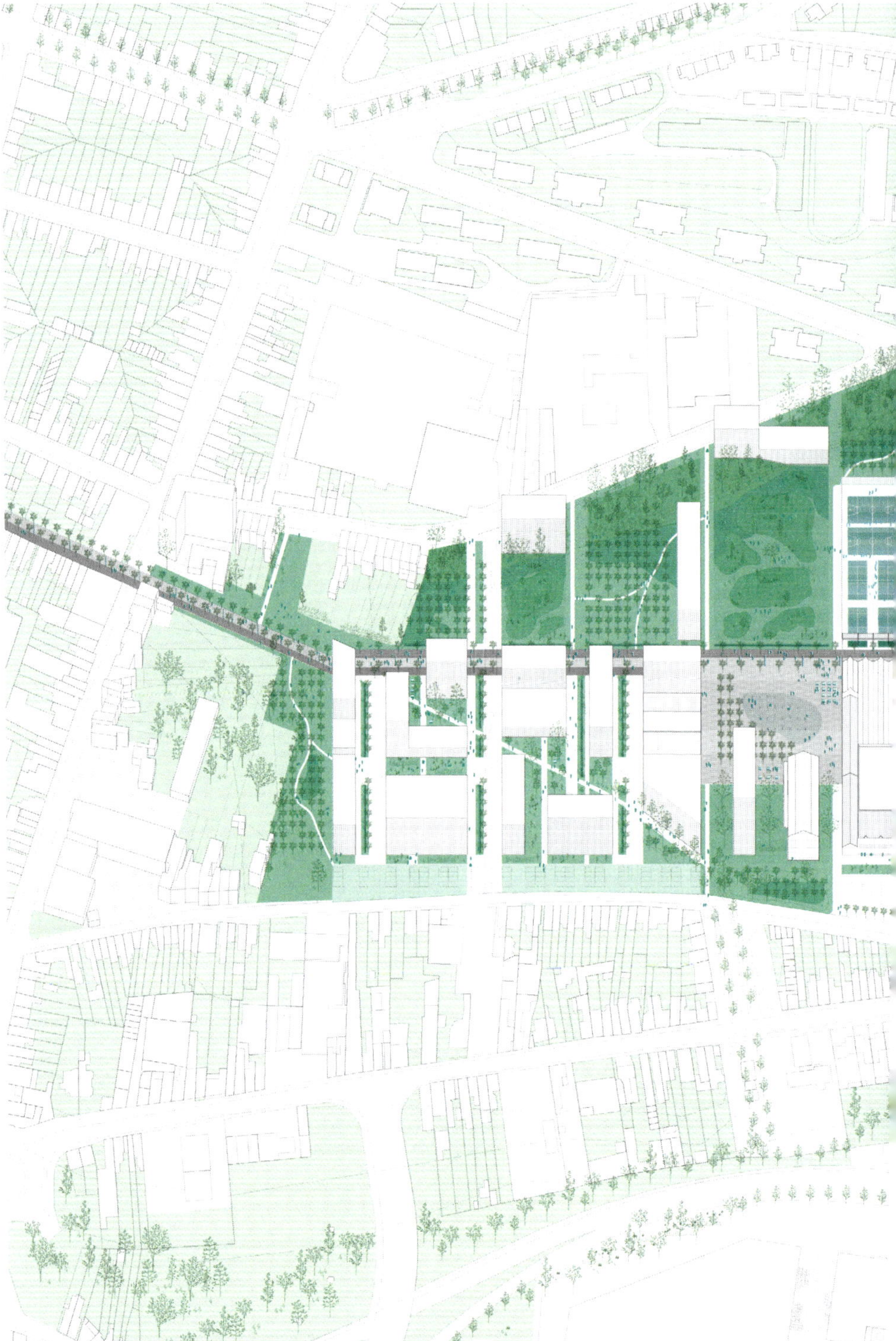

0
150
300m

Velaine
Keumiée
AUVELAIS
TAMINES
Oignies
Arsimont
Falisolle
Bois Casamagne

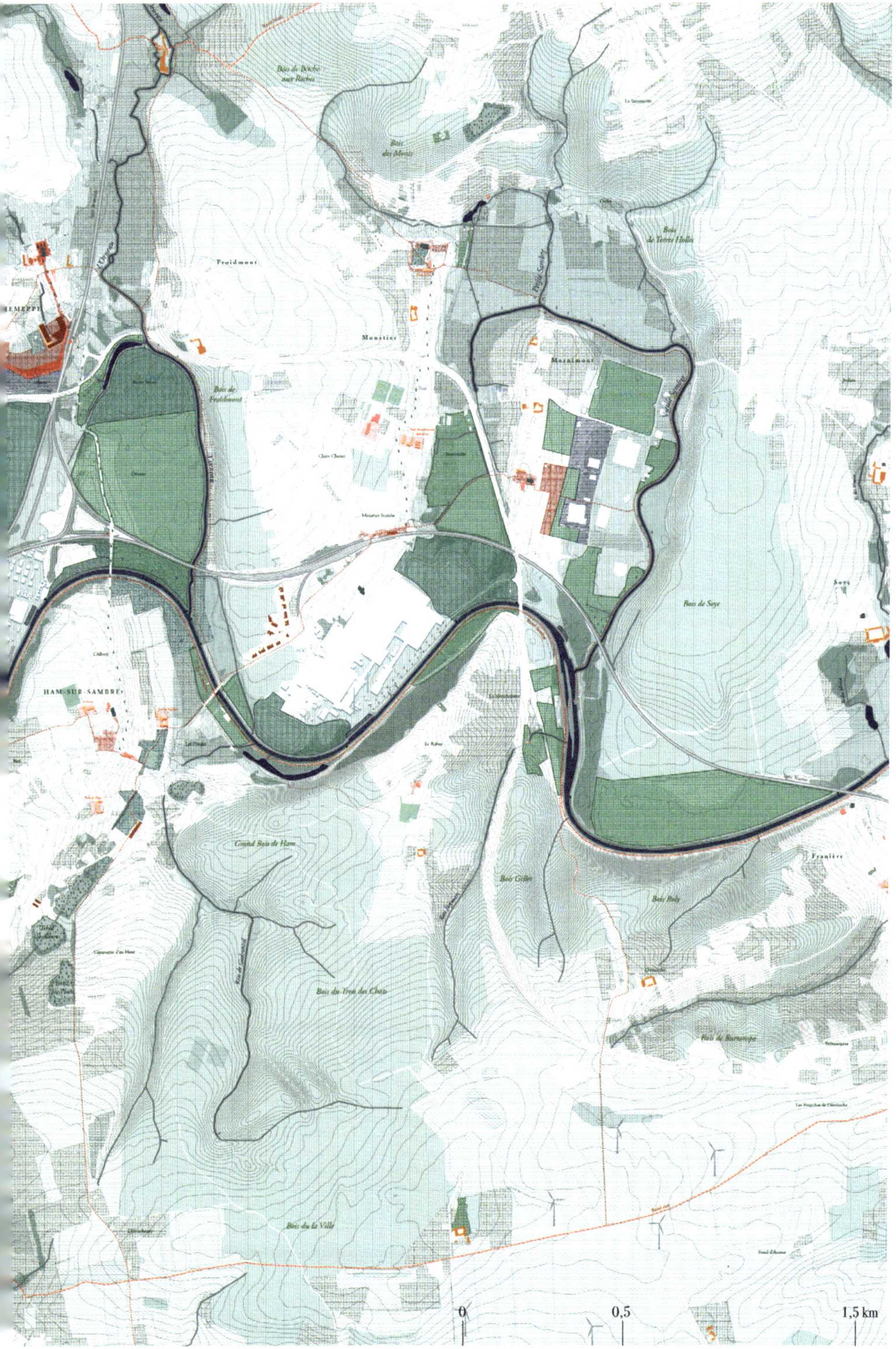

HAM-SUR-SAMBRE
Froidmont
Monstier
Mornimont
Bois de Soye
Soye
Franière
Grand Bois de Ham
Bois du Trou des Chats
Bois Ruly
0
0,5
1,5 km

Eurometropolis Lille-Tournai-Kortrijk: Blue Space

Established in 2008, the Eurometropolis Lille-Tournai-Kortrijk was the first European Grouping of Territorial Cooperation (EGTC) and comprises two countries, three regions, two languages, 147 municipalities and a population of 2.1 million inhabitants. Water, in all its forms, is the common, unifying element that provides continuity throughout the territory. Water does not care about borders: rivers, canals, minor watercourses, together with groundwater, flow through administrative and political territories.

Blue Space is a vision for the Eurometropolis that progressively reveals the space of water: "Là est le trait commun" wrote Paul Vidal de la Blache in Tableau de la géographie de la France (1903). A large, inhabited park connects and rationalises a multitude of urban landscapes, organising a multi-scalar succession of different habitats. While revealing three different spatial dimensions of water—longitudinal (watercourses), transversal (tributaries) and vertical (aquifers)—the Blue Space progressively describes the territorial park as a multi-dimensional project. A space of continuity, through 300 km of paths along canals and navigable rivers, interwoven with a reinforced railway network (corridors); a space of multiple ecologies, particularly along the numerous tributaries of the main watercourses, improving risk management strategies, strengthening ecological and open space networks (capillaries); a space of controlled infiltration within a collective governance of the common good (aquifers), at the same time thickening the space, expanding the roles and functions of the park. Blue Space is a vision and a political programme capable of re-structuring the extended city of the twenty-first century.

La Louvière: A project for the transition

After a long period of economic decline, La Louvière is currently in a historical context of transition and profound transformation. Climate change forces us to read and imagine the territory in different ways and to prepare it for ecological and social transition. The Projet de Ville develops a long-term vision to guide the city's transformation in the short and medium term and awaken a "dormant human capital" (Ferragina 2012). Its high quality territories (fertile soils, UNESCO-protected canals, remnants of ancient forests and industrial heritage, polluted areas to be regenerated) are at the heart of the La Louvière 2050 Ville Parc de Wallonie vision, along with the valorisation of its diffuse urbanity (the Civic Constellations) and the revival of the multiform and circular economies that can arise from the valorisation of the territory and its inhabitants: the residential, experiential, social and solidarity economy,

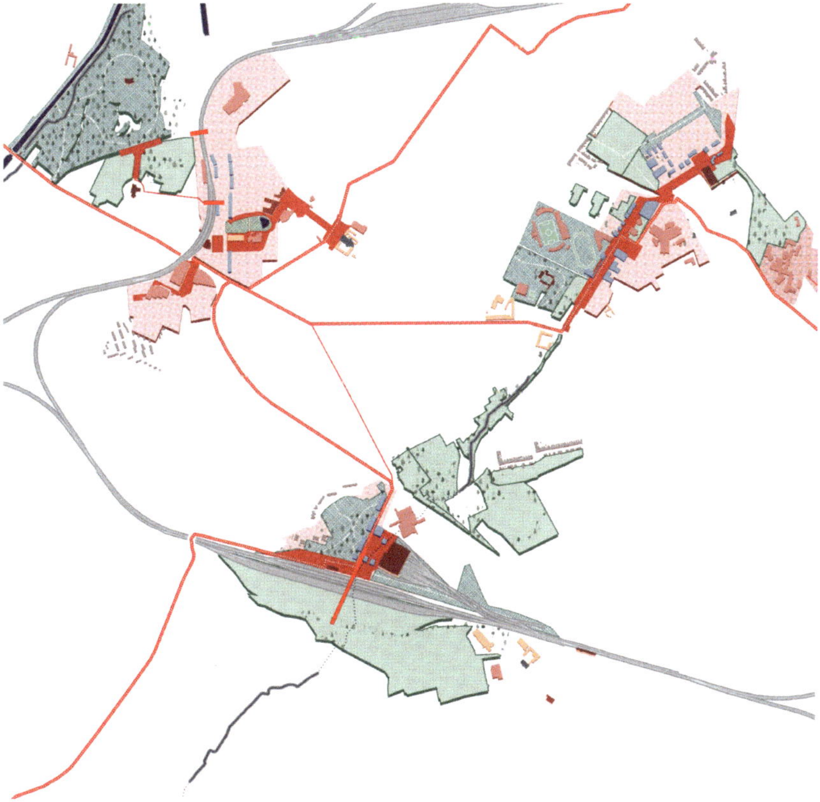

Fig. 83
Masterplan La Louvière Gare sud: scheme, 2021Studio021PaolaViganò. Paola Viganò, Achille Pelletier, Mathilde Meurice, Thomas Brun. With: Idea Consult, Arcadis, Saicom

together with the still existing industrial economy. The different forms of economy and capital (human, environmental, spatial, cultural, etc.) are mutually activated in a territory that retains enormous qualities, despite the exploitation to which it has been subjected. Its remains will require many decades to be tamed, neutralized or absorbed into a process of multi-scalar and multi-thematic regeneration that has enormous potential to increase their value.

Regionaal Landschap
West-Vlaamse Heuvel
Heulebeek
Neerbeek
Geluwebeek
Kapellebeek
Kortekeerbeek
Douvebeek
LEIE
LYS
Markembeek
Rekkembeek
Becque de Neuville
Becque De Bois
La Grande Espie
L'Esperlio
Becque Dewasiers
Becque du Plaque
DEULE
Becque de Corbeau
La Marque
Pas à Wasn
LILLE
ourant de la Libaude
don sainghin

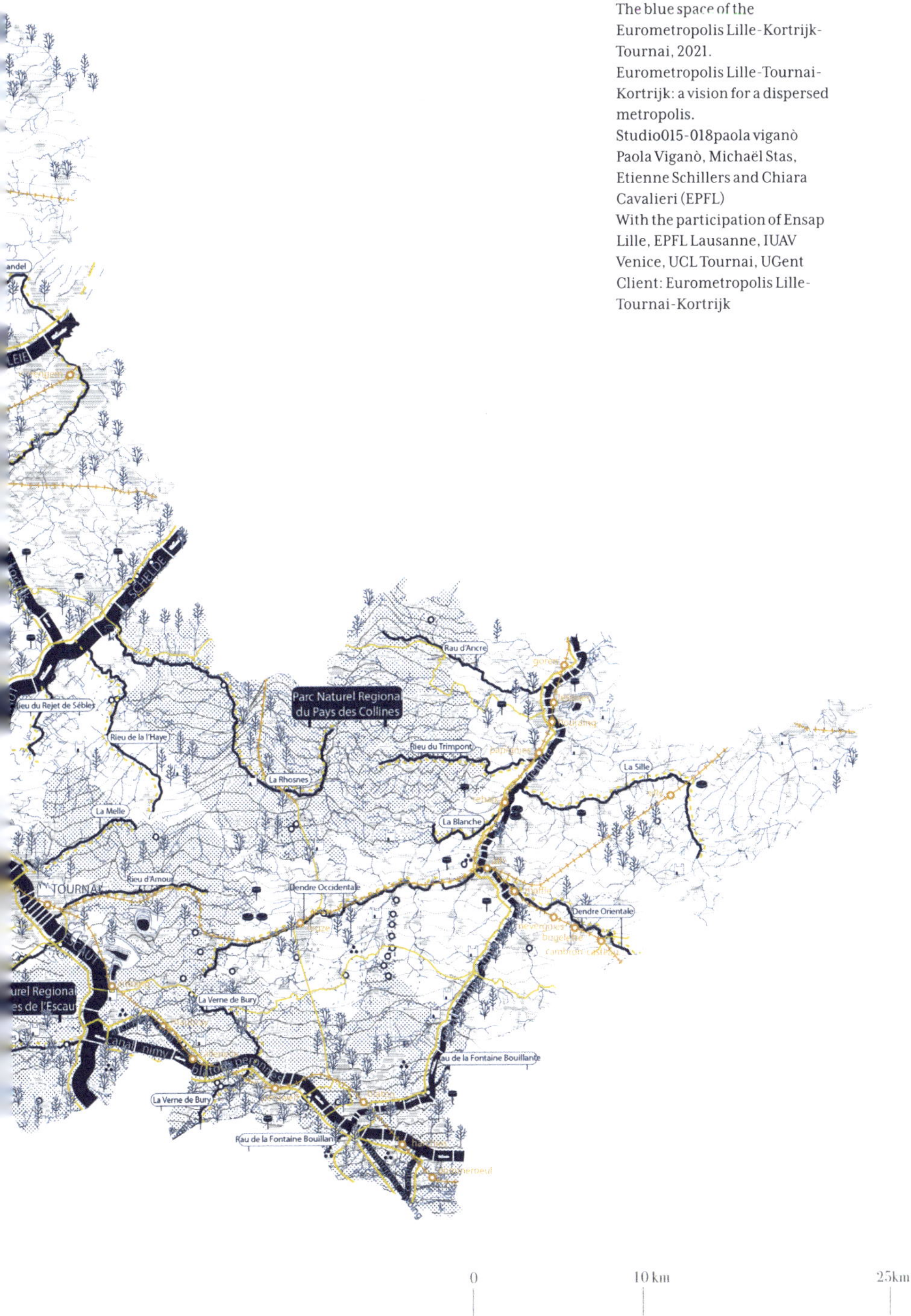

Fig. 84
The blue space of the Eurometropolis Lille-Kortrijk-Tournai, 2021.
Eurometropolis Lille-Tournai-Kortrijk: a vision for a dispersed metropolis.
Studio015-018paola viganò
Paola Viganò, Michaël Stas, Etienne Schillers and Chiara Cavalieri (EPFL)
With the participation of Ensap Lille, EPFL Lausanne, IUAV Venice, UCL Tournai, UGent
Client: Eurometropolis Lille-Tournai-Kortrijk

Fig. 85
La Louvière City Project 2050, 2020.

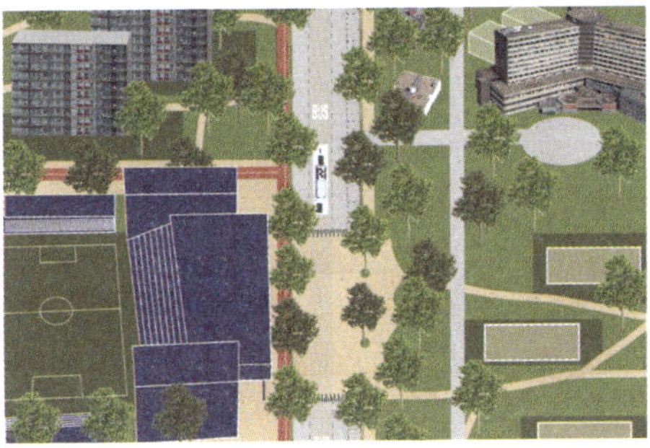

Fig. 86
Above: City-Park of Wallonia, 2020.

Fig. 87
Below, left: Space for Multiple and Resilient Economies, 2020.

Fig. 88
Below, right: Civic Constellations, 2020.

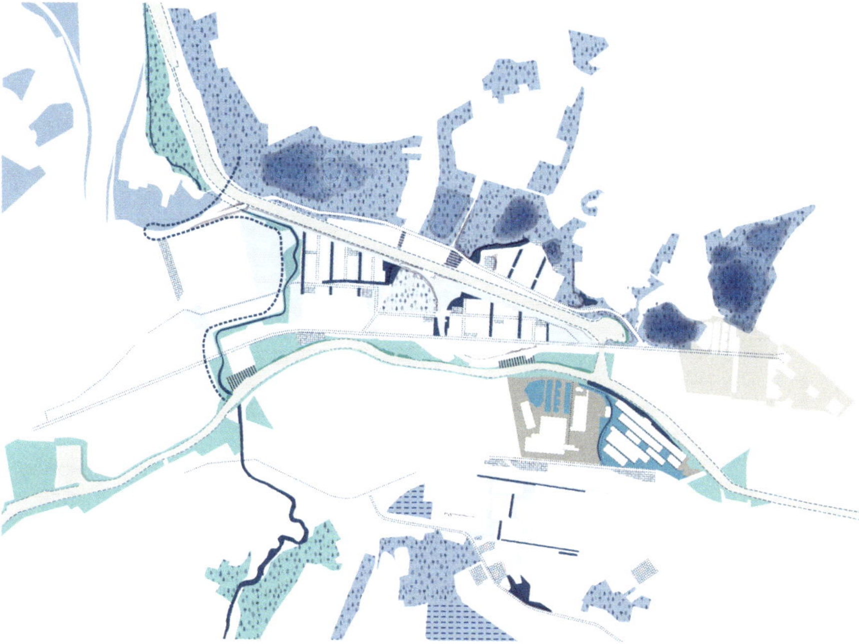

Fig. 89
Charleroi Landscape amplification and ecologic connectivity, 2021. Strategic master plan for the industrial and economic conversion of the Porte Ouest in Charleroi, 2021. Studio021paolaviganò. Paola Viganò, Achille Pelletier, Laure Thierrée, Morvan Rabin, Thomas Brun. With: Sweco and Idea consult, Origin architecture & engineering, tr@me. Consultants: Wim Timmermans, Cecilia Furlan. Client: Sogepa.

Fig. 90
Promoting heritage as a system, 2021.

Charleroi, Porte Ouest

A large, partially disused area close to Charleroi's main railway station, Porte Ouest occupies more than 100 hectares in which two heavy industries, a power station, dramatically polluted soils, abandoned buildings and infrastructures, and blast furnaces are still visible from a distance.

The master plan addresses at the same time, and not without difficulty, the recovery of the areas, new economic development and possible timeframes. It proposes strategies to be carried out always within different short-, medium- and long-term horizons (2026-2035-2050).

The first strategy concerns the attractiveness of the site, which is based on improving its habitability. It is impossible to change Porte Ouest's current image without addressing the problem of pollution. At the same time a new image is essential to attracting new businesses and users. The figure of an incremental campus is used to provide space for mixed activities, linked to existing economic hubs to transform Porte Ouest into a dynamic place for different activities and functions.

The second strategy proposes amplifying the ecological reinforcement and quality of space (built and unbuilt). On the 2028-2035-2050 horizon, the site regains a role of ecological connection at territorial scale (with the proposed opening of a disappeared watercourse), relations with the great terrils landscape, the reconstruction of typical wetlands on the valley floor, and the enhancement of ecosystems generated by abandonment.

The third strategy concerns the enhancement of a heritage system and not just a collection of objects. Porte Ouest is furrowed by narrative itineraries along which the long industrial history of the Charleroi region unfolds. The cultural axis that crosses the site (route de Mons) introduces an exceptionally rich heritage system. The master plan identifies different categories of elements: icons, buildings with potential for reconversion, infrastructures to be reused. A cultural system cannot be reduced to a mere collection of objects; it is the relationships between them that make a history legible, allowing for future integration and new uses. The living memory of a city of immigrant workers, of a political culture and solidarity, marks the places of the industrial revolution related to coal and steel production (Mitchell, 2013). It is represented in these objects and in their relationships.

The fourth strategy concerns mobility. Porte Ouest has dense infrastructure, not only in terms of the remnants of railways, bridges and footbridges, but an overland metro line connecting the site to the rest of the city, a road network serving the river port and providing access to the area, and a potential and extensive cycle and pedestrian network along the canals.

0
0,5
km

Fig. 91
Charleroi, Porte Ouest, the Masterplan, 2021.

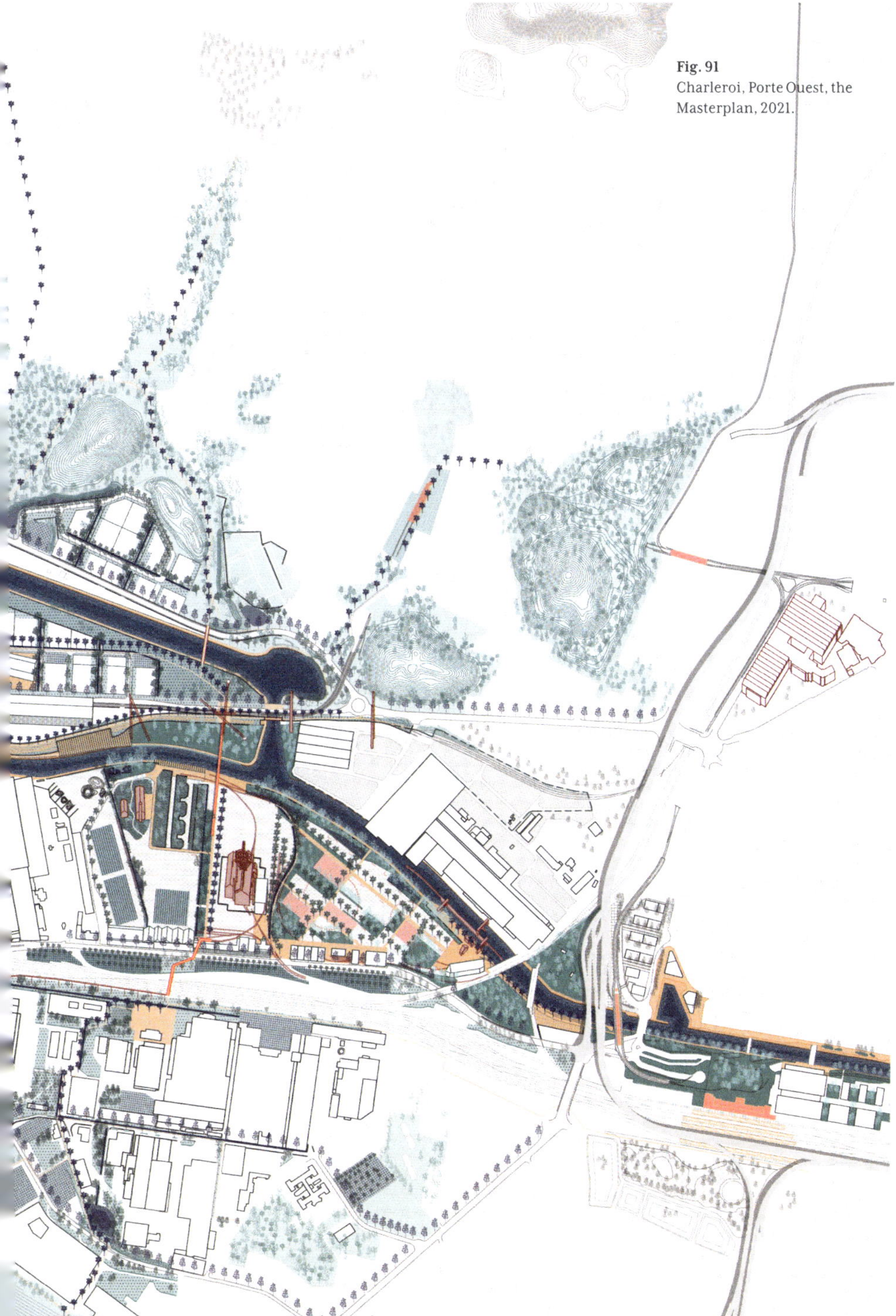

Fig. 92
Charleroi's West Gate Masterplan: Support Site Model, 2021. Strategic master plan for the industrial and economic conversion of the Porte Ouest in Charleroi, 2021. Studio021paolaviganò. Paola Viganò, Achille Pelletier, Laure Thierrée, Morvan Rabin, Thomas Brun.
With: Sweco and Idea consult, Origin architecture & engineering, tr@ me.Consultants: Wim Timmermans, Cecilia Furlan. Client: Sogepa.

Fig. 93
Below: Multidisciplinary strategic scheme for the Vesdre basin, representations. (From top left: Goffontaine, E. d'Hont 1920, Goffontaine, Today; La Nole, E. d'Hont 1920, La Nole, Today). Studio022-024PaolaViganò (ongoing). Paola Viganò, Etienne Schillers, Achille Pelletier, Stefano Gariglio, Maud Goossens and Uliège Team-Vesdre (Jacques Teller, Joel Privot, Martina Barcelloni Corte, Bruno Bianchet, Clémentine Schelings).
With: Yellow Window. Client: Région Wallonne.

Taken together, these infrastructures make it possible to envisage a transition project that will require little further investment to connect the site to the city and cross it.

Crossed by the Sambre and the endpoint of the Antwerp-Brussels-Charleroi canal, Porte Ouest is also strategic for river transport and for circular trade between industry and industry and between industry and the city. This circularity makes it possible to imagine carbon neutrality, the production of renewable energy within the framework of an energy community, establishing synergies between present activities and functions. The "zero-waste" logic can enhance the stock and material flows present. This is the fifth strategy.

The depollution of the area is the greatest obstacle to its development. The site awaits the refoundation of settlement rules to be imagined together with the soil reconstruction process. A "re-foundation grid", the sixth strategy—at the same time a device to organise drainage, soil depollution and new urban layout—provides structure to the project.

Finally, the master plan seeks to enhance the existing dynamics outside the area by providing space for public activities and cultural events, projects that tell of the city's progressive approach to Porte Ouest, in opposition to some of the dynamics within the area, which imagine the expansion of heavy industrial activities.

On the 2028 horizon, the project proposes accompanying the arrival of the "Quartier du futur" (a military area with strong ambitions to open up the city to technological innovation) with a first major transformation of the site. Its partial opening, starting with the Phare Ouest, a metropolitan park at present almost entirely covered with concrete slabs and overlooked by a blast furnace (HF4), will be possible with temporary and minor works. The former power station will be enhanced in the Clean-Tech Cluster of the new "Confluence Campus". This first stage will be taken up, continued and completed by subsequent ones in the medium and long term.

Vesdre Valley: The disruptive power of resilience

The Vesdre Valley was profoundly affected by the extreme floods of July 2021: at human, ecological, socio-economic and territorial level. The strategic scheme put in place by the Walloon Region, and which we are developing in collaboration with the University of Liège, reflects on new resilience at the scale of the basin slope, from the sources of the Vesdre, in Germany to its end in the Ourthe, itself a tributary of the Meuse and between the plateau and the valley floor. The valley is east-west oriented and lies between Liège and Aachen, bordered to the north by the plateau d'Herve and to the south by the Hautes Fagnes system. Faced with a persistent risk of flooding, the territory as a whole will have to share a future of solidarity in relation to climate change and the need to include the valley as a whole in a socio-economic transition process. It is a matter of considering new ways of inhabiting an area of ancient industrialisation that developed in the nineteenth century along the river and then, more recently, especially on the plateaux connected to the motorway and on the slopes. Through multi-disciplinary and multi-thematic approaches taken together with expertise gathered by the University of Liège, the strategic outline of the Vesdre basin is made up of an atlas ranging from direct observation and experience of the places to an in-depth examination of the variety of themes proposed by a territory undergoing socio-economic decline affected by an environmental catastrophe.

The description of the territory and the imagery surrounding it is constructed through studies by experts, numerous fieldworks and "stays" organised in order to listen to the sometimes-terrible experiences of its inhabitants, thanks to the in-depth knowledge gained at this juncture by each citizen. This approach, through scenarios building, always produces ideas for its future, the basis for an open discussion on the construction of a common vision.

The atlas is never just a collection of maps. Its construction is already the result of intentions regarding its use: in our case, it responds to the ambition of nurturing a vision for the entire river basin, bringing out the potential of a systemic and integrated approach and upstream-downstream solidarity—for example on the territories of the plateaux that have not been damaged, but may play a crucial role in controlling run-off flows.

The atlas concludes with an interpretative summary and a map highlighting the potential resilience to flooding, i.e. the territory's capacity to give space to water and not to be brought to its knees by episodic flooding, as well as to be able to overcome moments of severe drought, which, as climate change scholars since the last IPCC report have predicted, will take the place of major floods after 2050. The valley as a whole is the entity under study, to understand the interrelationships and synergies between the different parts upstream and downstream.

What interests us is connecting imagery of the flood, which emerged in numerous exchanges and interviews, and then adding to these voices the voice of the river, which is difficult to hear in the traditional sense, but which can be discovered and known. The different voices, contrapuntal or in unison, participate in the definition of a new perspective of resilience that inevitably involves territorial solidarity.

The river-stream as subject: Starting with the river and what the river wants.

Above all else, it seems important to me to take the liberty, for a few moments, of starting with the river-stream; that is to say, with its logic, rationality, spaces. Rivers (like other entities of the territory) are increasingly defined as "real subjects" with their own legal personality to be given a say

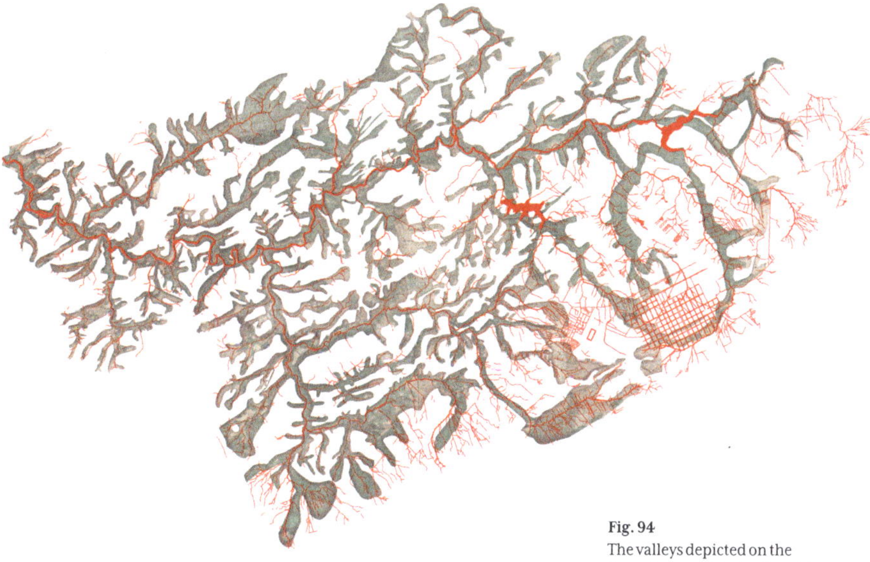

Fig. 94
The valleys depicted on the Ferraris map (1771-1776) and the Walloon hydrographic network, along with the area submerged in July 2021 and 2023.

at last. Some of the tables of the "diagnostic multihématique" can be used to extract the fundamental elements to bring out the Vesdre subject, its nature and ecology. But the subject is also made visible through representations that have accompanied it over time. The Vesdre was depicted by the Liège school of landscape painting (late nineteenth and early twentieth century). The railway line had already arrived, intertwining with the route of the Vesdre. The river, its riparian set-up and its relationship with the cultivated and wooded slopes depicted in these paintings can be compared with the current situation, where we still find intact, albeit episodically, the qualities of the places described by Victor Hugo in 1839. The valley is "la plus ravissante vallée qu'il y ait au monde. Dans cette saison, par un beau jour, avec un ciel bleu, c'est quelquefois un ravin, souvent un jardin, toujours un paradis".[44] All this

44. Victor Hugo, Le Rhin/VIII, (letter to a friend), Letter 8 (3 August 1839), Hetzel, 1842 (Tome I, p. 81-83). Hugo anticipates the arrival of the railway as the destroyer of the "douceur virgilienne" that characterises the valley and speaks about the mountain which seems to scream when the explosions linked to the works tear it apart: "On dirait que la montagne violée crie par cette bouche ouverte".

fed the image, still relevant today, of a natural Vesdre and valley, a gateway to the Haute Fagnes park.

The river/valley as an object of rationalisation

Over time and well before the eighteenth century represented in the Ferraris map, the Vesdre was moved, corrected and channelled. The many secondary canals, the biefs, served the textile industries and urbanisation. The forms of water have become complex: in addition to the downstream system (tributaries, confluence), the loss of wetlands along the river, the new ecologies created by the transformation of the great peat "sponge" of the Haute-Fagnes plateau (with great human effort at the time) into pine plantations, the hidden waters associated with karst valleys where water disappears but can arrive suddenly. The reduction of the bocages that held water on the slopes of the Plateau d'Herve impoverished the landscape and increased the speed of runoff. Urbanisation has gradually occupied large areas of the riverbed.

The Vesdre must be seen as the epicentre of an entire system where infrastructures operate, such as the railway, embankments, the main road, upstream dams, the transformation of the old branches, the reduction of the available space in the meanders.

The river/valley as socio-economic object

The floods occurred within a former economic corridor, long urbanised, affected by the deindustrialisation of the last century and the transfer of activities to benefit, in particular, the business parks developed on the Plateau d'Herve and directly connected to the motorway. The result is a socio-economically disadvantaged valley, both from the viewpoint of the inhabitants' standards of living and in terms of low employment. Moreover, the economic activities still found there—tradesmen, craftsmen, the self-employed, as well as small and medium-sized business owners—have been flood victims, with direct consequences in terms of employment and income flows. There is a great temptation for many of them to leave the valley. A culture, towns, heritage, traditions, and folklore have been created along the river. Towns moved closer to the water and houses, facilities, and some public spaces were built. At the same time, the rest of the territory has also developed, and this has speeded up in recent years: the relationship between the plateau and the valley floor has changed direction and the centrality of the valley floor (with Verviers as the symbolic place where wealth was created in a short historical period) has been much weakened; a comb-like urban and productive structure descends (or ascends) the valley. It is a total change in the settlement and urban organisation, the geography of wealth production and the economic weight of the valley floor, which increases the social divide and further reduces the visibility of the already marginalised parts.

First elements of a vision

What the Vesdre wants must be negotiated with what the citizens demand. Changes in agricultural, forestry and urban planning practices must accompany the valley and be deployed throughout the catchment area according to the principle of a new territorial solidarity.

The strategic scheme addresses the short and medium term by considering rapidly changing climatic conditions. Transformations that can help combat flooding will have to help overcome droughts and heatwaves after 2050. "New" forms of water (related to retention, accumulation, infiltration, etc.) must be brought up in conversation for extreme flooding and equally extreme drought conditions. Without imagining major new infrastructures, the map of resilience potential highlights the possibilities emerging from the valley itself (from its topography, lithology and land use), within coherent choices concerning the economy, society and the river-stream system. The question that this map raises is: to what extent can socio-economic choices strengthen the potential for resilience to floods and droughts and achieve both ecological and socio-economic resilience at the same time?

Or, conversely, to what extent can choices made in the name of resilience influence/guide socio-economic visions to restructure the economy (primary, secondary and tertiary) of the valley? The first scenarios explore the limits of what is possible: from the settlement rarefaction of the valley floor (what the Vesdre wants), to a future without fractures (what citizens want), to the possibility that from a confused and widespread situation perfect fragments may emerge, adapted to extreme flooding and drought conditions, or instead draconian limitations may have to be brought down from above in order to maintain large areas of continuity between the Hautes Fagnes Park and the Three Nations Park (between Belgium, Germany and Holland).

The designing of resilient spaces is a disruptive tool that allows us to review the order of things, the territorial organisation and its hierarchies, the established priorities. The map of resilience, and not of vulnerability, even before entering a discussion about the scenarios, is a way to start a collective debate on the future of the valley with a disruptive concept.

Designing resilient spaces in a resilient territory provides access to the heart of the all-modern mechanism of total resistance in the name of total and unattainable security. It dismantles it to regain it, possibly locally.

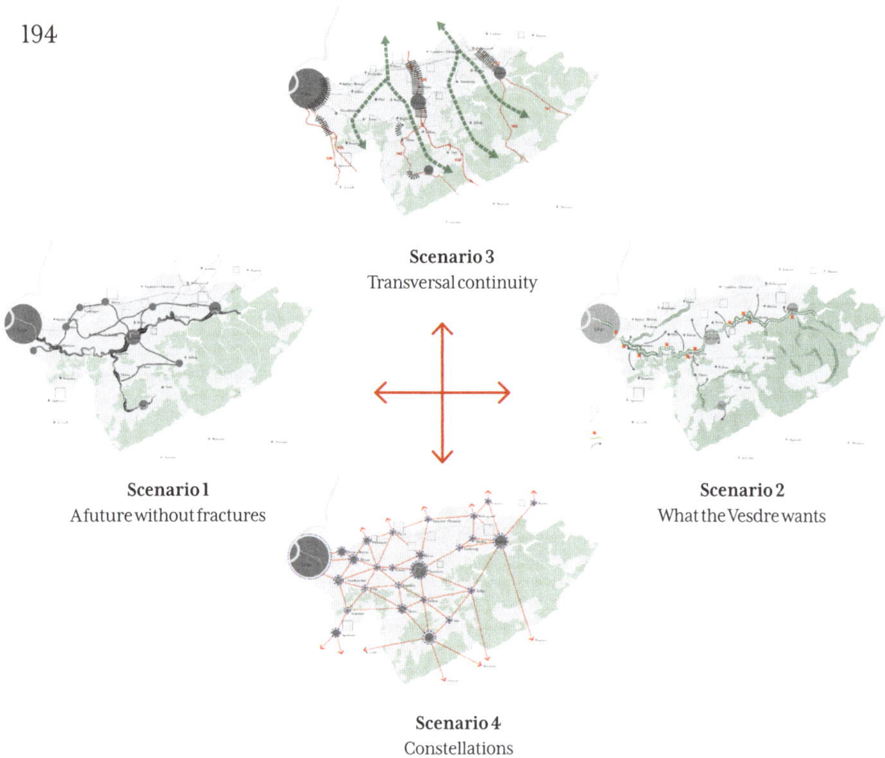

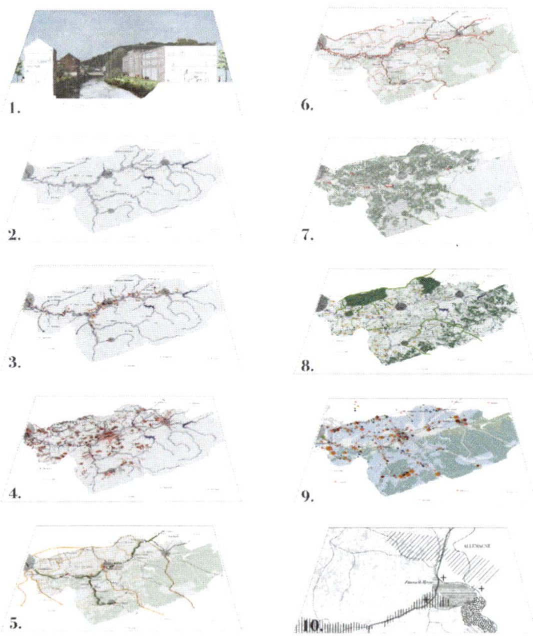

Fig. 95
Principles of the territorial vision. 2023.

1. Drawing the transition, a territory to regenerate and enhance.
2. Holding back, slowing down, delaying water
3. Making buildings resilient and transparent
4. Regenerating urban fabrics
5. Intensify public transport
6. Creating the Vesdrienne and the "strollers' route"
7. Adapting agriculture
8. Restore the Hautes Fagnes plateau
9. Imagining an intermediate scale of governance: the Constellations
10. Towards a park-valley, the extreme point of the great park of the Walloon furrow

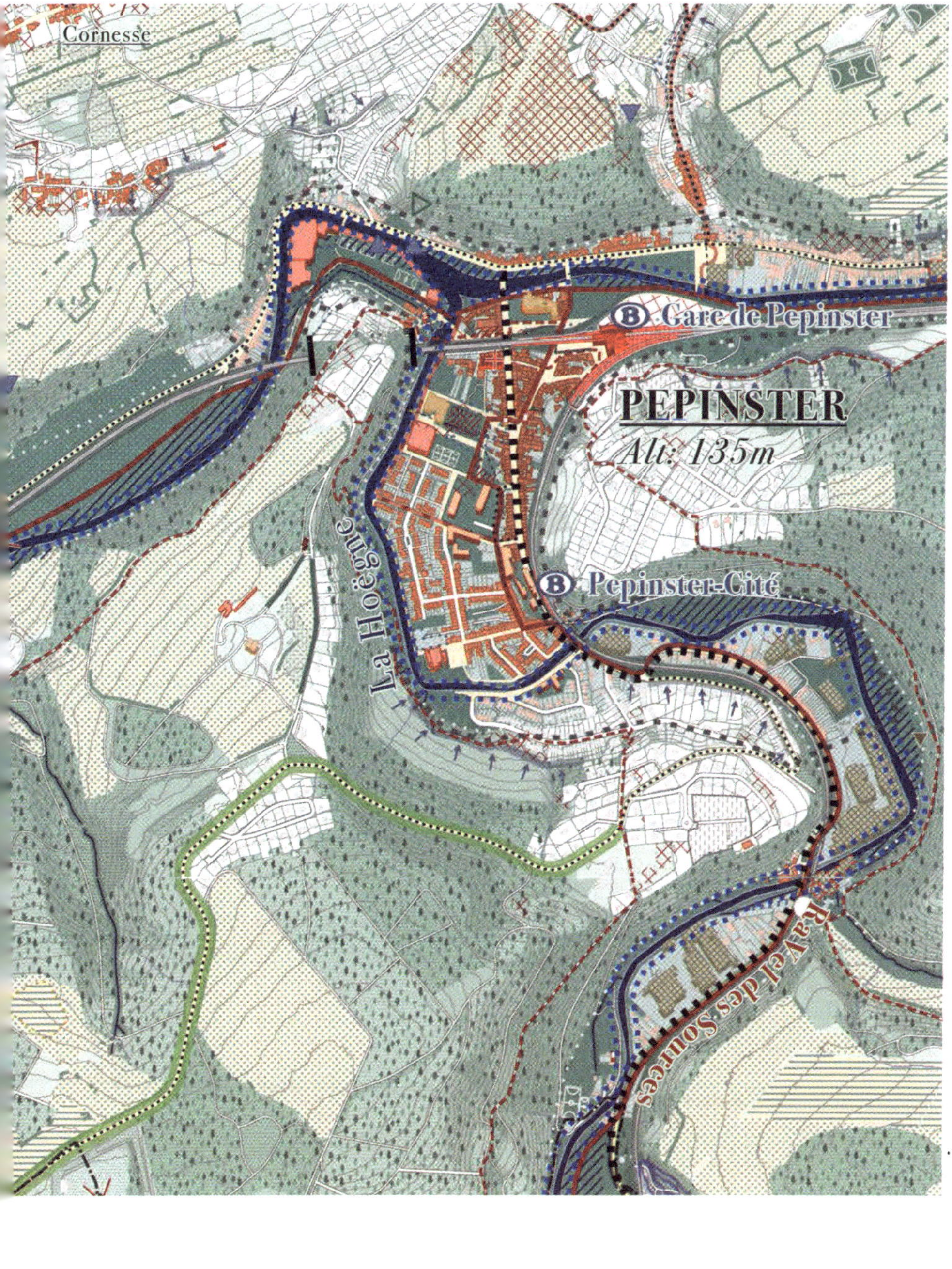

Fig. 96
Detail of the 1:10.000 map. 2023.

Fig. 97
Peterbos, Requalification of the public space: Between Monumentality and Domesticity, 2020. Peterbos, Anderlecht - Brussels Capital Region, public space masterplan and projects. studio019-021paolaviganò (ongoing). Paola Viganò, Bertrand Plevinski, Pietro Manaresi, Mathilde Meurice, Stefano Gariglio, Eugénie Laharotte. With: VVV - Nicolas Willemet, Guillaume Vanneste, Mathieu Auquier and with: Ara, Brat. Client: Anderlecht Municipality, Brussels Capital Region, Brussels.

Interior peripheries and public space: Peterbos, the Stone Guest[45]

The Peterbos district has the lowest force labour participation rates in the Brussels region and the highest unemployment rate, affecting, most of all, young people. It is an area marked by extreme poverty. These characteristics have made it a place where, as Pierre Bourdieu wrote, all "the misery of the world" has been concentrated (Bourdieu 1990). In such a context, it is legitimate to ask what the responsibilities of the space are and what kind of project could make sense here. A philanthropic and goodwill project? A veritable political project shared by all the actors sitting around the table (as we have indeed urged and partly obtained)?

Our aim as architects and urban planners and our only territory of action is, in this case, the open and public space: its quality and liveability. Bringing together architectural, landscape, urban planning, sociological, cultural and biopolitical issues, the project addresses public surfaces as possible, but not obvious, levers of action, and it does so through readings, interpretations and proposals.

The project starts with soil, water run-off and biodiversity, and proposes acting on the ground floors of buildings and their capacity to support programmatic diversity and enter into relationships with the rest of the city. It redefines openings and closures, transparency and opacity at all scales. It is a sufficiently wide space for manoeuvring as it satisfies a multitude of practices, both ordinary and extraordinary: the public space concerns everyone, without distinction. But it is terribly reduced if the project does not have the power to transform the inequalities found there, generated by decisions taken in the past to concentrate poverty, which has turned out to be ineffective in terms of social integration. Urban design and investments in the restructuring of the space are clearly not solutions that can exist on their own; they cannot be solely responsible in solving social and urban challenges. Interaction with economic policies and not just social ones is still too weak.

How can the design and restructuring of the Peterbos grounds transform them into a living and inclusive part of the metropolis? How can the public spaces of Peterbos be renovated to support residents in becoming part of a broader city, while at the same time strengthening the meaning of the park as an exceptional qualitative context in a rapidly growing metropolis, and establishing permeable boundaries with the rest of the territory, experimenting with new figures of public space? What are these figures unable to resolve

45. This text is a revision and summary of the article "Peterbos – Living in the park, inhabiting the city", Viganò, Plewinski, Vanneste, Willemet 2023, members of the team that won the competition for the recovery of the public spaces of Peterbos (StudioPaolaViganò, vvv architecture urbanisme, ARA, BRAT).

that could instead be addressed by structural changes and socio-economic political programmes?

Our conclusion revolves around three main aspects: 1) recognition of the richness of the original design of Peterbos, highlighting its potential qualities (a soil-monument); 2) addressing the need for closer alliance between the spatial design and economic development strategies (and between spatial design, public investments and urban regeneration policies); 3) viewing public space as an opportunity to reformulate deeper social issues and its design as a device to address the "stone guest" of social injustice.

A modern project: an unprecedented reading

The 1,600 apartments of the eighteen housing blocks of Peterbos were built between 1968 and 1980 under the driving force of the modernisation of Brussels. The first phase of construction (blocks 1 to 8) followed the project of the modernist and functionalist architecture firm Groupe Structures, established by architects Louis Van Hove, Raymond Steniers, Jacques Boseret-Mali and Jacques Vandermeeren. Some members of the group worked with the great representatives of the Belgian modernist era, such as Renaat Braem or the Groupe l'Equerre.

Contrary to other European countries and for reasons that we cannot go into here, modern residential experiments in Belgium were first concentrated in the garden city experiences; then after the Second World War they took place in the less hierarchical centre/periphery relationship of the French banlieues, with the formation of a specific widespread banlieue radieuse (Smets 1986), which only took the form of a large neighbourhood in the most important cities (Leloutre 2020). Largely unfinished, these developments often lacked sufficient community facilities or production spaces to become "parts of cities" to all effects and are now monofunctional enclaves (Sterken, 2013). Although some of these neighbourhoods were designed with great attention to ways of living, with high spatial and landscape qualities, they are marked by enormous social difficulties, low attractiveness and are stigmatised in the collective imagination.

The Peterbos landscape is extremely beautiful with its artificial plateau to the north, now connected to the Promenade verte, the large spaces between the towers with the various services (parking, football pitch, playground), and vegetation that has grown and diversified. The juxtaposition of different forms of soil constitutes the public space of Peterbos. The image of time is represented in these soils: the modern belvedere as a bastion against the ancient city at the end of the 1960s, and endless parking areas at the end of the 1980s and 90s. But other images can be conjured to describe the monumental soils of Peterbos: an original reading reveals the mix of unorthodox influences contained in the modern green carpet. Imagery inspired by the projects of

Fig. 98
The neighbourhood's new entrance, view. 2020.

Italian Renaissance villas and gardens emerge: the monumental staircases of the Boboli gardens (along the central path of Peterbos); the inclined green planes symmetrically framing the entrances to Villa d'Este in Tivoli (entrance from the western avenue to Peterbos); the staircases forming the backdrop to Palazzo Farnese in Caprarola, or the Villa Medicea in Castello (the staircases also at the entrance to Peterbos from the west). This imagery evokes another relationship with the land, beyond the functional and hygienic metaphor of the modern neighbourhood: the garden, a space of contemplation and symbolic representation, from which to extend one's gaze to the city, the space-monument. The topography is modelled through architectural devices: low walls, talus, slopes and monumental staircases.

On a broader scale, the landscape of Peterbos is part of the Anderlecht park system, a collection of public green areas sustained by the geography and part of the metropolitan green belt of Brussels, established at municipal level by Mayor Bracops (1947-1966) and implemented by the municipal engineer Georges Messin (Leloutre, 2017). This sophisticated approach is not surprising, even if it is rarely or never evoked in the reading of the urban and landscape structure of Peterbos: the late creation of the neighbourhood, the power of

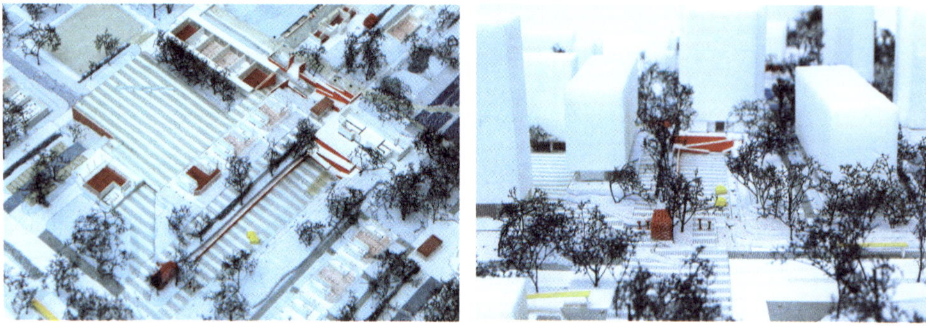

Fig. 99
Views of the model. 2020.

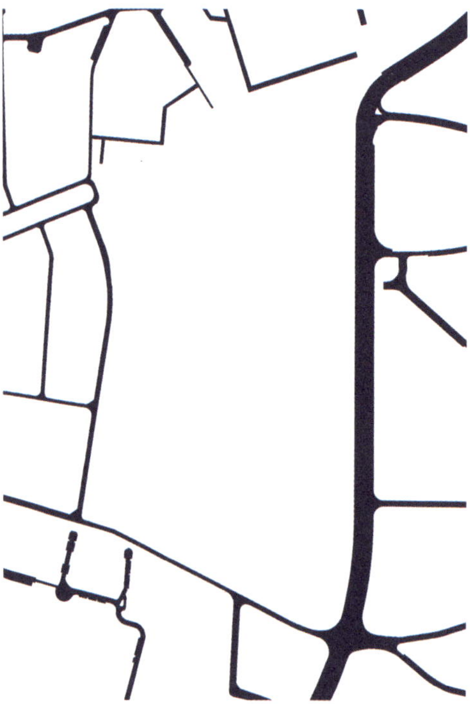

Fig. 100
Existing connections. 2020.

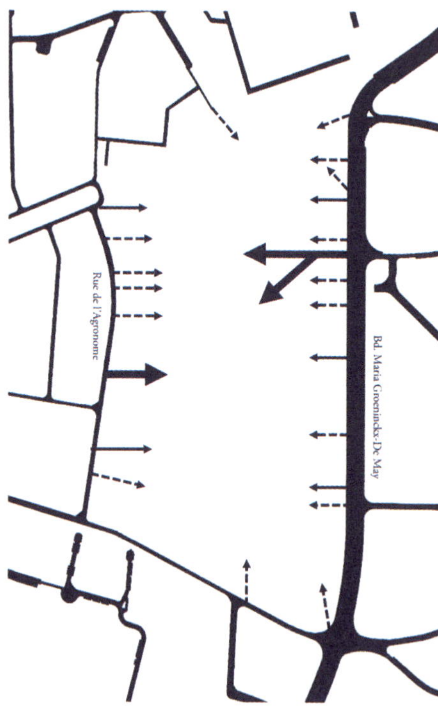

Fig. 101
New entrances of the neighbourhood. 2020.

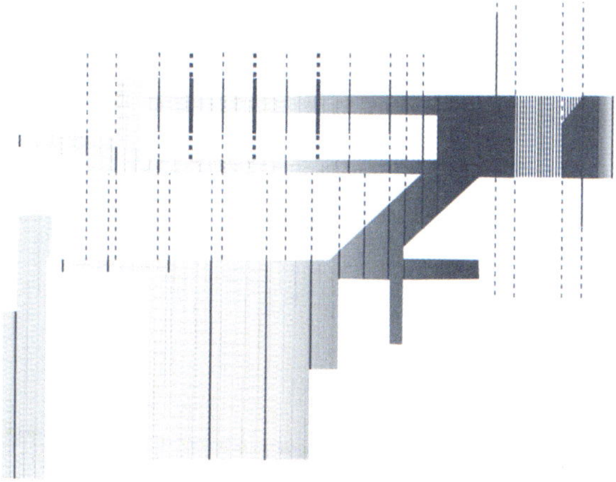

Fig. 102
Diagram of soil permeability in the new proposal. 2020.

historical and post-modern interpretation in Brussels and its role in the construction of the physical and cultural landscape of the city can provide some initial leads.

Today, car parks surround the housing blocks and can be accessed from a boulevard separating the neighbourhood (Boulevard G. de May) and from Rue de l'Agronome). A former motorway skirts the northern boundary, now transformed into a promenade verte encircling Brussels. The land at the foot of the towers is terraced and levelled to form a common floor housing 1 to 7 blocks, in some areas creating differences in height between the central pedestrian area and the parking areas. The central area was to be bordered by a canopy and water basin (not constructed but visible in the initial plans). The design radically applies the functionalist principle of the separation of flows.

From our point of view, it is above all the latent quality of the space that can become legible once more, today suffocated by changes to the proportions between green spaces and parking areas, and by the fragmentation of the space subsequent to the project which makes it impossible to grasp the scale of the park. It is the dignity of the designed space that still emerges, or could emerge, and the idea that this monument, even symbolically, could be one of the levers of the socio-spatial regeneration of Peterbos: to inhabit a place to which we collectively attribute value. This challenges the design: by reinterpreting the spatial devices of Peterbos in light of others that are better known from the history of architecture, a redevelopment strategy takes hold that seeks to transform the physical and visual barriers into potential places that reinforce the link with the natural terrain, the slope of the valley, thus defining urban thresholds and privileged places of relationship and representation.

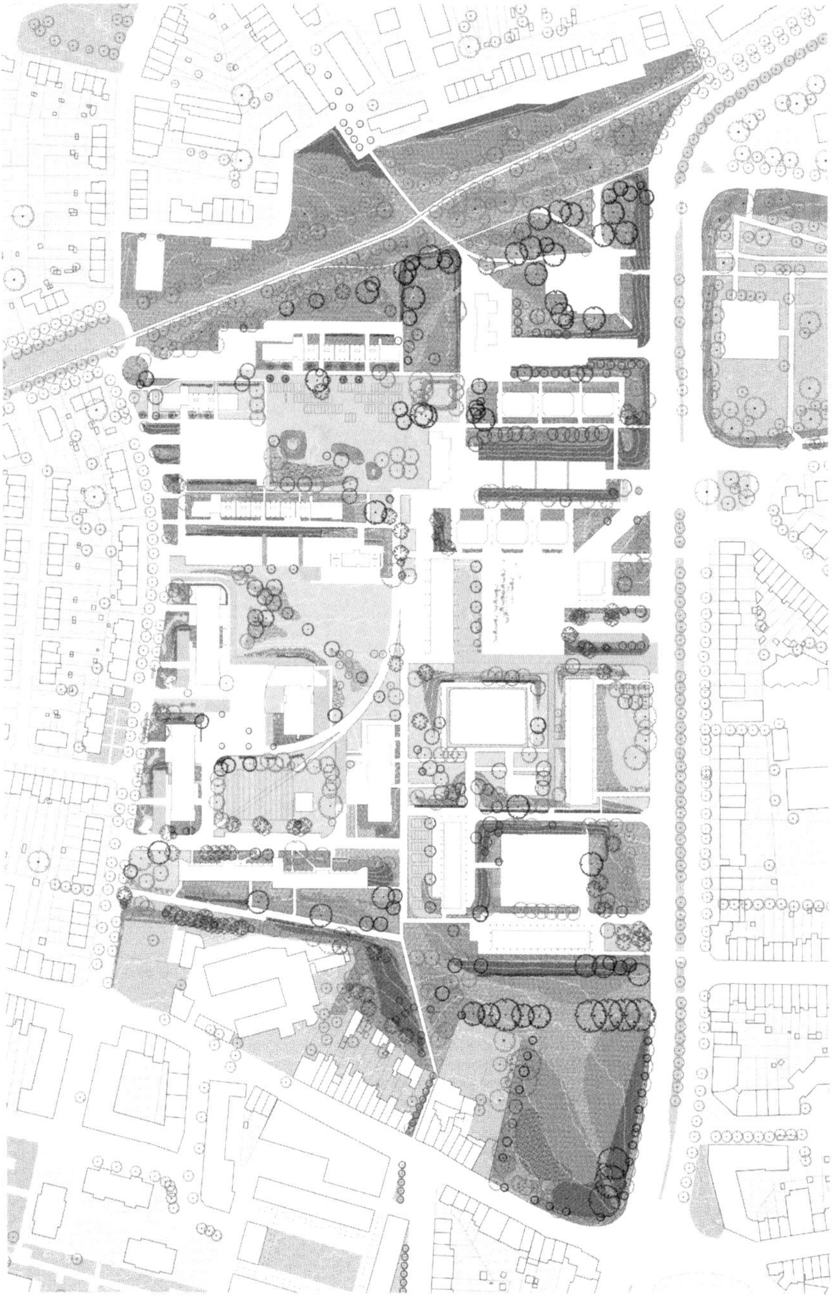

Fig. 103
Living in the Park: Master Plan, 2020..

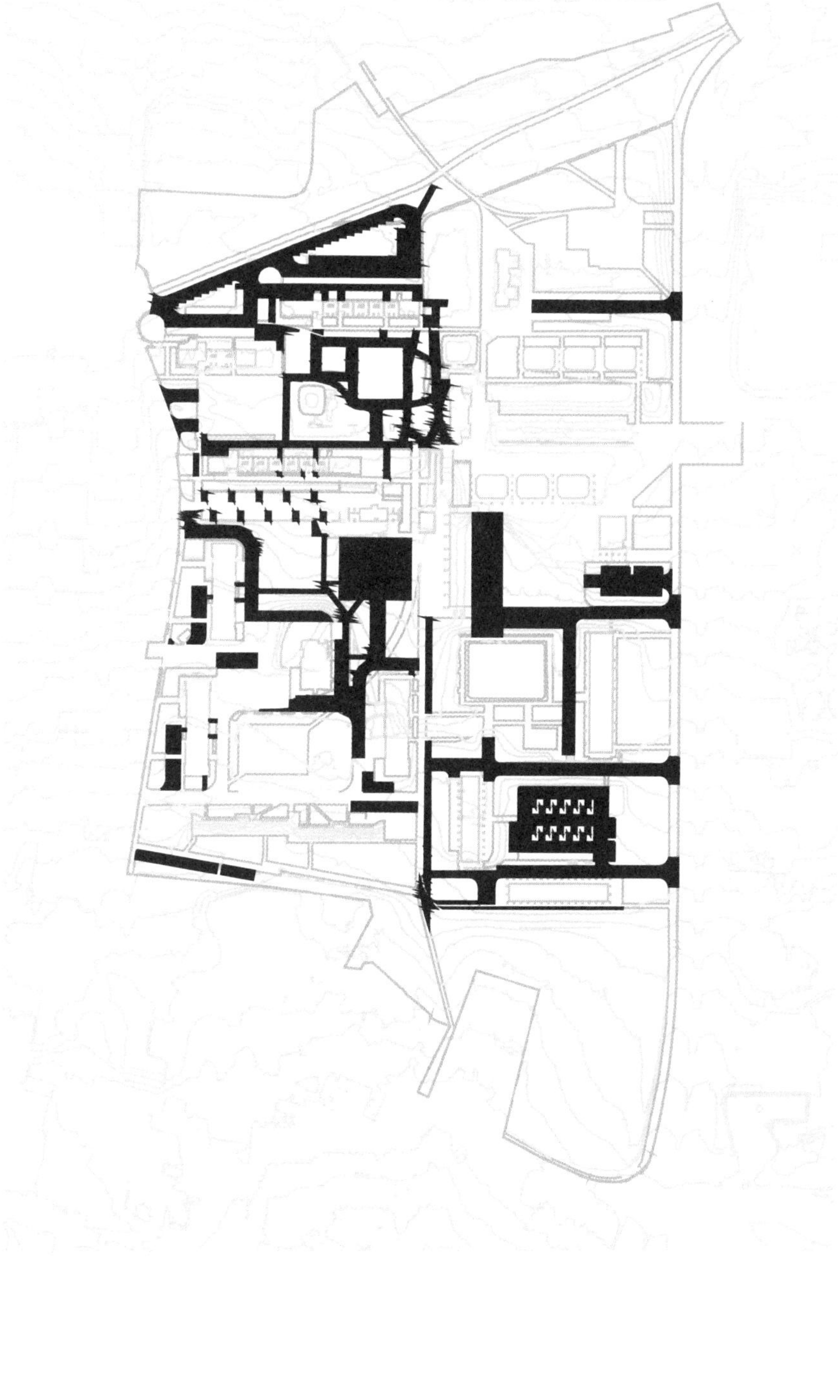

Fig. 104
Permeable surfaces and demineralization. 2020.

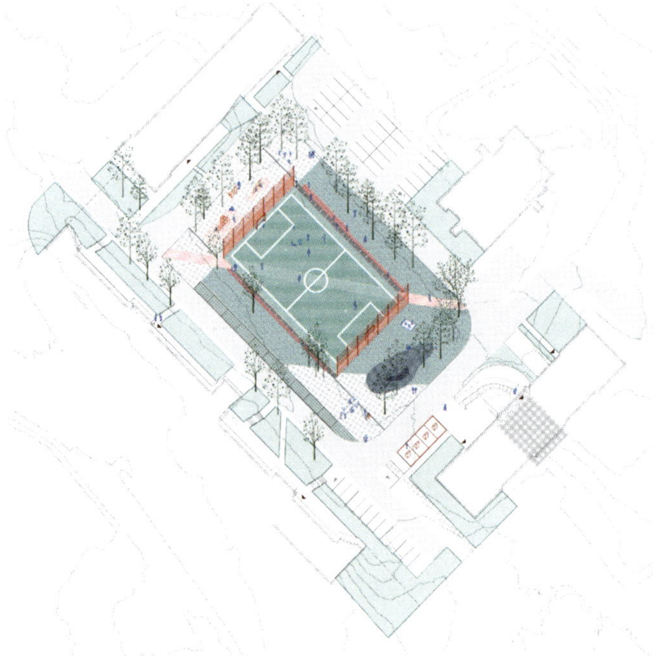

Fig. 105
Peterfoot, the sports field. 2020.

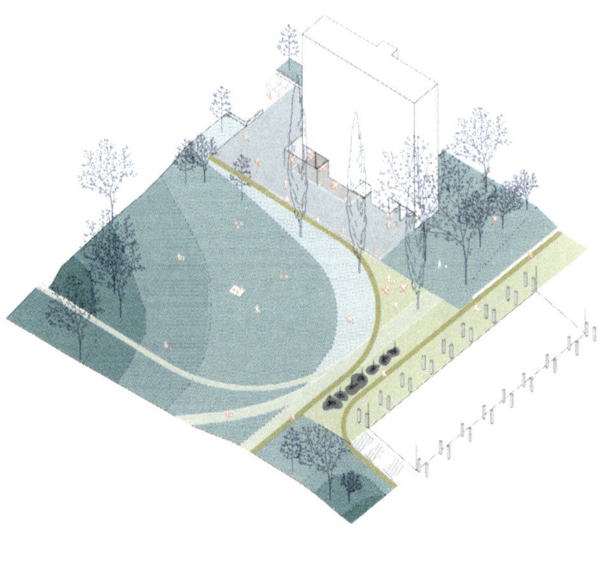

Fig. 106
Petertuin, the new green space. 2020.

Living the city, inhabiting the park

The design deconstructs the inverted figure of an exterior within the city, maintaining the qualities of the landscape and design of Peterbos. The challenge is to preserve what is dignified and beautiful about the enclave and, at the same time, open it up to the city, rethinking connections and thresholds to accommodate it within. A morphological, topological and social topic.

The project adopts approaches rooted in the strong figure of the continuity of the soil. It describes the geography of the valley of Broekbeek and enhances the monumental planes, while making them more fluid and permeable to paths. It extends the “centre” (now the realm of young drug dealers) towards the outside of the neighbourhood, crossing the large boulevard (now impassable) to create a porous threshold between the site and the city. It redevelops the plaines as complementary and more articulated spaces (not just green ones), proposing, lastly, that a name be given to the streets and squares/plaines in order to weaken the stigma of living in a numbered block in Peterbos.

1. Preparing the ground for ecological transition

Ninety percent of the surface area of Peterbos is open, potentially green and permeable. Here, the soil and water are two transformative agents that the design of the public space deeply embodies. The soil restructuring project is an opportunity to propose an eco-systemic and metabolic shift. What if Peterbos were actually better equipped than the traditional urban fabric to deal with climate transition? What if it could behave as a “climate body”? Could its large open spaces play a key role in supporting the ecological and urban transition?

Our approach is more metabolic than functionalist: it includes technical solutions, aims to meet the inhabitants’ requirements and is not afraid to be transformative and experimental. Peterbos, a large public property, represents a great opportunity to create a “Transition Landscape”.

2. Resizing the car parks and disaggregation

A fundamental evolution in parking areas is necessary. Today, Peterbos is a gigantic car park, a carpet of asphalt right down to the foot of its buildings. The project inverts the dominant status of cars and the design is geared towards a future of reduced car usage (in line with the Good Move regional plan). However, it maintains the accessibility of a limited series of parking areas close to each building, strongly requested by the residents, including the women of Peterbos, who drew our attention to danger felt by those moving around within their neighbourhood. It is a gender issue, but not only. The reduction of unnecessary parking spaces and roads is a preliminary step to allow other environmental strategies to take shape. Part of the parking areas will be allocated for other purposes.

Fig. 107
Entrance to the new kindergarten, as seen from rue de l'Agronome. 2020.

3. A climatic body

The image of the ground as a climatic body helps to reconnect elements that are currently disconnected: for instance, involving open and built spaces and their inhabitants/users, part of a common system. As a carrier of flows, matter, animal and vegetable species, and exchanges with the atmosphere, the soils of Peterbos can offer a transformative landscape of wet and dry areas, slopes and planes, maintained areas and others left fallow—from a reductionist, modernist vision of the soil as an inanimate carpet to a more aesthetic appreciation, a relational reappropriation of the resources and territorial subjectivity. Water management is part of the climatic and downstream risk reduction strategy. The terraces and slopes of Peterbos are enriched with water accumulation and infiltration spaces that generate new biodiversity, act on the micro-climate and introduce a different type of management and use of the open space. The transformation does not only concern the space, but the ways of inhabiting and maintaining it.

4. A soil that can produce

The heritage of community gardens and urban plots shows that there is a long history of family gardens as collective and social objects, constantly at risk and that have a dynamic geography (Cahn et al., 2018). The master plan collects the proposals of the associations and proposes the cultivation of some parts of the Peterbos park, creating new symbolic value: as a support for plant food and production, but also and above all as a social catalyst. Small structures, a greenhouse and apiaries will be developed in collaboration with local associations. New synergies with the ground floors of the buildings, now abandoned in most housing blocks or considered dangerous, will be possible.

5. Mixité: emancipation and initiatives

The case of Peterbos, with almost 3,500 residents, is no exception to the well-known imbalances found in large social housing complexes. Urbanity is excluded from the conditions of degradation and isolation sought by drug traffickers, giving way to forms of micro-tyranny and the gradual alteration of the identity of the neighbourhood through the media. The late arrival of urban renewal policies and a certain denial of reality by the public authorities have inevitably weakened the social links and the possibility of interaction with the residents also by the numerous associations that work in the neighbourhood. The inhabitants of Peterbos are somewhat resigned and indifferent to any initiative or participation developed by social policies and traditional planning, which often require a cultural and civic practice and codification that is not always shared (Pisecki, 2007).

The ground of Peterbos is a common surface of interaction among the different ongoing projects (the renovation of a large part of the buildings), the aspirations of the inhabitants of the neighbourhood and those of Anderlecht-Brussels. Through the fair distribution of functional programmes and accessibility to a multitude of social environments, the urban space can support emancipation possibilities through the development of individual or collective initiatives. The space is marked by roughness and omissions, and equity is not distributed in the same extent to the different parts of the city.

Living in Peterbos literally means living in a public "interior", and it is this that allows us to question our design practices and observe the limits of their ability to come up with a response, interacting with extreme contexts and modes of use consistent with them.

One of the missing dimensions we have worked on is the "intermediate urban grain": spaces that are not part of the private sphere of the building and are not the large public space, spaces that can encourage informal and working practices—a repair workshop, an ephemeral café, small-scale agricultural production and distribution. This idea is regularly excluded from policies, given the managerial, economic and even regulatory difficulties, with restrictions relating to the PRASS (Plan régional d'affectation du sol) on the possibility of using the ground floor of the buildings in public housing neighbourhoods. The frustration is even greater when we consider the number of people seeking work, the interest that emerged during discussions with the residents about

Fig. 108
A belvédère on the sports centre roof garden. 2020.

opening individual businesses, and the impact of inactivity on the vulnerable individuals of Peterbos. It therefore seems essential to rethink the possibility of an intermediate scale and "urban grain" and undertake initiatives that respond to the needs and desires of the inhabitants of these places. The intermediate grain is also absent at the social level: despite the large number of associations based in the neighbourhood and the social projects developed by urban renewal policies—the creation of a living lab managed by the university, the implementation of participation campaigns—interaction between the representatives and the represented is still very difficult. The sustainability of the socio-economic projects undertaken within the framework of "sustainable neighbourhood contracts" suffers from a lack of follow-up over time.

A provisional conclusion: the Stone Guest

Between the 1960s and 80s in Brussels, the debate on the city focused on the luttes urbaines. The term Brusselisation represented the vast, market-driven real estate operations of "modernisation" and regeneration with numerous building demolitions and the expulsion of inhabitants. Activists and residents decried the lack of a public voice in urban matters and claimed a "right to the city". The 80s ended with the creation of the Brussels Region, a regional institutional layer that covers and federates the nineteen municipalities of the metropolis. At this time the response to urban struggles culminated in the implementation of a renewal policy, the main result of which was the "neighbourhood contract" (Lenel, 2013; Van Criekingen, 2013).

According to Van Criekingen (2013), the institutional birth of the Brussels Region in 1989 led to a project that encouraged the return of the middle classes to the city, marginalising the objective of social cohesion in the working-class neighbourhoods. Another element in the context of access to social housing concerns management by the social housing companies, which in 1993 transitioned from a municipal to a regional level. The shift from an imperfect system—which left access to housing at the mercy of the contacts and spaces available, implicitly favouring a form of social mixite—to a more transparent system led to the concentration, homogenisation and impoverishment of the social strata present in the neighbourhoods. Moreover, the departure of the middle classes, ill-suited to the redefined categories, was experienced as class stigmatisation by those who remained (Schaut, 2017). Both elements suggest that the disinvestment of social housing in the neighbourhoods dates back to the turning point between the 1980s and 90s, and has worsened since then, despite the numerous reinvestment programmes.

The radical transformation of Peterbos is now a necessity and requires us to rethink social and physical contexts. The deconstruction of the implicit socio-biopolitical project derives from a series of probably good intentions, but it must now tackle the fundamental issue of the role, in our societies, of neighbourhoods that collect all the misery of the world. From this point of view it is important to recognise that the Peterbos neighbourhood contract was the first to encompass the entire perimeter within it, and is accompanied by actions that simultaneously address the quality of the buildings and housing, public space and social interventions.

The basic transformations we aim to initiate with the multiple themes developed in the project, as already mentioned, will never by themselves result in well-being, social cohesion, inclusion or jobs. But with its insistence on space as capital, agent and mediator, the project addresses the "stone guest" of spacial and social injustice. It clearly highlights the possible starting point for reform and the assumption of collective responsibility.

Fig. 109
The mystery of American reality: Towards research on Appalachia, territorial sections, University of Virginia, 2017.
Paola Viganò (Thomas Jefferson visiting professor), with Anthony Averbeck, lecturer at UVA, Roberto Sega, visiting PhD EPFL, and the students of UVA: Batul Abbas, Joshua Aronson, Joseph Brookover, Luke Harris, Laurence Holland, Jennifer Hsiaw, Elizabeth Kulesza, Lemara Miftakhova, Shannon Ruhl, Christian Storch, Xiang Zhao, Bonnie Kate Walker.

3.5 UTOPIA FOR OUR TIME

Some territories do not seem to have, nor to offer, a way out. We are faced with the inability of the territory and its communities to react to exploitation and impoverishment processes, and to an increase in ecological and social risk. The problem must be structurally redefined, and the project must tackle the complex terrain of seemingly unresolved issues: in areas that have always been in crisis or marginalised, subject to risks that can only increase and not decrease. In these cases, the narrative and design device of utopia structures criticism of the territory in the present—the here and now—while at the same time providing a projection similar to that returned by a mirror, in which topics and issues are transferred and resolved under conditions different from the current ones. The point of these explorations, beyond the often-fictitious field of problem-solving, is to provide radical and extreme keys to interpretation, which are important to clarify the gap between the current conditions and what could or should be. Such projects do not lead to an immediate alteration of reality, but they act as mediating elements between this and the action of change. Their ambition is to transform the contours of current discourse and establish new ones.

Faced with an uncertain range of variations and the possibility that there is no solution, many of the traditional tools of urban and territorial design seem to lose their usefulness. This difficulty prompts us to further explore the epistemological and ethical-political layer in order to define a position, albeit a provisional and contextual one. From this perspective, Appalachia touches on some important aspects. It is the result of a period spent at the University of Virginia in 2017 and enters into what Baudrillard referred to in the terms of the "mystery of American reality" (Baudrillard 1986) through the large region of the Appalachians.

The great mystery. Towards research on Appalachia[46]

The territory of the Appalachians coincides with a great mountain range several thousand kilometres long, a territory dense with issues, themes and problems that now seem to be worsening, despite in recent years having become increasingly diversified and structured with respect to a pure economy of resource exploitation. Appalachia is an area linked to mining and production, an industry that takes us back to the time of coal, an industry that apparently has never moved, but has refined and made its exploitation techniques even more destructive and invasive. Alongside them, specific and deep-rooted economies, populations and cultures are embedded in rapidly changing contexts.

Appalachia, the space within which tensions and relationships between people, things and imaginaries are increasingly divided, is all too transparent. Bewilderment and disbelief are felt in those who pass through this region as they find themselves in what until recently was the world's greatest economic power, the United States of America. Appalachia is a large territory inhabited by 25 million people.

Background

I have been reflecting on the relationships of dependence and autonomy within extended forms of urbanity, centres and suburbs, contemplating the great Megalopolis of the East Coast of the United States (Gottmann 1961), still one of the most interesting and significant conceptualisations to understand the North American city. However, it contains a bias concerning the primacy of coastal territories over inland territories, while highlighting the dependence of large coastal cities on inland territories that provide many of the resources necessary for their functioning, including water. In some large-scale infrastructure schemes, the dependence of the "strong" territories on what lies behind them emerges: the mountainous territories, which are less accessible and have fewer activities, but nevertheless allow the large centres to exist. Gottmann's interpretation is not taken for granted and is very precise. While maintaining the emphasis on coastal territories where population density, trade and the economy are linked to the presence of ports, he recognises the complexity of one territory adapting to the needs of another—an interior that allows everything else to function. The corollary of this dependence is a geography, not always clearly perceived, of barriers, dams, diversions, aqueducts, oil pipelines, and railway lines for the transport of coal, gas or extracted timber that have transformed the Appalachians,

46. The following text has been taken, with some changes, from an identically titled piece published in Cristina Bianchetti, ed., Territorio e Produzione. See: Viganò 2019.

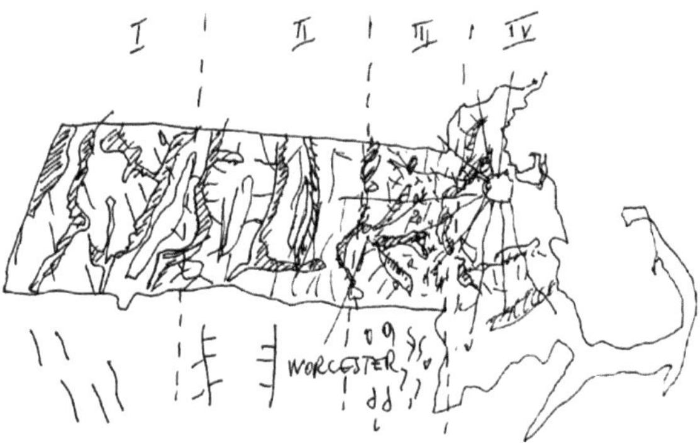

Fig. 110
Territorialism, Boston metropolitan area. Sequences of the "levees" (reinterpretation from Benton Mackaye). Paola Viganò, 2012. (Viganò 2014b).

heavily altering their ecological, cultural and social functioning, and their relationships with the plains and the sea.

Benton McKaye, a visionary and a member of the Regional Design Association, started with land construction and its landscapes to address design at all scales (McKaye 1928). He was behind the creation of the famous Appalachian Trail, a route that winds over the ridges and crosses the entire Appalachian chain. McKaye did not imagine the trail only as a tourist enhancement strategy. The project had more complex and profound ambitions. McKaye envisaged that by the mid-1920 the trail would be able to rebalance weights and territorial relations on/with the East Coast. Routes and infrastructures would organise new economies capable of exploiting the extracted resources locally, and enhancing them, without dispersing them, by sending them to the ports and coastal cities. For McKaye, the quantity of resources and the presence of infrastructures in the space (water, energy, large dams, etc.) fuelled the strength of the inland territory. The traditional image of that territory was turned upside down—and this is a strong hypothesis. Marginal territories are now the core of the system, instead of representing its edge, its frontier. But there is also extreme fragility: a fascinating hypothesis, which has not been implemented. What has been achieved, however, is the ridge path, maintained by many volunteers, often pensioners who have moved to this region to live cheaply and close to services. Once again, the issues that other mountain territories, or those in post-industrial crisis, have posed for a long time emerge: why can't their enormous resources be exploited locally to increase the well-being of the populations that inhabit them, without destroying the ecosystem, and instead increasing the wealth of other territories? Why do they always remain on the margins?

The above are rhetorical questions, the only ones possible in the face of assumptions that seem beyond questioning. They are, however, important questions to consider and to leave in the background in order to proceed towards a first reading.

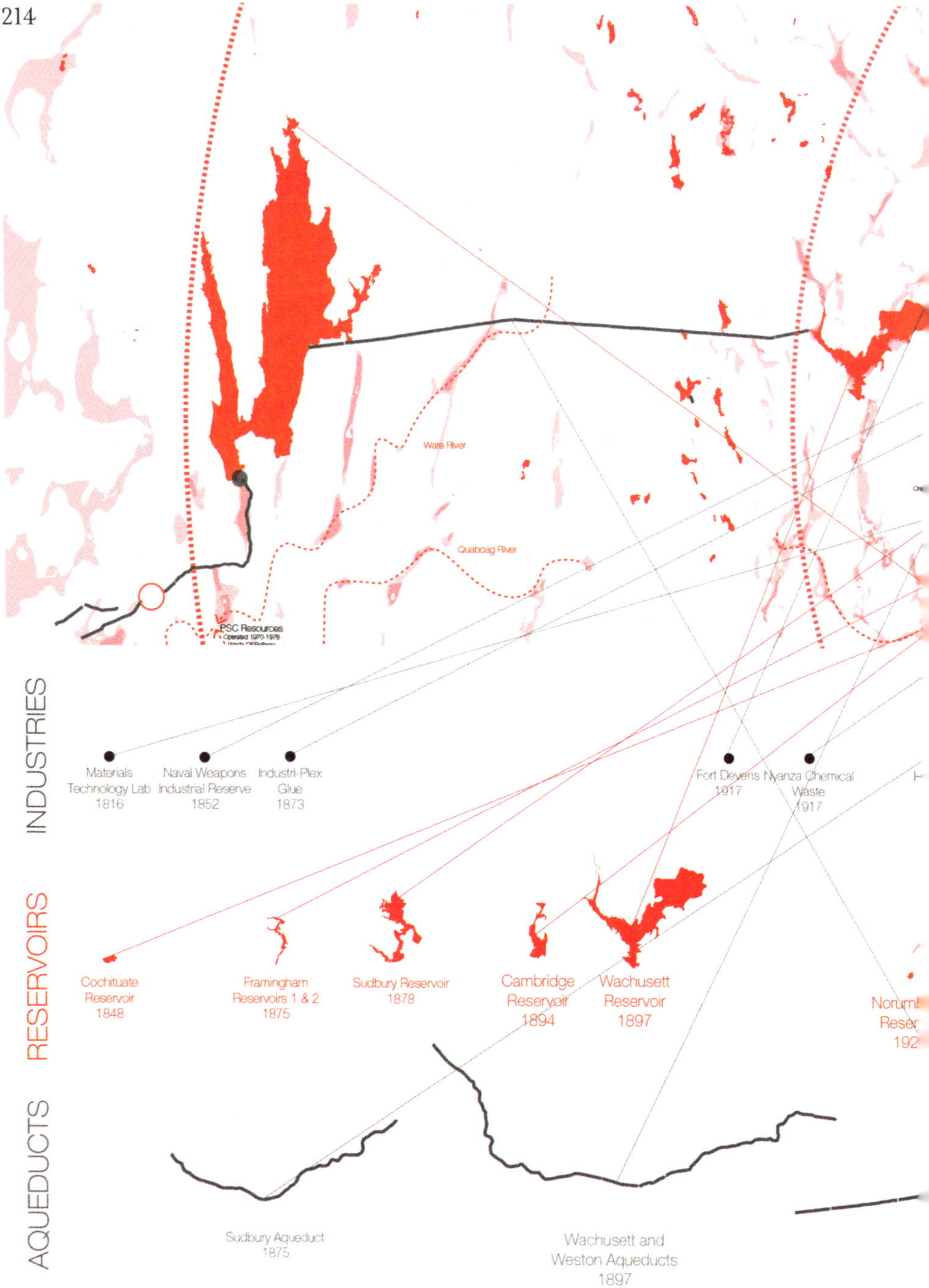
Ware River
Quaboag River
PSC Resources
Operated 1970-1978
INDUSTRIES
Materials Technology Lab 1816
Naval Weapons Industrial Reserve 1852
Industri-Plex Glue 1873
Fort Devens 1917
Nyanza Chemical Waste 1917
RESERVOIRS
Cochituate Reservoir 1848
Framingham Reservoirs 1 & 2 1875
Sudbury Reservoir 1878
Cambridge Reservoir 1894
Wachusett Reservoir 1897
AQUEDUCTS
Sudbury Aqueduct 1875
Wachusett and Weston Aqueducts 1897

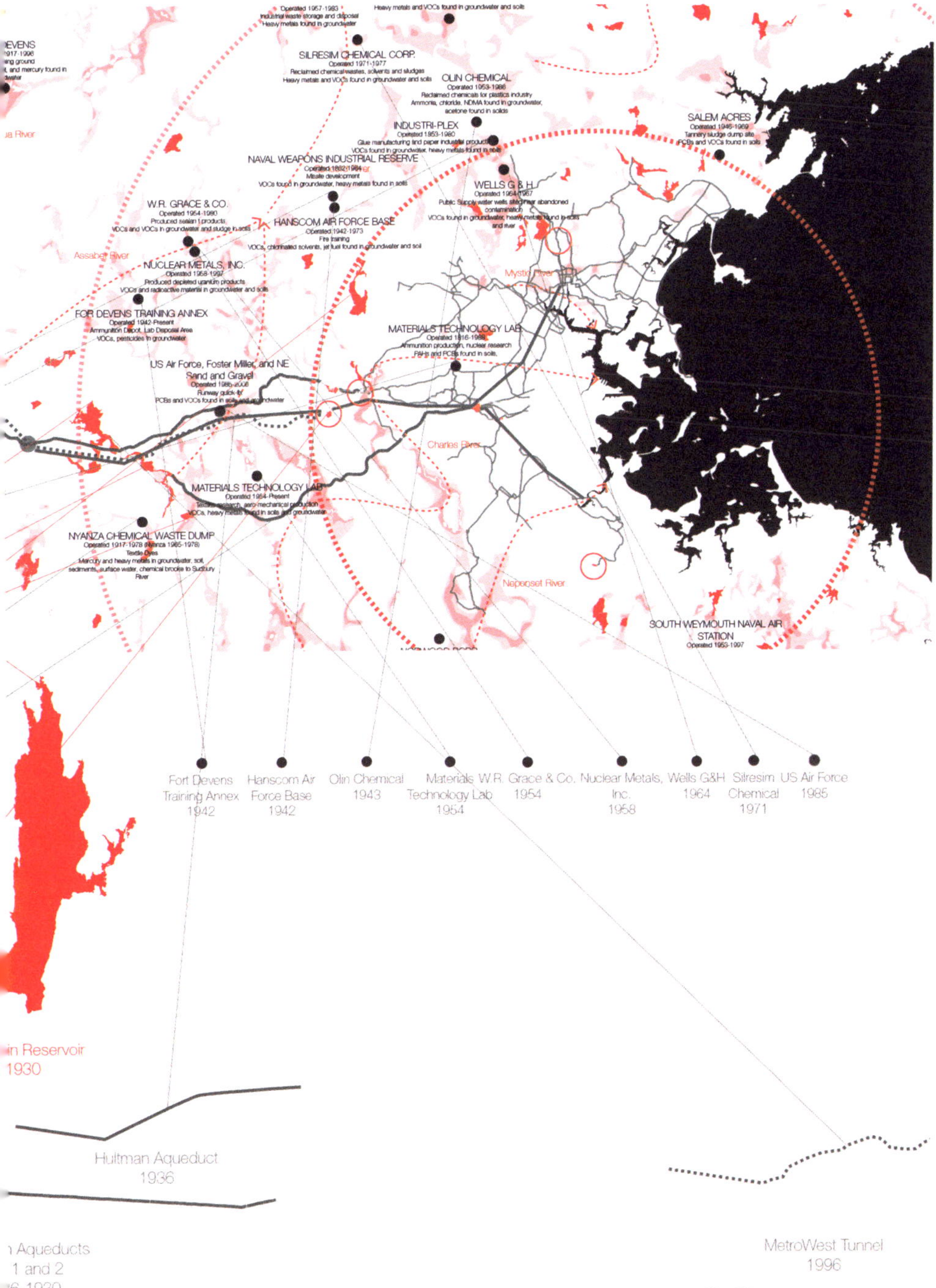

Fig. 111
Territorialism, Boston metropolitan area. Map of the Evolution of Aqueducts. Student: Phoebe White, GSD, 2012. (Viganò, 2014).

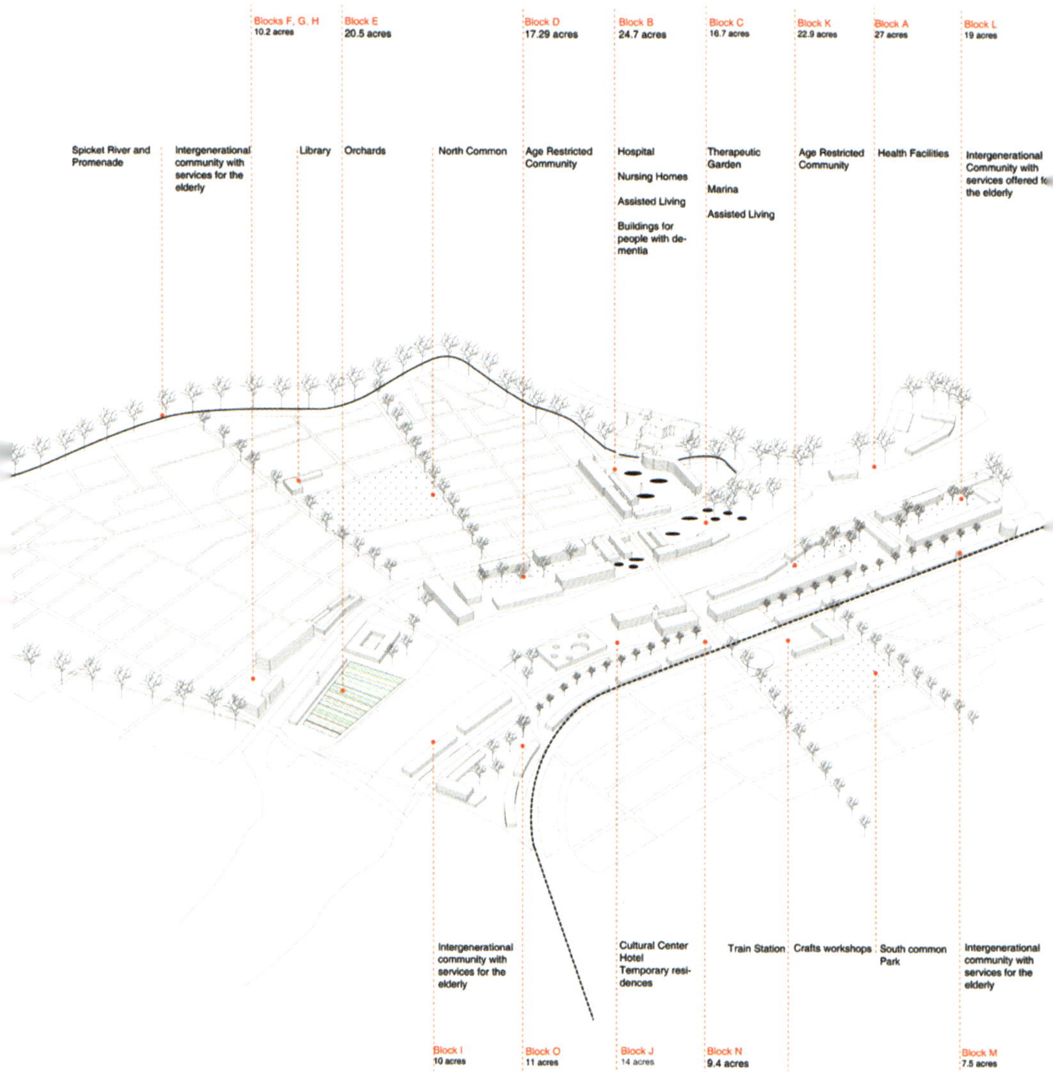

Fig. 112
Above: Territorialism, Boston metropolitan area. Lawrence, the campus scenario: Pedro Bermudez, Hugo Colon, James Whitten, GSD, 2012 (Viganò, 2018b).

Fig. 113
Opposite page, above: Territorialism, Boston metropolitan area. The Big Lawrence factories on the River, 2012. (Viganò 2018b).

Unresolved crises

Within Gottmann's Megalopolis, a large-scale urban continuum, there are numerous fractures, lacerations, socio-spatial gaps, and inner suburbs located along or within the Appalachian Mountain range, but also close to the coastline and more densely populated cities. In the Boston metropolitan area, where I have been with groups of students on previous occasions,[47] and along two north-south and east-west axes, lies Berkshire, part of the Appalachians, a few hundred kilometres away from the coastal megalopolis and the mill towns that mark one of the great manufacturing seasons of the East Coast: urban centres planned on the basis of the textile industry, along waterways channelled to exploit the water resources. Impressive complexes that are now often abandoned, or reused by new immigrant and marginal populations, are the result of great territorial transformations that leave behind monumental spaces, residential fabrics, hydraulic rationalisations and a heritage of collective memory. This is the case of Lawrence, just north of Boston, a planned city founded in 1845, an inner suburb that has become a ghetto limited by spatial barriers, with the materiality of heavy infrastructure, not the invisible walls that emerged from Mario Gandelsonas's maps of Chicago. The highway separates the city along the valley—impoverished and racialised (the populations are Latino and their economies exist on the fringes of legal ones)—from the affluent suburbs and prestigious colleges that dot the hills and forests.

To describe these spatially legible contrasts and therefore to emphasise their inherent spatiality (Soja 2000), I have used strong terms, taking them in

47. GSD, Fall 2012 and Fall 2013. See also: Viganò 2014b.

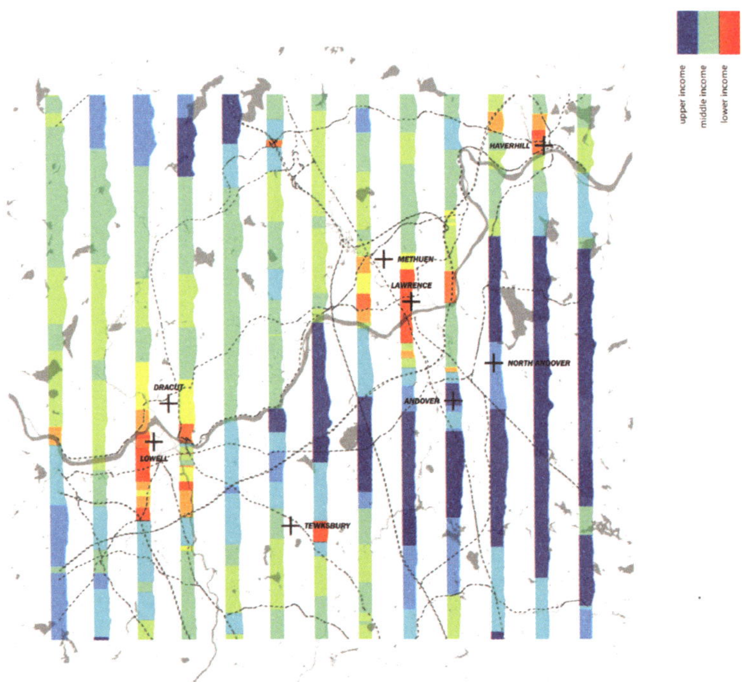

Fig. 114
Above: Territory of Andover-Lawrence. Student: Pedro Bermudez, 2012. (Viganò, 2018b).

Fig. 115
Below: Territorialism, Boston metropolitan area. Wealth disparities within a 25x25 km geographical area. The study was conducted by James Whitten, GSD, in 2012 (Viganò, 2018b).

Fig. 116
Territorialism, Boston metropolitan area. The Big Lawrence factories on the River, 2012. (Viganò 2018b).

part from the reflections that in Greater Paris[48] led us to speak of "evil places". Places that are perceived in the collective imagination as highly problematic, the presence and proximity of which arouses concern and results in stigma. I found almost the same terms in the press in metropolitan Boston about the city of Lawrence. What interests me here are both the inertia and the malleability of space in the construction of places of ethnic and social exclusion, the power of the images that are deposited on them, and finally the responsibilities of urban design in their definition and sedimentation, themes that Bernardo Secchi forcefully recalled in La città dei ricchi e la città dei poveri, as did Edward Soja around the same time (Secchi 2013; Soja 2009). Different types of cities contain contrasting and distant social morphologies, as shown by maps connecting topography, water, incomes and ethnic groups. Certain elements clearly divide and organise relationships between different parts and in space. The effort to build infrastructure, railways, canals, and new towns produced wealth for a few decades—in Lawrence up until the 1950s. By the 1970s failed renewal policies and the large-scale arrival of Latino populations put an end to this growth. Today growth is linked to gentrification in places with good rail accessibility from downtown Boston. This is a crisis that will not be resolved, and this is an important point. People live their lives in the midst of these unresolved crises.

48. I am referring to the maps and collages "The Properties of Lucifer" contained in Secchi & Viganò 2011 and Kaveh Rashidzadeh's doctoral thesis, "The Geography of Evils in the Paris Region", IUAV University of Venice, 2014.

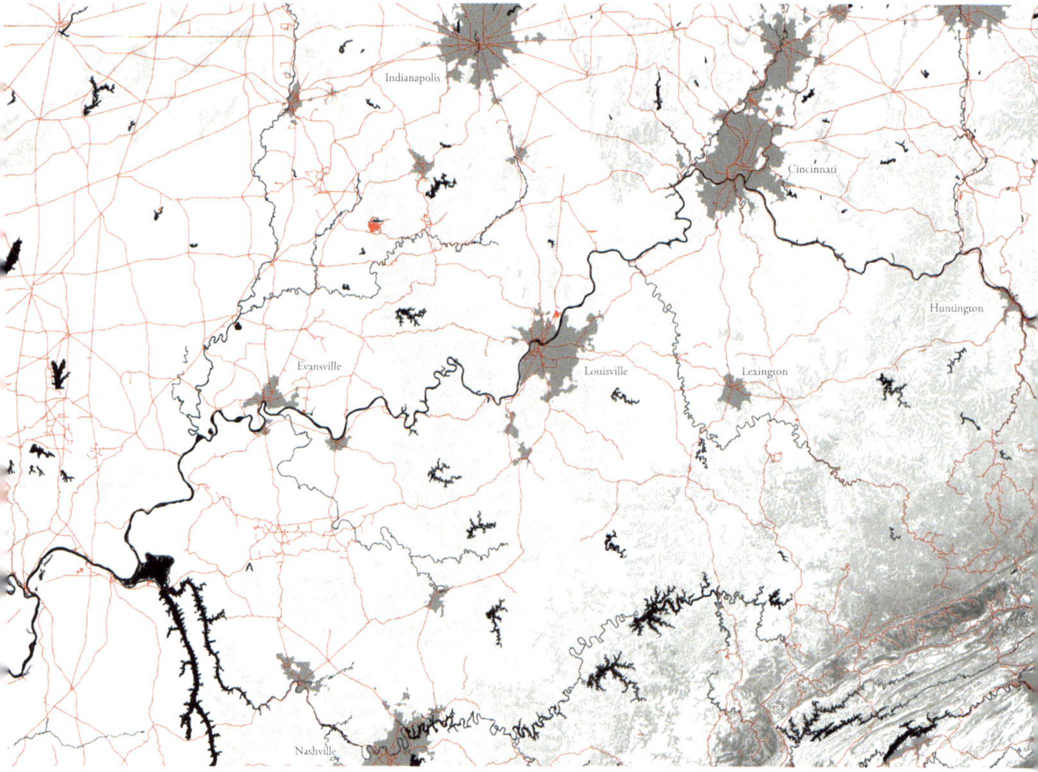

Fig. 117
The Mystery of American Reality: Towards Research on Appalachia, Between the East Coast and the Great Plains. UVA, 2017. Paola Viganò (Thomas Jefferson Visiting Professor), with Anthony Averbeck (Lecturer, UVA), Roberto Sega (Visiting PhD, EPFL) and the UVA students Batul Abbas, Joshua Aronson, Joseph Brookover, Luke Harris, Laurence Holland, Jennifer Hsiaw, Elizabeth Kulesza, Lemara Miftakhova, Shannon Ruhl, Christian Storch, Xiang Zhao, Bonnie Kate Walker.

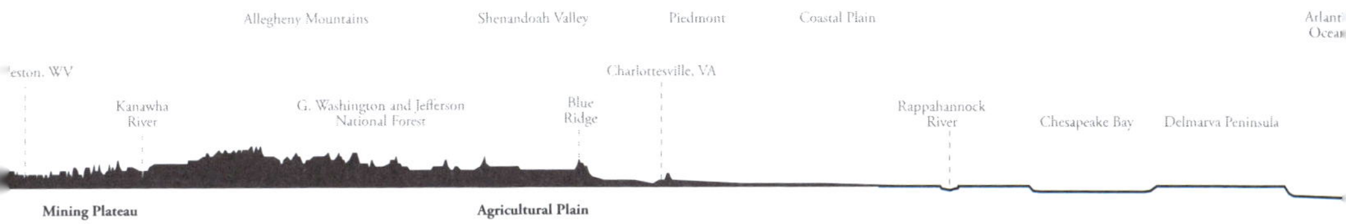
Allegheny Mountains
Shenandoah Valley
Piedmont
Coastal Plain
Charlottesville, VA
Kanawha River
G. Washington and Jefferson National Forest
Blue Ridge
Rappahannock River
Chesapeake Bay
Delmarva Peninsula
Mining Plateau
Agricultural Plain

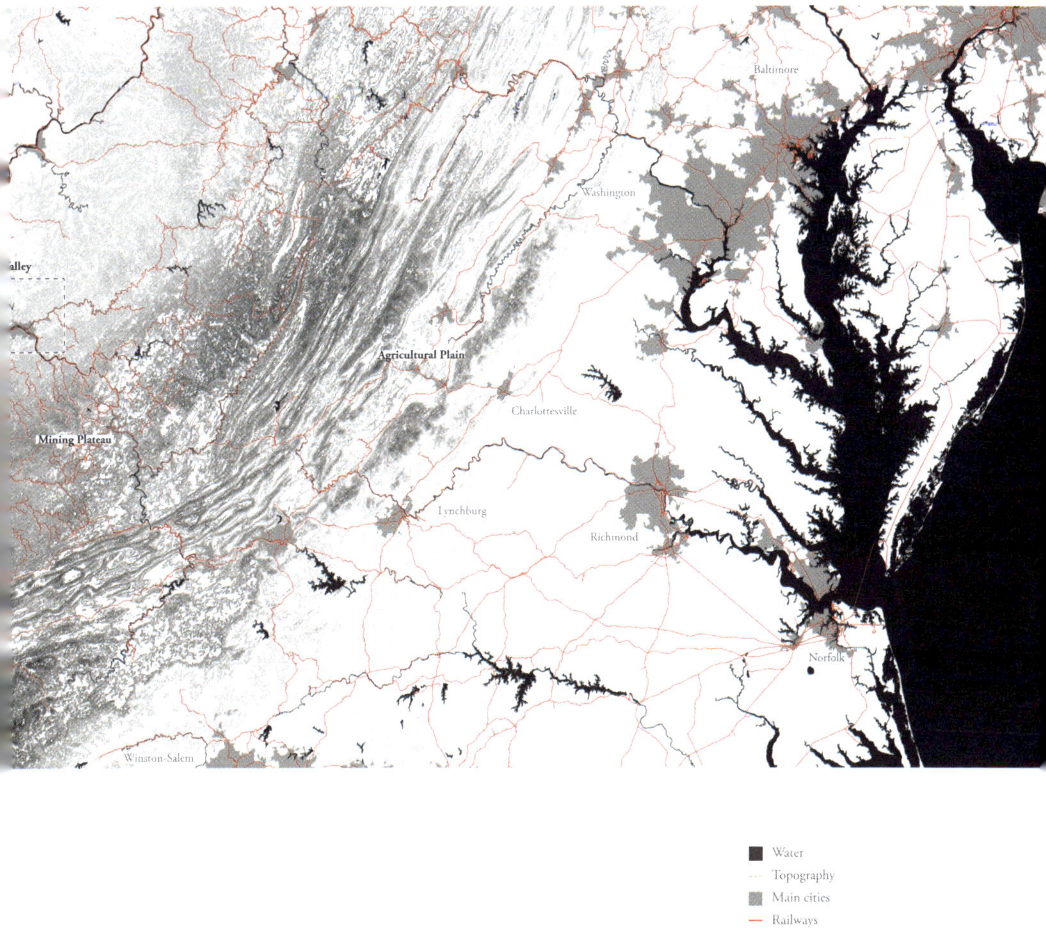
Baltimore
Washington
Agricultural Plain
Charlottesville
Mining Plateau
Lynchburg
Richmond
Norfolk
Winston-Salem
Water
Topography
Main cities
Railways

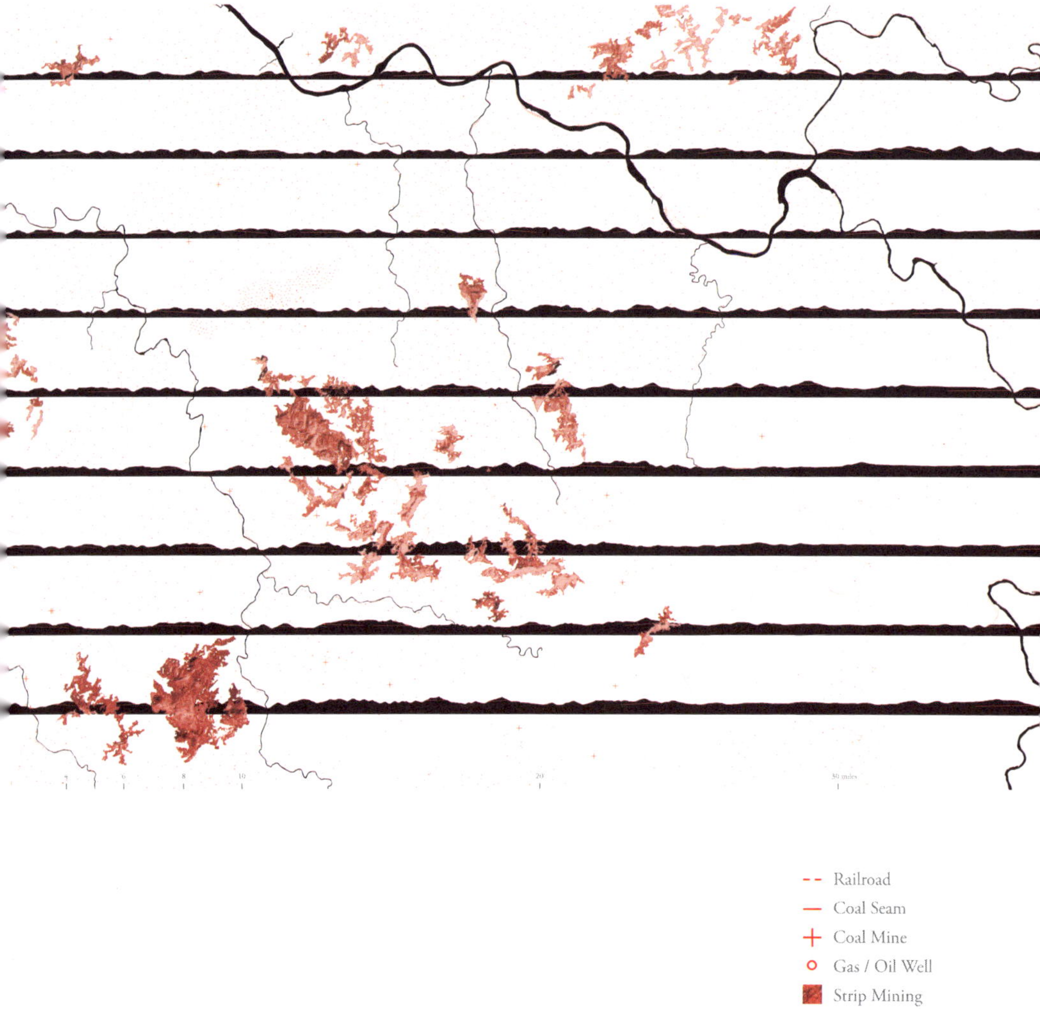

Fig. 118
Plan and sections: Quarries. Uva, 2017.

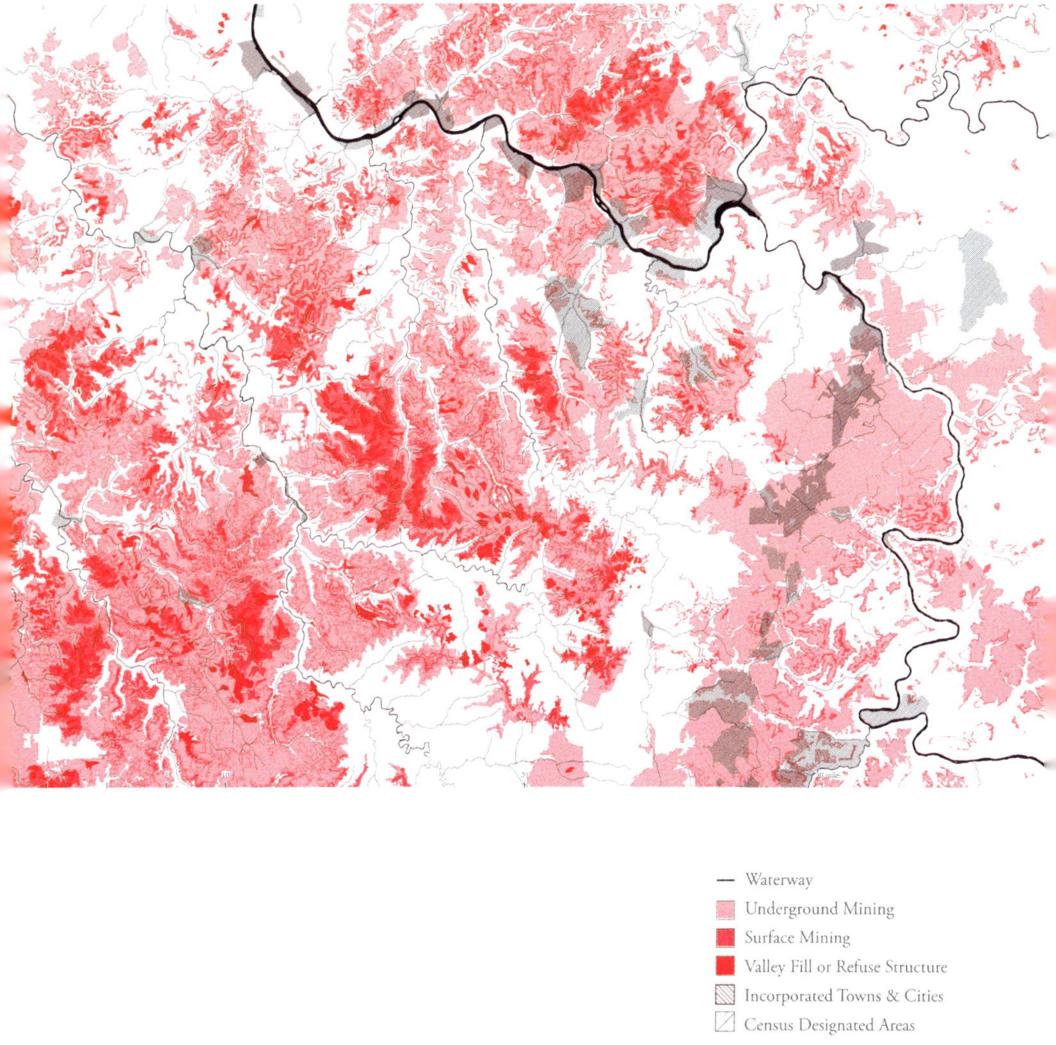

Fig. 119
Surface mining and quarries in UVA, 2017.

Faced with cases such as these, is it possible to come up with an improvement and emancipation project starting with the space, its qualities and potential? How can we maintain our ability to imagine a different future, knowing that the very inability to think about change plays a negative role in defining expectations? What is the role of spatial capital in the opening of new economic and social cycles? Among the relevant design tools, I would place not only the traditional device of the scenario, as an exploration of possibilities, but also its translation/breakdown into exercises that could be ascribed to an effort of utopian imagination: prefiguration conceived outside the current conditions of achievement and at the same time capable of enlightening certain aspects of the problem to be made manageable.

For example, while in the United States there is an increasing number of gated communities reserved for the elderly, the mill town can be imagined as an equipped enclosure, a spatial device that could usefully be employed within a project that connects local populations without work to new elderly populations in need of services and space, and that could, in the large flexible brick buildings of the mills, host new phalansterical forms. Or within Boston Bay, the serving territories between the airport, city and port, where the periphery seems to have an unresolvable destiny, where there is a clear lack of environmental and spatial justice (air pollution linked to heaps of salt ready for the winter and not sufficiently protected, the presence of heavy traffic and barriers to movement, polluted areas, the risk of explosions due to the presence of airport-related fuel depots, the rise in the sea level due to climate change, etc.). Here it is important to take the time to map the places of spatial and environmental injustice; it is especially important to connect spatial injustice to environmental injustice, through specific representations. The two often follow each other and overlap with relationships that are not easy to decipher. This type of periphery cannot be eliminated simply as it has been produced by the rest of the city for needs it cannot otherwise solve within the current socio-economic model. These spaces are uninhabitable and yet densely lived in. The idea of decommissioning a part of the port, due to the rise in sea level that will alter the uses and characters of Boston Bay, makes it possible to imagine a return to the sublime landscape, the fantasy landscape depicted in the maps of explorers of the New World. The project rethinks the original territorial conditions and transfers them to a utopia in which the new relationships between land and water define a different habitability.

The question raised by exercises of the imagination and ideas far removed from current possibilities concerns the construction of alternative futures. It is a return to utopian thinking, which is not meant to provide the high road to transformation but allows for critical reflection on issues that should be addressed in order to move towards a concrete and radical transformation.

 There is no linear relationship between vision and utopian construction other than the common need to imagine a better future, to strengthen the social construction of hope through the potential contained in each space.[49]

Returning to the United States for a new experience in 2017, I thought that the best way to resume that reasoning was to start with the "mystery". Baudrillard uses this term to describe the "reality" that the North American city continues to represent, even in my eyes. As far as I am concerned, it is about the difficulty of understanding how a country as important and rich as the United States can be marked by such desolately marginal territories, great voids of meaning and marginalisation in which, nevertheless, lives take place and powerful exploitation economies unfold. It is also about the urgency of reconnecting the profession of the urban planner and architect with reality and its profound mysteries, particularly at a time of such accelerated transition, ecologically, economically and socially.

Readings: Towards research on the Appalachians

In Amérique, a text published in the mid-1980s, Baudrillard contrasts the European utopian tradition with the "empirical radicalism" of the United States (Baudrillard 1986). The great frictions and imbalances that mark the Appalachians give dramatically concrete form to this radicalism in which the violence of contrasts is expressed, along with the pioneering and experimental spirit and the detachment from the smooth European space (as seen from a distance).

Looking once again at the great Appalachian mountain range in its relationships with the coastal centres has been an inspiring exercise,[50] guided by three main interpretative categories that structure the project of an atlas of the Appalachians: the physiography (because the shape of the territory is crucial), the palimpsest (described as a palimpsest of exploitation, because these territories are conceived as places to be impoverished and abused) and the resource (to highlight the presence of resources denied over time, such as agriculture, and ones that are intensively mined today, such as coal).

The question I raised, starting with the few cognitive elements at my disposal and an awareness of the enormous economic, geographical, and

49. I dealt with this theme in Viganò 2018b.

50. "The Mystery of American Reality" is the title of the exploratory design study, condensed into five weeks, that I held as the Thomas Jefferson Visiting Professor at the School of Architecture of the University of Virginia. I thank Inaki Alday, Ed Ford, Margarita Jover, Alex Wall, and all the colleagues who supported it. In particular, I would like to thank the group of good students (Batul Abbas, Joshua Aronson, Joseph Brookover, Luke Harris, Laurence Holland, Jennifer Hsiaw, Elizabeth Kulesza, Lemara Miftakhova, Shannon Ruhl, Christian Storch, Xiang Zhao, Bonnie Kate Walker) for their strong motivation; and lastly, for their essential help, my thanks goes to Anthony Averbeck, lecturer UVA and Roberto Sega, visiting Ph.D. EPFL. The five weeks were accompanied by a series of lectures divided into two parts: the first on the role of design and the second on space and biopolitics.

Fig. 120
Micro-stories of Appalachia.
UVA, 2017.

 cultural literature that exists on the Appalachians, concerned our ability to read and interpret, within a limited time, a vast territory of such complexity. At the same time, I also noted the lack of studies and research on the Appalachian space, in which its different roles (as capital, support and agent) were treated and represented. The risk was having to recognise that this was an impossible exercise and territory: to read, describe, imagine, design.

In this context, a "literary gaze"[51] made it possible to connect the first explorations and to design a journey through Virginia and West Virginia, along an East-West transect, rediscovering the places narrated by Breece D'J Pancake in his short stories about Appalachia, published posthumously in 1983. We mapped the writer's world, his hometown of Milton, and the ancient Teays River described in the short story "Trilobites" in West Virginia. Each of the tales and almost every sentence of them highlighted a stage in Appalachia's path towards dependency, although significant efforts have been made nationally to eradicate poverty.

The literary gaze, coupled with the construction of maps inspired by the research carried out by Franco Moretti (Moretti 1997), revealed correlations and connections that were otherwise invisible, and allowed insights often taken for granted. On the role of maps and representations, we must agree with Moretti, an important professor of literature, who extols their usefulness. On the other hand, in our job as explorers of space, novels and short stories complete the vast arsenal of references that allow us to go beyond conventional gazes and customary images, even risking outdatedness. The literary gaze has played a fundamental role in the construction of many of the projects we have worked on, even in the past.[52] The effort made with this brief but intense exercise has been to open up partially unprecedented cognitive paths and new points of view on Appalachia.

In contrast to a past in which the Appalachians were interpreted as a boundary and frontier, they are now located between two large portions of American territory, both dynamic and megalopolitan: the large cities on the coast and, beyond the Appalachians, the metropolises that have developed around the Great Lakes or to the south of the mountain range. Benton McKaye's reading, which still pointed to the Appalachians as the conclusion of a geographical system (a complicated set of ridge lines, watersheds and valleys), or Gottmann's, which pushes the megalopolis to its "natural"

51. I would like to thank Alex Wall for inviting me to the Waltz Symposium, co-coordinated with Margarita Jover in Charlottesville, where I came upon Jedediah Purdy, his denunciation of the environmental havoc underway in the Appalachians and his text After Nature: A Politics for the Anthropocene, 2015. After listening to him, I proposed to the school the topic I would have discussed. I would also like to thank Alex Wall for having written to me at Christmas time in 2016 to give me some fundamental literary advice.

52. See for example Bernardo Secchi, Paola Viganò, "Étude pour le Val de Durance", completed in 2012, Région PACA, France.

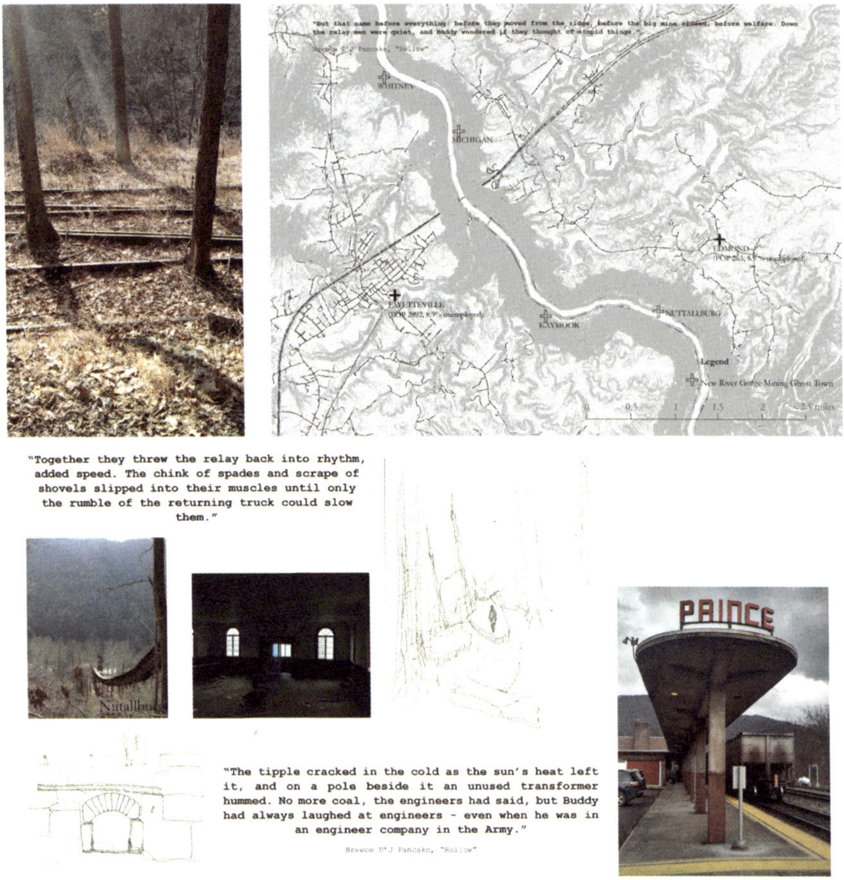

Fig. 121
Micro-stories of Appalachia. UVA, 2017.

frontier, the ridge line, should be definitively overturned. Observing the Appalachians as a space in the middle, and not on the edge, substantially changes the possible interpretations. This is particularly interesting when, through the spatial sections, we read about the relationships they establish with neighbouring territories.

The settlement system and the small towns described by Breece D'J Pancake, with their weak and modest centralities, rest lightly on the territory. They are uncertain towns, on the ground of which almost nothing is founded.

 City-camping ground. Many families live in caravans, if not in shacks. And even when they do live in houses, the houses are not served by the infrastructure bands to which even the widespread European city has accustomed us, they seem destined to be short-lived. The stories of Breece D'J Pancake, a young writer who committed suicide at the age of 26 in Charlottesville, are useful to understand these small towns. Written in the late 1970s, they speak about the small towns linked to coal and its extraction, and describe their physical, economic and social space. Breece's writing is in/about space: his stories formed the basis of a special set of maps that we made by selecting the places mentioned in the texts and the relationships established between them. It is amazing how these maps give us a different view of what is described in words and the territory of which we can only have a limited experience.

In one of these stories, "Trilobites", Pancake describes the Teays River, a vanished river whose presence he imagines he can feel through the sound of pebbles being moved by groundwater. This is now an extremely fertile area, under which the river actually flows. The geological dimension and the long timescale are often present in the tales allowing us to understand the shapes of the land, the main valleys and the great plateau, which is by no means flat but hilly, dense with reliefs and infertile forests, which we have attempted to represent through diagrammatic models. This great space, always understood as indifferent and available, is in fact a set of corrugations and incisions. Each of them, wrote Breece D'J Pancake, has its own story.

Over the course of our journey we heard many opinions, all converging on the question of whether or not there is a vision for the improvement of the area. There is no future, no hope here, was the response. Even those with more affluent living conditions seem to be there temporarily, having just returned, just arrived, or about to leave for other destinations. Some of Breece D'J Pancake's sentences had prepared us for these atmospheres; they had already taken us there. We chased some of these stories. Those of pensioners who moved at the foot of the Blue Ridge Mountains where the Appalachian Trail runs—not exactly the worst part of the Appalachians because of the low cost of living and presence of health facilities. We discovered, then, that this territory can be attractive to ageing populations seeking quality landscapes, low costs and the necessary services. Physiography and micro-histories intertwine in the territory's narrative.

Following pages:

Fig. 122
Left: Hollows; UVA, 2017.

Fig. 123
Right: Soil fertility in the Teays Valley and Kanawha River; UVA, 2017.

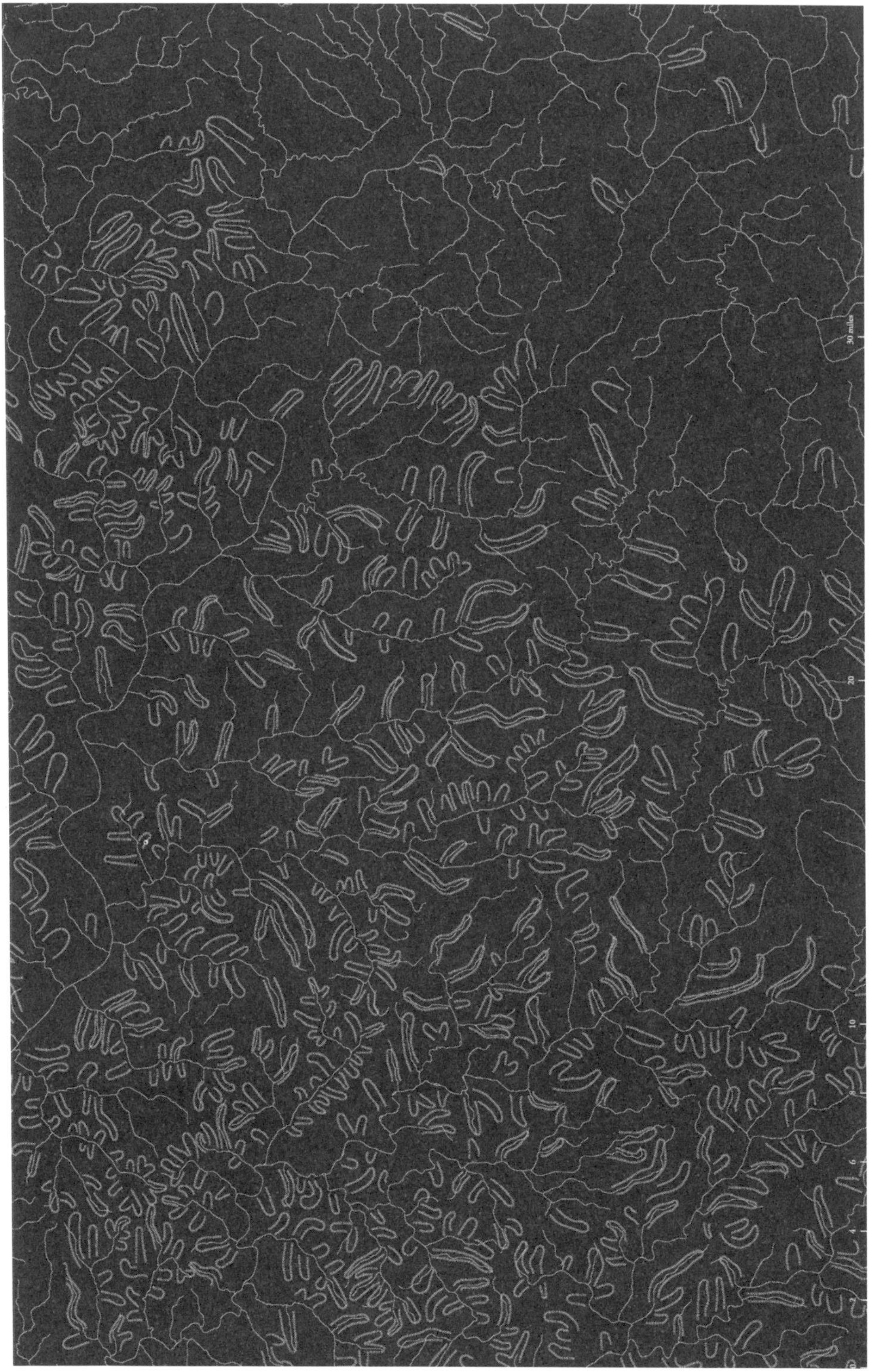
30 miles
20
10
8
6
4
2
0

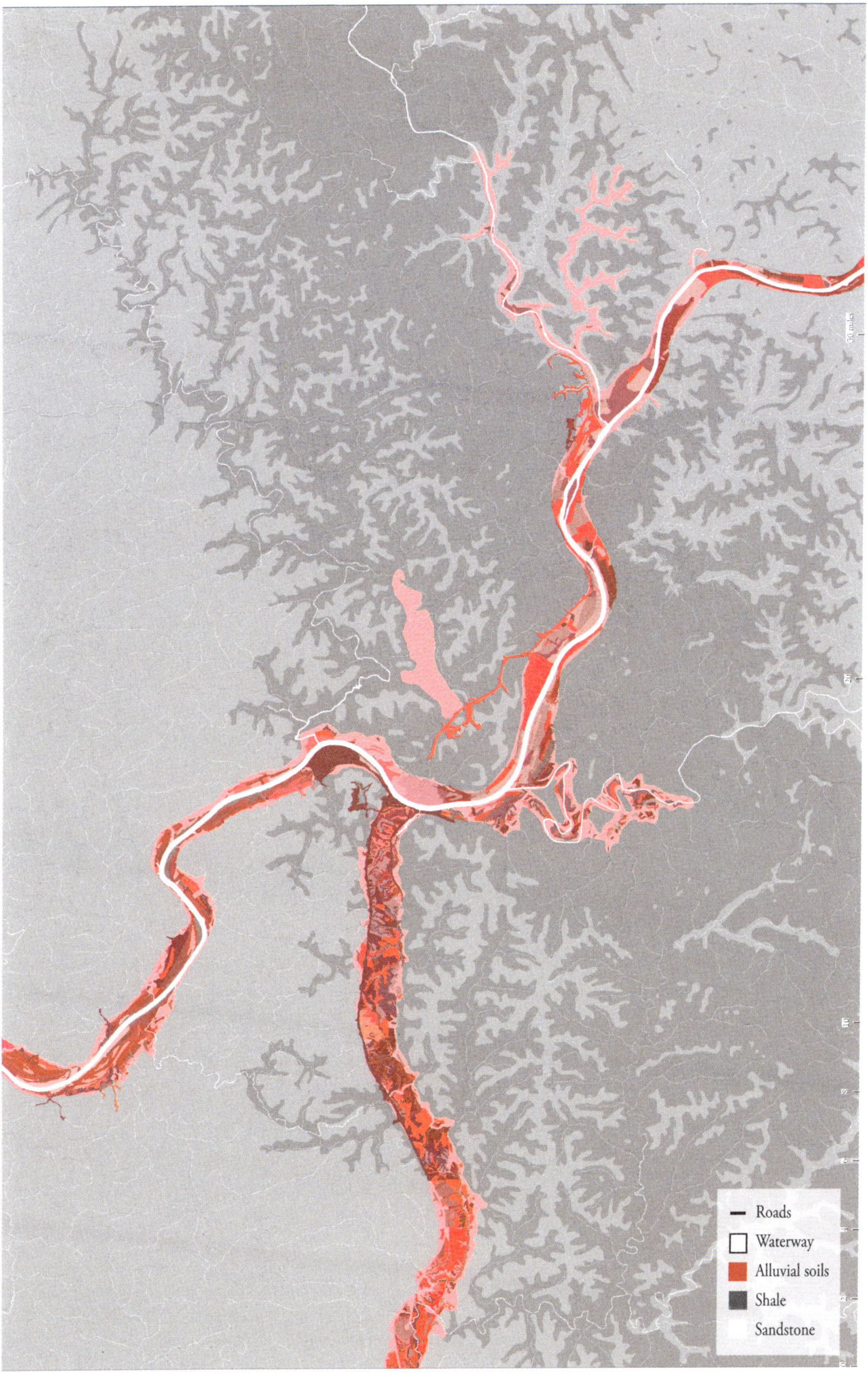
Roads
Waterway
Alluvial soils
Shale
Sandstone

Palimpsest of exploitation

The central theme of this part of the atlas is the palimpsest of exploitation. We are inside a territory that in the collective imagination is reduced, almost uniquely, to a place of extraction and exploitation, and it is difficult to escape from this image as new ones would have to replace it, facing the inertia of sedimented images. In The Land as Palimpsest, André Corboz asserts that there is no territory without an imaginary of the territory (Corboz 1983), and when one touches on territories so deeply marked by negative and stigmatising images, the truth of this sentence becomes very real.

The negative image of the Appalachians, as of other territories overlaid by images of poverty and exploitation, is perhaps one of the most obvious problems to be reconsidered, especially when it is precisely because of these images that they have been the subject of major political attention. It can be said that the imaginary of the Appalachians is welded to the entire history of the United States. I recall two episodes. John Kennedy visited them and initiated the great project of the President's Appalachian Regional Commission.[53] After Kennedy's death, Johnson identified this territory as one of the pivotal places for welfare policies, where the efforts of "his" war against poverty could be concentrated, the frontier.[54] In Pancake's stories we find criticism of that welfare state conceived to solve poverty problems, which produces more degradation without solving the widespread condition of social and territorial marginality.

The picture that emerges from these few lines should not lead to misunderstandings about the social, cultural and environmental qualities of the Appalachians. Appalachia is culturally rich, producing literature, music, art, economies. Pride in the specificities of these mountains is found in those who labour there: the miner, first and foremost, the symbol of a great past and still capable of exerting strong political pressure on contemporary politicians. At the same time, however, the population is prisoner to these images in a territory designed as a great mining machine, furrowed by an infinite number of railways linked to the transport of materials which today have largely lost their use.

In the atlas we find pipelines, railways, places that have been transformed and destroyed by mountaintop removal techniques (removal of the top of the mountain to reach the coal deposits) which change the topography of the country by pouring the remains of rocks into the valleys after extracting the valuable material, thus filling and flattening them. These operations

53. See also the study prepared in 1964 which honours the request made by John F. Kennedy ("Appalachia: A Report by the President's Appalachian Regional Commission," *https://www.arc.gov/noindex/aboutarc/history/parc/PARCtoc.pdf*) and presented to the new president Lyndon B. Johnson.

54. "War on poverty" informally defined the welfare policies undertaken by Johnson. See also Precourt 1983: 86-110.

 produce very few jobs and destroy huge portions of the plateau in a very short time, creating new serious problems for the environmental system, related to water, groundwater pollution and so on. It is the systematic destruction of the land to extract limited quantities of high-quality coal. Mountaintop removal replaces the traditional techniques of underground mining, whose access points were at the end of inhabited valleys. Mining systems are intertwined with settlement forms: in the hollows (small valleys), the paths flanked by homes lead to the mouths of the old mines. This is a place for locals, not tourists. Everything points to a territory radically subjugated to mining.

Resources

This part of the atlas avoids mentioning coal, timber or water, but describes some of the soils of Appalachia and discusses their fertility. A rare but present resource, the arable soil of Appalachia could play a role in the recovery of economies that existed in the past. Some economists argue that part of its dependence on the outside world is linked to the destruction of agriculture.[55] The Appalachians are dependent on the outside world for food production, whereas in the early days of industrial mining they were self-sufficient territories capable of feeding their populations. Some valleys, especially the larger ones such as the Shenandoah Valley, are still partly cultivated; the plains are used for breeding livestock, although the most fertile territories are others, those on the slopes, which are now often abandoned due to the difficulties posed by mechanised agriculture.

Together with the contradictions mapped in the palimpsest of exploitation, this part of the atlas highlights some potential uses in an area in search of new definitions.

A different image

Moving towards a conclusion that opens up the future, it is still important to return to the large space of Appalachia, which is not very dense but bordered by a series of megalopolises (to the east, the Gottmann Megalopolis; to the northwest, the Great Lakes area; to the south, the Piedmont Atlantic), and place it within the whole North American context. Some maps, at the scale of the United States, propose unusual juxtapositions and overlaps, such as that between political choices and geology. The entire Appalachian chain is Republican, far from the East Coast cities and the southern Black belt of Democratic tradition. From the start, there was a direct line of communication between Donald Trump and the Appalachians. His deal with residents of Appalachia was a promise to reopen the mines, which he implemented.

55. The dependency also concerns the loss of food self-sufficiency (Salstrom 1994).

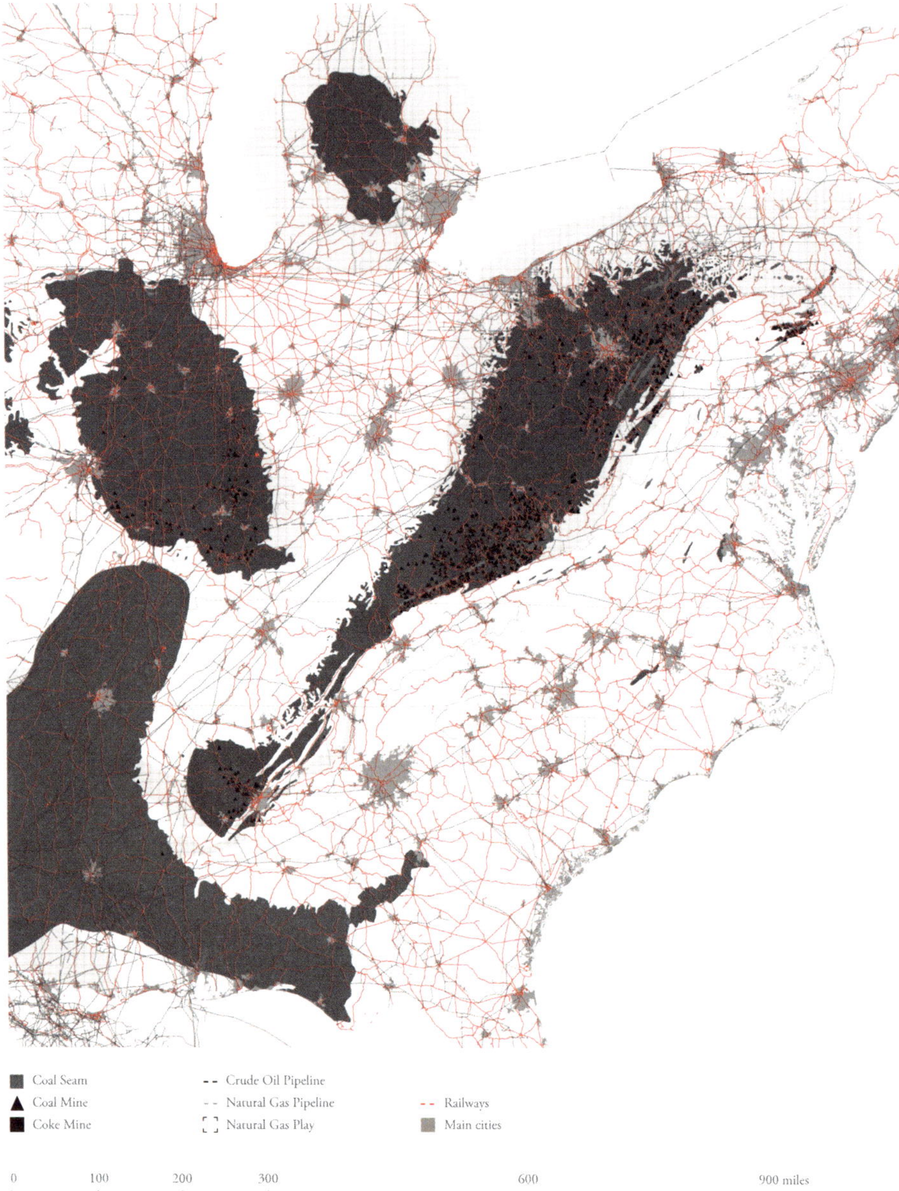

Fig. 124
Above: A palimpsest of exploitation. UVA, 2017.

Fig. 125
Scenario 1: «Extracting Appalachia. The paradox of plenty». UVA, 2017.

The maps show that conditions in the Appalachians are now getting worse, not better. Drug abuse is on the rise. The crisis of the late 1990s is even deeper today. The indicators of social malaise, population loss, as well as job losses, are only slightly mitigated by the proximity to the large megacities. The economy is struggling to restructure itself by opening up to the public service sectors, and in particular the health and care sectors, which are rapidly expanding today. In this weakness, which is becoming increasingly rigid, lies the utopian imagination or, perhaps better, the "empirical radicalism" of three scenarios[56] that add some projections and points of view to the atlas and the micro-stories, each of which, in addition to opening up a discussion, could constitute the beginning of possible research.

These are the three scenarios:

1. Extracting Appalachia. The paradox of Plenty

The scenario perhaps closest to Baudrillard's idea of "empirical radicalism" starts with the inevitable paradox that arises from the wealth of resources, their exploitation and therefore the presence of the extractive machine. He imagines that the current process continues, but inserts the possibility, now non-existent, of its design in space, in the landscape. This scenario contains some very realistic and concrete elements to reckon with. What if this is really how it should end? If this really were the future of Appalachia, would we still have to deal with an extreme condition of exploitation that alters and redesigns the whole territory? This is not a rhetorical scenario to be

56. The scenarios are represented in a video, unsophisticated in terms of workmanship but weighty.

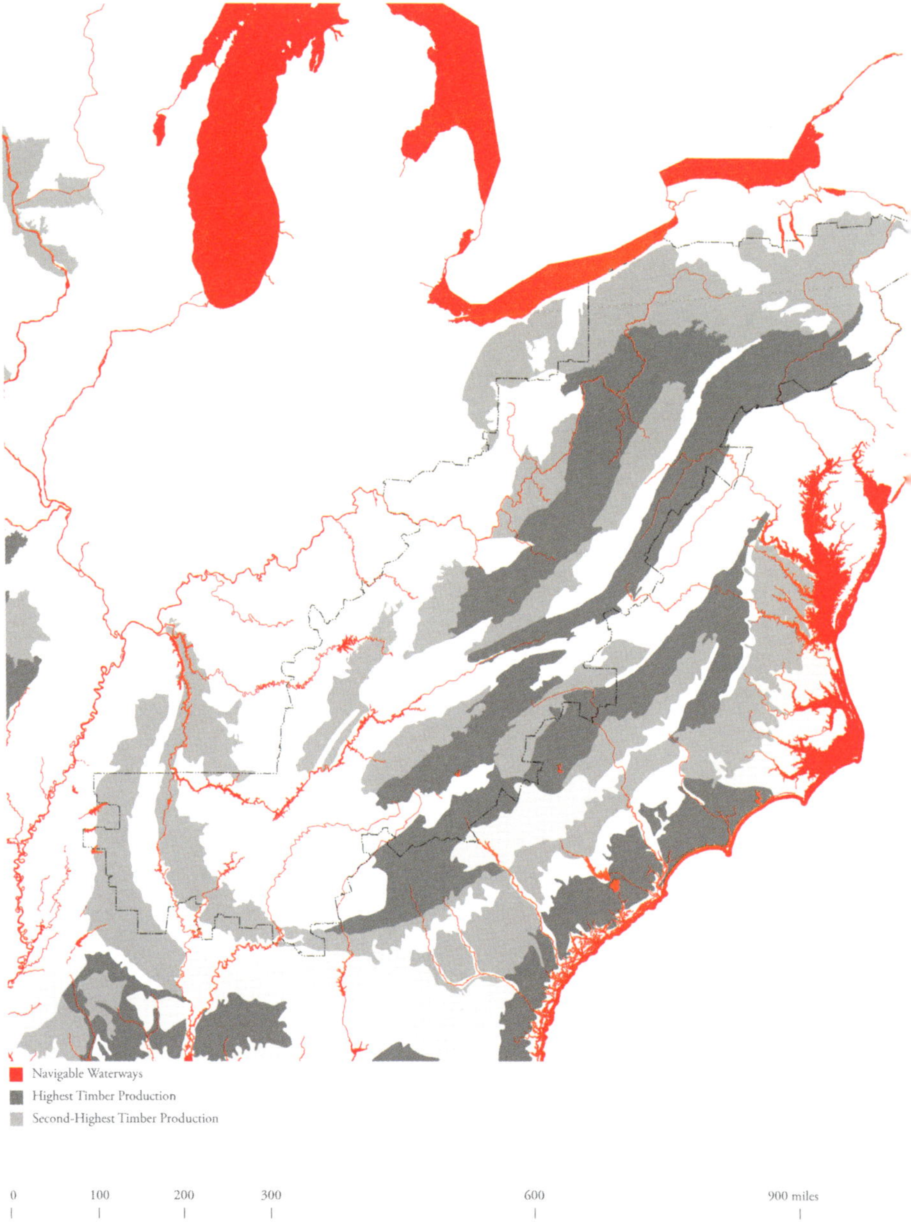

Fig. 126
Above: Resources: Forest biomass. UVA, 2017.

Fig. 127
Right page, above: Scenario 2: «Autarchical Appalachia». UVA, 2017.

disregarded immediately after having stated it, but a possible future, which drags with it a series of inescapable issues, including many biopolitical and environmental ethics questions and their relationships with a socio-spatial project.

2. Autarchical Appalachia

The second scenario overturns the previous interpretation, imagines the decline of non-renewable energies: natural gas and coal. It raises the issue of territorial self-sufficiency, the need of strengthening different economies starting with other Appalachian resources, such as biodiversity or agriculture. The region's lower risk of destruction from rising seas levels, compared to the more precarious position of coastal cities, contributes to a new attractivity. An experimental terrain (empirical radicalism again) for exploring new forms of coexistence between humans and non-humans, Appalachia sees itself as a place to survive catastrophe.

There are many "Preppers" or survivalist movements in the United States, stemming from the risk of nuclear war, that seek protected and disconnected spaces where the catastrophes that await us cannot reach us. In this scenario, the Appalachians, one of the oldest mountain ranges on our planet, and one of the most important biodiversity hubs in the United States, becomes the space for a radical social and ecological experiment: one that concerns life and the protection of life.

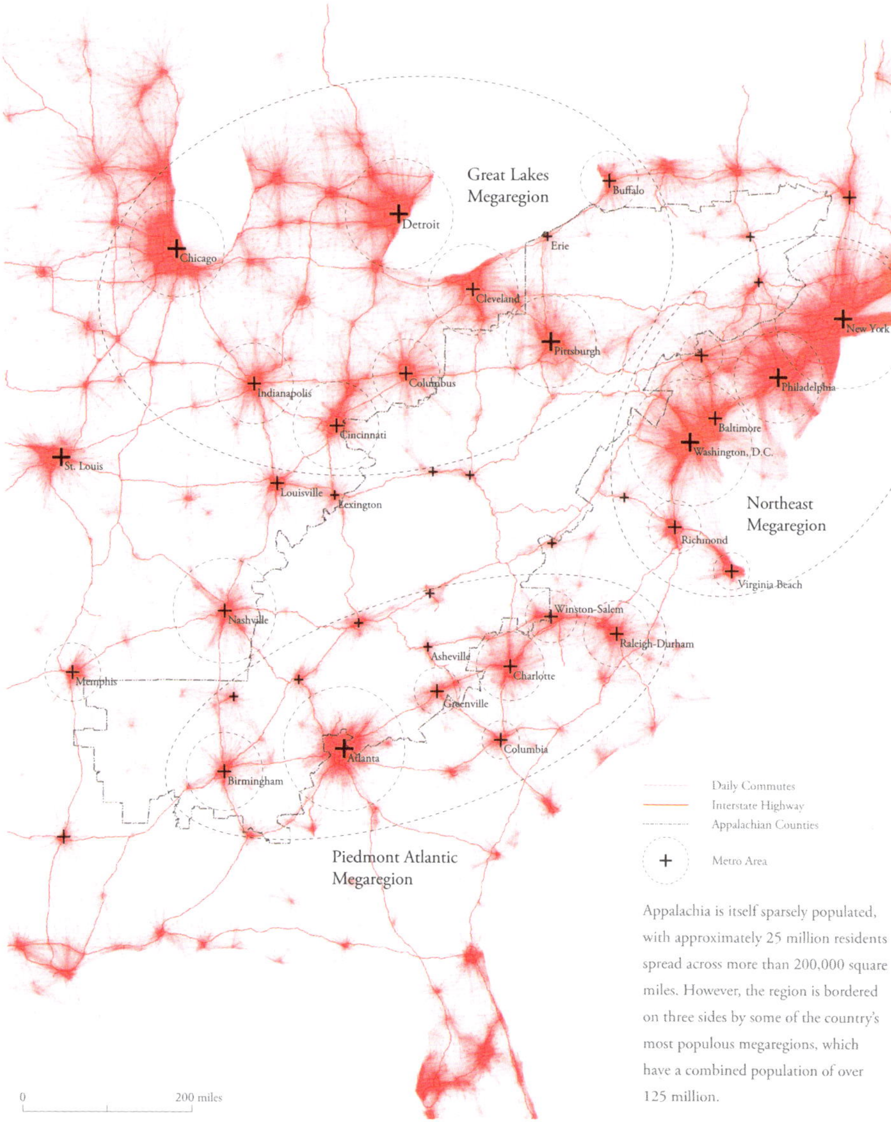

Appalachia is itself sparsely populated, with approximately 25 million residents spread across more than 200,000 square miles. However, the region is bordered on three sides by some of the country's most populous megaregions, which have a combined population of over 125 million.

Fig. 128
Above: Settlements and connectivity. UVA, 2017.

Fig. 129
Right page, above: Scenario 3: «One, no one, one hundred thousand». UVA, 2017.

3. One, No One, One Hundred Thousand Appalachia

The third scenario, One, No One, One Hundred Thousand,[57] starts with the need to deconstruct, disrupt, and destroy the unitary image of Appalachia, which is one of the region's fundamental problems—the one perhaps best to start with. To do this, the scenario questions the Appalachians' "natural" existence by emphasising the variety of landscapes, including urban ones, which comprise it. This scenario considers the proximity of the different parts of Appalachia to mega-cities and distinct metropolitan areas as a great potential for its future. Within a non-trivial idea of metropolisation, within a process of inclusion and not selection, of integration into a horizontal metropolis, places with strong economies will be able to extend benefits and new cultural and economic relations to the Appalachians. Cultivating an extended heterogeneity may reveal the multiplicity concealed by the big picture of Appalachia, the many opportunities that exist along its edge and in relation to it. Appalachia is not, as the narrator of the video we made tells us, "a special and mystical region", but a region inhabited by those who demand living conditions similar to those permitted by other territories.

The third scenario rejects the hypothesis of the great project/great policies for the Appalachians, its unified representation. It imagines that contributing to the revelation of the differences, the hundred thousand Appalachia, could be a way of unhinging the fixity of the great space and an important role for architects.

The three scenarios could form the starting point for research on Appalachia and at the same time research on a renewed relationship between the design of space and the mystery of reality.

3.6 FRAGMENTS OF A DISCOURSE

The Biopolitical Garden contains fragments of a new discourse on space, life and design. Taking up the three fields discussed in chapter two—biopower, deep ecology and the emancipation of the subject—it encompasses an epistemological, ontological and ethical shift.

The territory subject

In the mid-80s[58], André Corboz highlighted a passage that is fundamental today: "... Étant un projet, le territoire est sémantisé. Il est « discourable ». Il porte un nom. Des projections de toute nature s'attachent à lui, qui le transforment en un sujet" (Corboz 1983). The territory has gone from being an object, a "subjugated" entity, to a subject with a name or names; it is named. It is endowed with meaning and is not merely a dead and insignificant accumulation; it participates in the construction of discourses as it is the recipient and inspiration behind projections and imaginaries (il n'y a pas de territoire sans imaginaire du territoire). The territory as a subject is an agent territory and not a mere support.

Corboz's theory contains many implications. The understanding and consideration of its implications are not yet complete; territorial research and current policies have not adequately absorbed and reformulated them. The ecological, social and economic transition instead calls for the construction of a new outlook, a new epistemology of the territory starting with the territory-subject. This is my hypothesis.

The analogy Corboz established between the idea of the subject (therefore endowed with rights and duties) and that of the territory likely contributes to the difficulty in understanding and assuming responsibility. To simplify things and support the start of a discussion, I will attempt to remove the how, for a moment leaving the "territory-subject" to take shape in the open field of our imagination. More than subjectivity or identity, a process is represented in this territory-subject, namely subjectification, that is to say the production, conscious or not, implicit or explicit, entirely internal or imposed from the outside, of a subject. In this case the territory in all its parts.

The territory-subject (or the subjectification of the territory) has some important epistemological and ontological implications, as well as very profound

58. Paragraphs one and two take up some considerations developed in Viganò (2020b).

ethical and political ones. The subject is a single, unique individual, but it is also, and in any case, the result, expression and product of relations and logics of power (Foucault 1994b; Revel 2014). Piero Bevilacqua spoke about the non-obviousness of this shift, which considers "nature", even that transformed by human activity, to be a historical product endowed with "relative autonomy with respect to the action of individuals..., a dynamic existence, free and pre-existing to the very conditionings of technology" (Bevilacqua 1996:10). He goes on to say that nature is the "active partner" and second subject "in the process of wealth production" (Bevilacqua 1996:10). The centrality of productivity for human purposes and of the concept of resource, if useful to overcome the myopic or blurred gaze of traditional economic thought "which at least from Adam Smith to Marx has in fact consecrated human labour as the sole protagonist of the process of enhancement, and therefore itself as the only thing responsible for the creation of wealth" (Bevilacqua 1996:10),[59] is not sufficient to bring us into the world of the territory-subject. While in his writings he remained focused on the idea of the active partner, Bevilacqua evoked this different ethical and research dimension when he spoke of the other: "...it really is the start a cultural revolution that has just begun." (Bevilacqua 1996:11). From commodity and resource, the territory becomes subject.

In the literary experiences—reading, interpretation and design—which I have conducted in recent years and covered above, the questions raised by the idea of the territory-subject and their controversies have emerged regularly and with severity, without ever retreating, as if it were no longer possible to go backwards but only to advance, even with difficulty, within the radical recontextualisation of the territory-subject and territorial subjectivation. In this approach I include all the indeterminacies and problematic issues contained within the process and that emerge with the ambiguity of the very term subject (sujectum-subjectus, as Étienne Balibar recalled) (Balibar 2012). At the same time the subject is individual, anthropological-political, but also subjugated, placed underneath.

I will focus on just some of the methodological and design consequences that the idea of territory-subject has generated, and among them the assumption of the reasons for the territory as a critical object of investigation. Territorial rationalities—the long-term construction processes that have transformed natures, economies and landscapes by developing new ones—have entered in a clearer and more fundamental way into the revision of the idea of the

59. Bevilacqua cites Hans Immler (Natur in der ökonomischen Theorie, Opladen 1985) and his "Nature and work. Analysis and reflections on a book", in Meridiana 1994, 20. The notion of labour-value, argues Bevilacqua, does not allow for the inclusion of the physical world, which escapes the process of transformation into a commodity, albeit actively participating in the production of wealth. These are themes that have their roots in the 1970s and 80s and that in the 90s and, especially, the first decade of the 2000s consolidated around the idea of ecosystemic services and the economic value of natural resources (Valencia Torres et al. 2021).

city, its form and structure and its design, for example by enhancing the widespread and isotropic networks that, as we have mentioned, have an ecological, economic and political rationale (Viganò 2008; Viganò, Secchi, Fabian, 2016). After a few seasons with almost no spatial memory, attention is once again placed on the material construction of the territory which is necessary to decipher the logics that form and transform it, the adaptations, abandonments and recoveries.

Through these readings and interpretations, the ideas of capital space, support and agent have fostered the revision of the territorial project, restoring to the territory the position of a subject around the table of the choices that concern it. However, the subject-territory—with its characteristics and qualities, states and dynamics—and the agent territory that can perform actions, can also suffer them: it is weak, manipulable and violable. It is indeed "subject to", subjugatable and subjugated. Here too, an understanding of territorial rationalities—and among them the complex, ancient and recent sphere of rationalities related to the organisation of agricultural, proto-industrial and industrial production—reveals the countless paradoxes that constitute our late and tired modernity. Even if each of the recognised rationalities has at some time in human history had a collective, political and social meaning, or performed essential functions for our survival and the development of territorial habitability, this does not prevent us, today, from measuring with ever greater precision and knowledge the distance that separates us from them and their internal contradictions, especially those that respond to strong, destructive and hegemonic rationalities, the expression of resistance logics that are the most difficult to adapt and rethink. In the case of the Vesdre Valley, which concludes the series of projects presented, the search for territorial resilience involves the idea of the territory-subject and is disruptive as it compares different logics within a common and equal dialogue. At territorial scale, the transition project implies the extensive and pervasive revision of agricultural, hydraulic and production models, the circularity of production, a different mobility, etc.—a different ecological and socio-economic model.

In the light of climate change and the rarefaction of resources, the reflection on territorial rationalisations is part and parcel of the criticism of modernity and modernisation: processes and transformations that today pose fundamental problems.

Weak structures

To discuss the paradox of the subject-territory, simultaneously endowed with rights and subjugated, I am assuming that the structuring capacity of some of its elements and of the territory as a whole is not only pertinent to strong structures representing the development ambitions of a region, town or city (for instance, large infrastructures). There are structures that are less capable of imposing their point of view, "weak structures", terms I have taken from the debate on post-modernity in which they originally arose (Vattimo 1985). Weak territorial structures, incapable of resisting, which are often violated and rejected—what interests me about these structures is their pervasiveness, their capacity to organise contemporary extended urbanity to question the current development models, and lastly, their ability to adapt. In order to fully appreciate them, however, we must return to the territory-subject and its rights.

Confirming that environments and pieces of territory are legal entities, as occurred for example in New Zealand with regard to rivers and natural areas (Iorns Magallanes 2015), has been considered an important achievement, even if this once again locks nature into a cage of precise social or common values and precise hierarchies that are culturally and historically determined. Similarly, consideration of the value of the soil, a weak structure par excellence, does not seem to be able to escape the mechanism of monetising its fundamental functions (a controversial topic that is not agreed on, even at the European level). We are far from Aldo Leopold's Land Ethics.

Two questions emerge. They concern the sense of extending rights to the entire territory, beyond the wilderness and sphere of nature protection and conservation—this is the first question—and the possibility of going beyond the utilitarian dimension, imprinted into the term resource (the territory as a resource or as capital), especially when we speak about the "vocations" of a territory. This is the second question: attributing value to the territory-subject for what it is and not only for the reserves/resources/capital it contains, thus also to its less useful, impressive and trivial portions.

Reflecting on the weak character of the structure calls into question the concept of order and with it the foundations of modern thought and its totalising rationalities. Attention to weak structures reveals latent coherences and reconnects what has been separated and fragmented, often rediscovering conceptual trajectories that have subconsciously traversed victorious modernity, proposing alternative paths (Audier, 2017; Barcelloni Corte, Viganò, 2022). The aspect of weak territorial and spatial structures that interests me is that they continue to be devices of emancipation in a context of crisis and transition, and to cross it a high level of widespread infrastructure must be maintained. I am interested in the weak subject's ability to pose questions and upset the balance of traditional relationships of power. In the field of urban and territorial design it means abandoning the omni-comprehensive claim, unless it provides a common vanishing point, and instead highlighting possibilities set in motion, demanded with "gentle nudges" (Thaler, Sunstein, 2008) that do not avoid facing up to the need for extensive structural changes. This point of view also has consequences for "strong structures", indicating the possibility of new relationships between them and the various "subjugated" territorial strata.

Space and economy

The focus on territory-subjects and weak structures overturns current development models and makes it necessary to build new alliances between economy and urban/territorial design. This should not come as a surprise: after years of criticism and condemnation of the new urban question, after a number of important texts have revealed its extent and seriousness, after new marginalities and imbalances have emerged and pre-existing ones have deepened, it is clear that the territorial and urban development project must reposition itself and redefine its role within different and alternative paths compared to the past. In a new biopolitical discourse (in which the Foucauldian themes, discipline and security, are extended to deep ecology and the emancipation of the subject), talking about development requires a joint effort, a renewed alliance between the economic thought/discourse of development and the thought/discourse on the city and the territory.

While, in the past, architecture and town planning assumed without or with little critical distance the idea of progress as continuous growth; and while the exploitation of resources was the inevitable condition for the development of many territories along with their forced specialisation, regardless of their capacity for self-regeneration; and while human capital was at that time fluid and easily available and disposable; and, finally, while the project of space was part of this vision, giving shape to its design—today this path must be profoundly reinterpreted. The difficulty, if not the impossibility, of following the trajectories of the past and the need to reformulate new development logics, starting with space, economy and society (i.e. starting with spatial and environmental, cultural and human capital), emerged in the initial research on the Appalachians and in the urban and territorial projects for Wallonia.

It should be made clear that the logics of the past are not entirely absent in the places observed. They have not disappeared: they persist and, in part, delay our awareness of the environmental and social problem underlying the need for new economies. Research on space must position itself, bring out the contradictions present and the possible alternatives, "[produce] a language of economic difference", emphasise practices obscured by traditional economic forms and help to broaden "the economic imaginary" (Gibson-Graham 2006:x) beyond the alternative ways of conceiving work, wages or the market, and through an understanding of space. It is here that the subject-territory takes on its full meaning. In fact, new forms of subjectivity can emerge from this process: in the rejection of preformed individualities linked to traditional economic practices (Foucault: 1983).

In other words: "sustainability is inextricably entangled in the construction of alternative production paradigms and political orders." (Escobar, 2008:103). Alternative development, alternative modernity and alternatives to modernity are three "coexisting processes and political projects" (Escobar

2008: 162) that can foster reflection. It is the complex and unprecedented relationships that can develop between the three processes (from the search for non-exclusive well-being, to food self-sufficiency, to radical new visions of world reconstruction) that foster the hypothesis of the formation of a new biopolitical project.

Biopolitical (eco-socio-spatial) prototypes

The transition project is a vast project made up of countless small and large transformations and will only have a chance of being implemented if it is supported by broad consensus, since it is about adapting and changing our way of life. It is a project that is both decentralised and centralised at the same time, which challenges the simplified bottom-up rhetoric as well as the already widely criticised top-down rhetoric. A largely unknown terrain lies before us, to be approached with an experimental attitude and at all scales of the project. Thoughts will inevitably return to the great season of the American counterculture (Maniaque 2021), with its attempts to reconstruct the world, as well as to certain imaginative efforts of the 1970s that reveal the proximity between distant ideas and authors: films such as Alain Tanner's Jonas Who Will Be 25 in the Year 2000 (1976), and utopian novels such as Ecotopia (Callenbach, 2009). In the former case, the themes of soil and labour unleash all their utopian force which reverberates on every aspect of social life and human-nature relations. In the latter, the biopolitical component is clearly stated. The protagonist, a journalist, says: "There is no doubt, I have been forced to conclude, that the risky social experiments undertaken here have worked on a biological level" (Callenbach, 2009:163 ff.), an awareness that goes beyond the boundaries of Ecotopia.

Prototype design has an important tradition behind it that belongs to the culture of design and problem solving, and this might make its use unconvincing, at times marked by doubts concerning the very meaning of problem solving design, even before considering its solutions (Viganò 2018). The development of prototypes is nonetheless appropriate for inevitable experimentation in a transitional period with a strong social and biopolitical dimension in space. Here again there are two stories: the first, the role of a weak space that is prototypical in reorganising a territory starting with soil and work (a vision for Greater Geneva); the second, an experiment in which the entire city space becomes a laboratory, using every occasion and minute on a daily basis to translate a vision up to the 2040 horizon: the adaptation prototypes in the reconstructed centre of Brest. In the latter case, synergies between urban and metropolitan services, and between forms of citizen participation are set in motion to conceive, achieve and maintain projects with different timeframes, from the most minor ones that act in the short term and announce change, to definitive ones that must last. The resources are recomposed by using the available funds in different ways, in the end creating spaces that play a role in the social and ecological transition of the city.

Production of urban space and production of ecologies

Relations have always been difficult between soil and city, between soil and urbanisation. In modern design, the city is associated with the destruction of soils and their qualities. Today, natural soil and urban soil are both a three-dimensional body evolving over time, a "living soil" with vital functions, a living entity among other living entities. The project for a new part of the city, in Rennes, presented on the previous pages and started in 2003, is now more than half-way concluded. The project was accomplished along with the regeneration of its soil, reusing a partially disused and polluted industrial and military area. Here it was possible to tangibly measure and explore urban transformation as an opportunity to overcome the traditional antithesis between the city and natural dynamics.

The project is the same: regenerate city and nature. The soil, watercourses, large trees or younger ones that have great hopes for life form the basis of choices about the type of space in which to live. The project becomes idiography, it brings out different histories and completes them with the most recent, a new layer from which uses, proximities and relations will develop. The production of inhabited space represents the possibility of new ecologies and the strengthening of existing ecologies, in some cases the outcome of the transformation itself. "Urbanisation" is no longer synonymous with the destruction of ecosystems, but a rethinking of the conditions that allow life in a milieu that is defined together with its transformation.

Fragments

The territory-subject composed of subjects (not only human, not only animal) definitively criticises the categories of "object" and "resource" territory. Criticism of the strong structures of modernity, its "integral" rationalisations, reveals the weak territorial and social structures that have been denied and subjugated. A new alliance between economic and spatial forms follows alternative development trajectories. Eco-socio-spatial prototypes explore their interrelationships, simultaneously regenerating nature and the city, accommodating the complex ecologies of the technonatures produced by each transformation.

They are fragments of a project: an epistemological, ontological, ethical and, of course, (bio)political shift.

CONCLUSIONS

Heterogeneous and varied as gardens are, the Biopolitical Garden is a space of coexistence and concerns the design of spaces within which bodies, lives, and desires are shaped and interact.

The garden metaphor has a long history even within biopolitical thinking. Bauman wrote about it, recalling its use from Frederick the Great up to the socialist programme of H.G. Wells: a garden is designed for the growth of humans, to care for them with the same care devoted to plants and flowers (Bauman 1991), carefully separating them from things that can harm them, watching over their purity and safety, taking the immunity paradigm described by Roberto Esposito to its extreme consequences (2004). This is of course not the meaning of the book's title, in which coexistence, ambivalence, ambiguity, heterogeneity and mixing constitute the sense of an ecological and social transition project, in contrast to the thought of separation, selection and homogeneity evoked in the borrowing of a biopolitical metaphor. The distance between the present and future city will be the result of an excavation into new ways of co-existing, the redefinition of boundaries, distances, porosity: between contrasting proximities in the space of individuals, groups, societies, species and practices. Questioning these modes implies reopening the debate on the role of architecture, urbanism, territorial and landscape design within a broader biopolitical project that concerns a life in common: its sharing through a complex system of relationships between living and non-living entities that form spaces and shape/are shaped by different forms of power.

The Biopolitical Garden, as should be clear by now, is not only imagined as a coercive tool, an apparatus of control exercised over a population. In its positive meaning, it is a reservoir of emancipation possibilities for different subjects, it is a place for the profound redefinition of relationships between humans and non-humans, and it is a social and ecological space at the same time. It is also an opportunity to address the depth and infinite ambiguity of the biopolitical reflection initiated by Foucault, without shyness tinged with hypocrisy: the urgency lies in the era we are living through, in the ecological, social and economic transition which, redefining the modern biopolitical project, leads us to rethink the role of space in the process of improving the quality of life, of lives, and of forms of life. Space is the collective capital of this transition, a fundamental support and agent.

The design of space is covered above all in the first and third parts of this book. The first part deconstructs modern and postmodern experiences that are now classics but always rediscovered and reread with different eyes (in Calvino's definition of the classics)—space function, space nature and social space. The third part reflects on experiences of the present; here biopolitical issues surface with great clarity and open up paths that are still too narrow to redefine the project, although it has the merit of anchoring ideas to overcome the current limits of design practice. At the centre of the book lies the hard core of the confrontation with biopolitics: I reread some of the relevant authors and approaches and suggest some ways to penetrate and cross it. In this section I proposed three working hypotheses/fields of research that attempt to clarify in what sense the project of space can face the challenge of an affirmative biopolitics (Esposito 2004). The three hypotheses/fields have accompanied me for years in attempting to discern the meaning of my action and run in plain sight through the last part of the book together with the three spaces of the first part.

In thinking and designing the city and the territory I have used, without too much sophistication, the term life with the double meaning of biological life, the life common to all those who live (the Greek term zoé), and life in the sense of bíos, which indicates the life proper to an individual or a group, the forms of life (Agamben, 1995). On closer inspection, while for the philosopher the two terms now seem increasingly difficult to separate and isolate (Esposito 2004:5), this is also the case with the design of space, for which the technical and political dimensions of governing life in both senses mentioned above cannot be foreign.

The delicacy of the shift contained in the frequent use, within the Biopolitical Garden, of the words project or design does not escape anyone: it indicates the shift from the plane of being to what ought to be, from critical analysis to the propositional and normative plane. I hope I have not crossed these planes, this shift, in an excessively crude way. It is this, however, that I am concerned with and it is for this reason—to be able to design—that I had the absolute and unmediated need to write this book.

Luckily, the biopolitical discourse is unstable and open; it has gone through different variations over time and, as I have already mentioned, it is a very useful theory-building device that allows us to clarify the renewed centrality of "life"' in every reflection and project on the future of space, extended to all forms that planetary urbanisation has developed in different contexts. The hypothesis of a "new biopolitical project" broadens the picture, reformulates the priorities of design research and provides a new direction to our gaze and imagination.

The themes I have touched upon do not end there. The theme of the relationship between soil, the city and its design, for example, re-emerges cyclically, even in the arduous elaboration of interdisciplinary, multidisciplinary and transdisciplinary thinking, an epistemological shift that shakes modern Western thought to its foundations and which will not happen by chance.

Many expectations are now focused on urban soil, an unbuilt space that shares the fact of being part of the city. However, the full urgency of the centrality of this issue is not yet recognised. Two debates prevent it from being entirely understood: the first concerns the assumption of the compact city as a unique model of a sustainable city. In this case, the enclosed areas are primarily the space of densification and compaction of the city. I do not think it is necessary to dwell on the arguments and rhetoric developed for a model that is often nostalgic, abstract and distant from the actual conditions in which many territories find themselves. It is too well known: for several decades it has been the debate held by institutions, academies, and important authors.

The second line, not opposed to the first, indeed often in direct continuity with it, does not consider the diffuse urban space, in which the majority of the European and world population lives, to be a case that should be the focus of policies and institutions at various scales. This debate focuses on global cities and slums[60] where the increasingly marked divide between rich and poor and, at the same time, the new ambitions of "emerging" countries are represented. Unlike the first debate, which aims to standardise intervention strategies in favour of a single urban model, the second line simply forgets the existence of other forms of urbanity where people live and coexist, use public transportation, services and space, create new economies, and where many of the risks that could endanger "cities", understood in a more traditional sense, are absorbed, and where the ecological and socio-economic transition requires specific projects.

60. This is, for example, the line taken at the Urban Age conference in July 2016, coordinated by the London School of Economics at the 15th Venice Biennale.

The cultural hegemony found in the two debates cannot be underestimated. We are dealing with systems of exclusion (Foucault 1970), and this is why, despite the now vast literature on settlement situations that cannot be absorbed within the categories of core city or slum planet, a counter-debate is still necessary today. This is also why the production of new interpretative and design images of urbanity in the making—in light of the hypothesis of a new biopolitical project—is a necessary exercise and a fundamental part of a common discussion between civic society, geographers, sociologists, architects, urban planners, landscape architects, economists, natural sciences scholars, agronomists and agricultural economists, and scholars of ecology and political economy.

The hypothesis of a "horizontal metropolis" that we have put forward on several occasions, an oxymoron that combines metropolitan conditions and the horizontality of relations, which values heterogeneity instead of condemning it, only partly deals with a physical object. Despite the similarities and characteristics that we have recognised in the widespread territories, it is still above all an ecological, social and political project to be finely articulated. The soil is an active and indispensable agent of this project.

A final note on the three hypothetical fields contained in the central part. The first field: a full consideration and assumption of the biopolitical viewpoint in the project of architecture and the city. The second: integration of the thought of deep ecology and political ecology within this same approach. The third: resumption of the theme of emancipation of the subject (also part of a possible meaning of positive biopolitics), downstream of the extension to humans and non-humans (the "subject territory").

The most general hypothesis contained in these three fields concerns the possibility of establishing direct, mutually enriching relations between them, and of being able to find in these relations a coherent politics of the space of a life in common. For this reason, space, the problematic category I introduced at the beginning of this book, its design and the research that uses it seem highly strategic to me. While the biopolitical space project has focused on the protection, security and stability of individuals and populations—and consequently has taken on coercive characteristics and certain contradictory conditions of individual and collective freedom based on mechanisms of controlling those same supposedly free individuals and communities—the risk is to exasperate these devices and their contradictions. Not only by continuing the separation and distancing of one from the other, but also by establishing new hierarchies between community and individual, between holistic thinking and individual appreciation. This is why the three fields cannot be separated: separating them would shatter their mutual contradictions. Instead, a dialogical area opens up, within which each project is an opportunity to test the coherence and flexibility of the relationships between deep ecology, nature space and emancipatory biopolitics, social and functional space. The eco-socio-spatial prototypes I have discussed, and among them, for example, the weak structures of the socio-ecological continuity infrastructure, reflect the dialogical experience and test the substantial change in point of view. According to Escobar, "design is ontological" because it always implies particular and specific ways of being, knowing, and acting (Escobar 2018:X),[61] and the environmental crisis is a crisis of "design" itself (Escobar 2018:44).

The transition project is not just a new focus on consumption and emissions, it is a new reflection on existence, on the life we have in common, on the forms of life and their acting spaces. It is a new project of space, inescapably biopolitical.

61. Escobar refers to and has contributed to the ontological turn, which emphasises questions of existence and the importance of different worlds constructed by different representations. "To nourish design's potential for the transitions, however, requires a significant reorientation of design (...), toward a type of rationality and set of practices attuned to the relational dimension of life." (Escobar 2018:X). According to Escobar and many other authors linked to the ontological turn (from Descola to Dona Haraway, Viveiro de Castro or Latour), the theme is breaking out of the dualistic system of Western rationality (nature/culture, us/them, subject/object or mind/body) and its hierarchies. For Escobar, the theme is also the disjunction of "design" from the current economic system in order to learn from other worldviews and regain an understanding and acceptance of the radical interdependence of the whole. This approach is the basis for the "autonomous design" he proposed.

Fig. 130
The Biopolitical Garden, 17th Venice Architecture Biennale, 2021.

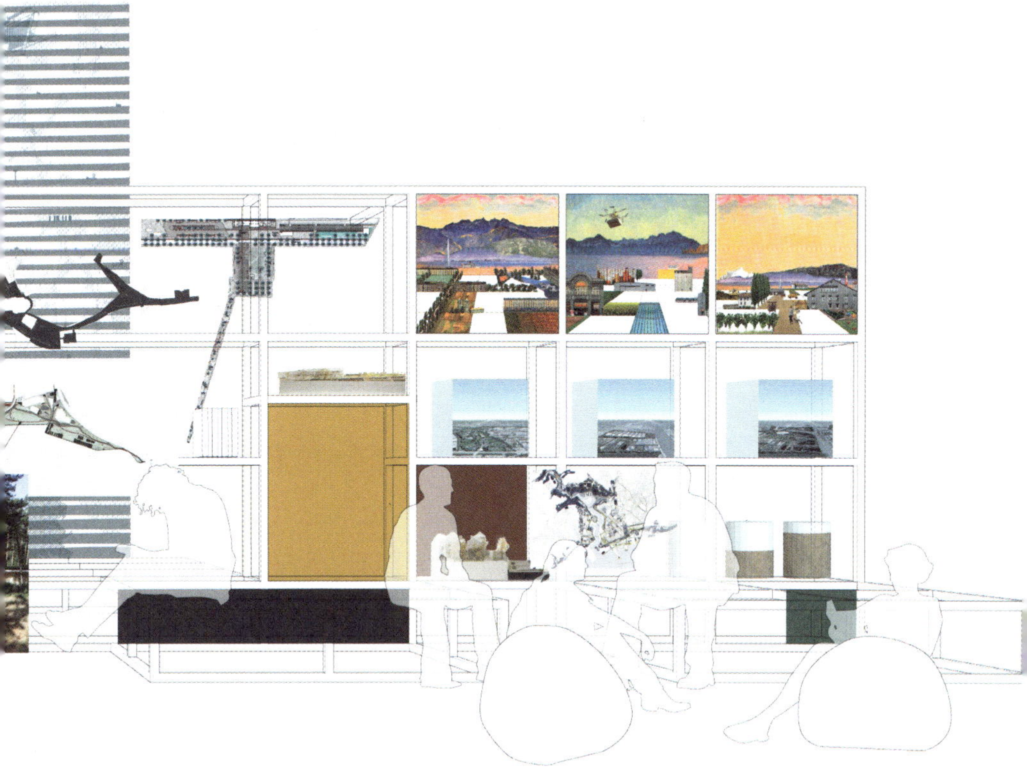

BIBLIOGRAPHY

Abrahamsson, Christian. 2013. "On the genealogy of Lebensraum." *Geografica Helvetica* 68:37-44.

Agamben, Giorgio. 1995. *Homo Sacer: Il potere sovrano e la nuda vita.* Torino: Einaudi.

Aggéri, Gaëlle and Pierre Donadieu. 2003. "Le retour du sauvage dans les parcs publics: un nouveau jardinage." *Les carnets du paysage* 9(10).

Aggregate Architectural History Collaborative. 2012. *Governing by Design. Architecture, Economy, and Politics in the Twentieth Century*. Pittsburgh: University of Pittsburgh Press.

Alberti, Marina. 2016. *Cities that Think Like Planets*. Washington: University of Washington Press.

Anderson, Stanford, Gail Fenske, and David Fixler. 2012. *Aalto and America*. New Haven: Yale University Press.

Andersson, Thorbjörn. 2002. *To Erase the Garden: Modernity in the Swedish Garden and Landscape*. In *The Architecture of Landscape 1940-1960*, edited by Marc Treib. Philadelphia: University of Pennsylvania.

Audier, Serge. 2017. *La Société écologique et ses ennemis; pour une histoire alternative de l'émancipation*. Paris: La Découverte.

Austen, Jane. (1814) 1996. *Mansfield Park*. New York: Penguin.

Avermaete, Tom. 2004. "Stem and Web: A Different Way of Analysing, Understanding and Conceiving the City in the Work of Candilis-Josic-Woods." In *Team 10: Between Modernity and the Everyday*, edited by Dirk Van den Heuvel and Max Risselada. Delft: Delft University Press.

Aymonino, Carlo. 1965. *Origini e sviluppo della città moderna*. Venice: Marsilio.

Balibar, Étienne. 2012. *Citoyen-sujet et autres essais d'anthropologie philosophique*. Paris: PUF.

Banham, Reyner. 1966. *The New Brutalism: ethic or aesthetic*, Architectural Press, London.

Barcelloni Corte, Martina, and Paola Viganò, eds. 2022. *The Horizontal Metropolis. The Anthology*. New York: Springer.

Barthes, Roland. 1994. "Sémiologie et urbanisme." In Œuvres *completes II (1966-1973)*. Paris: Seuil.

Baudrillard, Jean. 1986. *Amérique*. Paris: Grasset.

——. 2007. *Forget Foucault*. Los Angeles: Semiotext(e).

Bauman, Zygmunt. 1991. *Modernity and Ambivalence*. Cambrige: Polity Press.

Bellamy, Edward. 1888. *Looking Backward, 2000-1887*. Boston: Houghton, Mifflin and Co.

Bennet, Jane. 2010. *Vibrant Matter: A Political Ecology of Things*. Durham: Duke University Press.

Bergdoll, Barry, and Peter Christensen. 2008. *Home Delivery: Fabricating the Modern Dwelling*. New York: The Museum of Modern Art.

Berlin, Isaiah, 1969. *Four Essays on Liberty*. Oxford: Oxford University Press.

Bevilacqua, Piero. 1995. *Venezia e le acque. Una metafora planetaria*. Rome: Donzelli.

——. 1996. *Tra natura e storia*. Rome: Donzelli.

Bianchetti, Cristina. 2016. *Spazi che contano. Il progetto urbanistico in epoca neo-liberale*. Rome: Donzelli.

——. 2020. *Corpi tra spazio e progetto*. Milan: Mimesis.

Bianchettin Del Grano, Monica. 2015. "Lo spazio fra le cose. Learning from the existing landscape is a way of being revolutionary for un urbanist." PhD dissertation. Iuav University of Venice.

Borsi, Katharina. 2015. "Drawing the Region: Hermann Jansen's Vision of Greater Berlin in 1910." *The Journal of Architecture* 20(1).

Bourdieu, Pierre. 1986. *The Forms of Capital*. In *Handbook of Theory and Research for the Sociology of Education*, edited by John Richardson. New York: Greenwood.

——. 1993. *La misère du Monde*. Paris: Seuil.

Braudel, Fernand. 1958. "Histoire et Sciences sociales: La longue durée." *Annales. Économies, Sociétés, Civilisations*. 13(4):725-753.

Butor, Michel. 1982. "La Ville comme texte." In *Répertoire V*. Paris: Minuit.

Cahn, Livia, Chloé Deligne, Noémie Pons-Rotbardt, et al. 2018. *Terres des villes: Enquêtes potagères de Bruxelles aux premières saisons du 21è siècle*. Paris: Éditions de l'éclat.

Callenbach, Ernest. 2009. *Ecotopia*. New York: Bantam Books.

Cambi, Enrico, Benedetto Di Cristina, and Giovanna Balzanetti Steiner. 1980. *Tipologie residenziali a schiera*. Milan: Be-Ma Editrice.

Cambi, Enrico, Michele Di Sivo, and Giovanna Steiner. 1984. *Tipologie residenziali in linea*. Milan: Be-Ma Editrice.

Candilis, Georges. 1972. *Planning and design for Leisure*. Stuttgart: Karl Kramer Verlag.

——. 1977. *Bâtir la vie*. Paris: Stock.

Candilis, Georges, Alexis Josic, and Shadrach Woods. 1962. "A la recherche d'une structure urbaine." *Architecture d'Aujourd'hui* 101:50-51.

——. 1975. *Toulouse Le Mirail, la naissance d'une ville nouvelle*. Stuttgart: Karl Kramer Verlag.

Canguilhem, Georges. 1966. *Le normal et le pathologique*. Paris: PUF.

Carini, Alessandra, and Roberto Farina. 1979. *Housing in Europa*. Bologna: Edizioni Luigi Parma.

Carter, Ian, and Mario Ricciardi, eds. 1996. *L'idea di libertà*. Milan: Feltrinelli.

Cassin, Barbara, ed. 2004. *Vocabulaire européen des philosophies: dictionnaire des intraduisibles*. Paris: Le Seuil.

Cavalieri, Chiara, and Paola Viganò. 2020. *The Horizontal Metropolis. A Radical Project*. Zürich: Park Books.

Cavalletti, Andrea. 2005. *La città biopolitica. Mitologie della sicurezza*. Milan: Bruno Mondadori.

——. 2019. "Potere sovrano e nuda vita, l'indagine di Agamben lunga vent'anni." *Il Manifesto*. March 17, 2019. https://ilmanifesto.it/potere-sovrano-e-nuda-vita-lindagine-di-agamben-lunga-ventanni/.

Caye, Pierre. 2020. *Durer. Éléments pour la transformation du système productif*. Paris: Les Belles Lettres.

Châtelet, Anne-Marie, Luc Lerch Dominique, and Noël Jean, eds. 2003. *L'ecole de plein air*. Paris: Edition Recherches.

Chombart de Lauwe, Paul-Henry. 1952. *Paris et l'agglomération parisienne - Méthodes de recherches pour l'étude d'une grande cité (écologie, statistique, expression graphique) II*. Paris: PUF.

——. 1965. *Paris Essai de sociologie, 1952-1964*. Paris: Les Editions Ouvrières.

Clarisse, Catherine. 2004. *Cuisine, recettes* d›architecture. Paris: Éditions de l›Imprimeur.

Clevenger, Samuel M., and David L. Andrews. 2017. "A Peaceful Path to Healthy Bodies: The Biopolitics of Ebenezer Howard's Garden City." *Urban Planning* 2(4):5-9.

Cogato Lanza, Elena. 2003. *Maurice Braillard et ses urbanistes*. Geneva: Éditions Slatkine.

Coles, Romand. 2016. *Visionary Pragmatism. Radical and Ecological Democracy in Neoliberal Times*. Durham: Duke University Press.

Collina, Vittore. 2003. "L'attenzione agli spazi." In *La politica e gli spazi: Prima giornata di studio "Figure dello spazio, politica e società*, edited by Bruna Consarelli. Florence: Firenze University Press.

Conrads, Ulrich. 1970. *Programs and Manifestoes, on 20th-century architecture*. Cambridge: The MIT Press.

Corboz, André. 1983. "Le territoire comme palimpseste." *Diogène* 121.

Cosgrove, Isobel, and Richard Jackson. 1972. *The Geography of Recreation and Leisure*. London: Hutchinson University Library.

Cutro, Antonella, ed. 2005. *Biopolitica. Storia e attualità di un concetto, ombre corte*. Verona: Ombre Corte.

Daalder, Remco. 2003. "The Amsterdamse Bos: the Definitive City Park." In *Planning Amsterdam. Scenarios for Urban Development, 1928-2003*, edited by Allard Jolles, Erik Klusman, and Ben Teunissen. Rotterdam: NAi Publishers.

de Certeau, Michel. 1980. *L'Invention du Quotidien*, 1, *Arts de Faire*. Paris: Union générale d'éditions.

Deland, Mats. 2001. "The Social City: Middle-way approaches to housing and sub-urban governmentality in southern Stockholm, 1900-1945" PhD dissertation. Stockholm University.

Dixon Hunt, John. 1991. "The Garden as a Cultural Object." In *Denatured Visions: Landscape and Culture in the Twentieth Century*, edited by Stuart Wrede and William Howard Adams. New York: Museum of Modern Art.

——. 1993. "Nel concetto delle tre nature." *Casabella* 597-598: 98-101.

——. 1996. *L'art du jardin et son histoire*. Paris: Editions Odile Jacob.

Eleb, Monique, and Anne Debarre-Blanchard. 1995. *L'invention de l'habitation moderne, Paris 1880-1914*. Paris: Hazan.

Escobar, Arturo. 1999. "After Nature: Steps to an Antiessentialist Political Ecology." *Current Anthropology* 40(1):1-30.

——. 2008. *Territories of Difference: Place, Movements, Life, Redes*. Durham: Duke University Press.

——. 2018. *Designs for the Pluriverse. Radical Interdependence, Autonomy, and the Making of Worlds*. Durham: Duke University Press.

Esposito, Roberto. 2004. *Bíos. Biopolitica e filosofia*. Turin: Einaudi. (English translation: *Bíos: Biopolitics and Philosophy*, University of Minnesota Press, Minneapolis 2008).

Eugenides, Jeffrey. 2002. *Middlesex*. London: Bloosmbury.

Ferragina, Emanuele. 2012. *Social Capital in Europe: A Comparative Regional Analysis*. Cheltenham-Northhampton: Edward Elgar.

Fatio, Guillaume. 1899. *La campagne genevoise d'après nature*. Illustrated by Frédéric Boissonnas. Geneva: Société Auxiliaire du Musée de Genève.

Forti, Simona. 2012. *I nuovi demoni. Ripensare oggi male e potere*. Milan: Feltrinelli.

Foucault, Michel. 1966. *L'Archéologie du savoir*. Paris: Gallimard.

——. 1971. *L'ordre du discours*. Paris: Gallimard.

——. 1975. *Surveiller et Punir. Naissance de la prison*. Paris: Gallimard.

——. 1976. *Histoire de la sexualité, La volonté de savoir I*. Paris: Gallimard.

——. 1983. "Afterword." In *Michel Foucault: Beyond Structuralism and Hermeneutics*, edited by Hubert L. Dreyfus and Paul Rabinow. Chicago: University of Chicago Press.

——. 1994a. "Qu'est-ce que les Lumières ?" In *Dits et Ecrits 1980-1988, IV*: 562-578. Paris: Gallimard.

——. 1994b. "Le sujet et le pouvoir." In *Dits et écrits, 1980-1988, IV*. Paris: Gallimard.

——. 1997. *"Il faut défendre la société". Cours au Collège de France (1975-1976)*. Paris: Gallimard.

——. 1999. *Les Anormaux. Cours au collège de France (1974-1975)*. Paris: Gallimard.

——. 2002. "Spazio, sapere e potere." In *Spazi altri*, edited by Salvo Vaccaro. Milan: Mimesis.

——. 2004. *Sécurité, territoire, population. Cours au Collège de France (1977-78)*. Paris: Gallimard. (English translation 2007, *Security, Territory, Population: Lectures at the Collège de France, 1977 78*, London: Palgrave Macmillan

Friedland, Roger, and Deirdre Boden, eds. *NowHere. Space, Time and Modernity*. Berkeley: University of California Press.

Friedman, Yona, and Manuel Orazi. 2015. *Yona Friedman: The Dilution of Architecture*, edited by Nader Seraj. Zürich-Lausanne: Park Books-Archizoom.

Gandelsonas, Mario. 1991. *The Urban Text*. Cambridge: MIT Press.

Gandy, Matthew. 2003. *Concrete and Clay: Reworking Nature in New York City*. Cambridge: MIT Press.

——. 2014. *The Fabric of Space: Water, Modernity, and the Urban Imagination*. Cambridge: MIT Press.

Gibson-Graham, J. K. 2006. *The End of Capitalism (As We Knew It): A Feminist Critique of Political Economy*. Minneapolis: University of Minnesota Press.

Giedion, Sigfried. 1941. *Space, Time & Architecture: The Growth of a New Tradition*. Cambridge: Harvard University Press.

Goldscheid, Rudolf. 1911. *Höherentwicklung und Menschenökonomie: Grundlegung der Sozialbiologie*. Leipzig: Verlag von Dr. Werner Klinckhard.

Gottmann, Jean. 1961. *Megalopolis: The Urbanized Northeastern Seaboard of the United States*. New York: The Twentieth Century Fund.

Grassi, Giorgio. 1975. *Das Neue Frankfurt e l'architettura della nuova Francoforte*. Bari: Edizioni Dedalo.

Gruet, Stéphane, and Rémy Papillault, eds. 2008. *Le Mirail, Mémoire d'une ville*. Toulouse: Editions Poiésis – A.E.R.A.

Gunneflo, Markus. 2015. "Rudolf Kjellén: Nordic Biopolitics before the Welfare State." *RETFÆRD ÅRGANG* 38(3):24-39.

Gutkind, Erwin A. 1962. *The Twilight of Cities*. New York: MacMillan.

Habermas, Jürgen. 1986. "Taking Aim at the Heart of the Present." In *Foucault: A critical reader*, edited by David Couzens Hoy, 103-108. New York: Basil Blackwell.

Habraken, J. Nicolas. 1972. *Supports: An Alternative to Mass Housing*. London: Architectural Press.

Hache, Émilie, ed. 2012. Écologie politique. Cosmos, communauté, milieux. Paris: Éditions Amsterdam.

Halbwachs, Maurice. 1950. *La mémoire collective*. Paris: PUF.

Haney, David. 2010. *When Modern was Green: Life and Work of Landscape Architect Leberecht Migge*. London-New York: Routledge.

Hardt, Michael, and Tony Negri. 2000. *Empire*. Cambridge: Harvard University Press.

——. 2004. *Multitude: War and Democracy in the Age of Empire*. London: Penguin.

Hayden, Dolores. 1981. *The Grand Domestic Revolution*. Cambridge: MIT Press.

Hertzberger, Herman. 1991. *Lessons for Students in Architecture*. Rotterdam: 010 Publishers.

Huizinga, Johan. 1997. *Homo Ludens*. Turin: Einaudi.

Iorns Magallanes, Catherine J. 2015. "Nature as an Ancestor: Two Examples of Legal Personality for Nature in New Zealand." *Vertigo* 22.

Jencks, Charles. 2000. *Le Corbusier and the Continual Revolution in Architecture*. New York: The Monacelli Press.

Jesi, Furio. 2000. *Spartakus*. Turin: Bollati Boringhieri.

Juvonen, Helvi. (1958) 1992. *Bedrock*. In *A Way to Measure Time*, edited by Bo Carpelan, Veijo Meri, and Matti Suurpää. Helsinki: Finnish Literature Society.

Khan-Magomedov, Selim O. 1987. *Pioneers of Soviet Architecture*. London: Thames and Hudson.

Keck, Frédéric. 2008. "Les usages du biopolitique." *Revue L'Homme* 187-188: 295-314.

Kelly, Michael. 1994. *Critique and Power. Recasting the Foucault/Habermas Debate*. Cambridge: MIT Press.

Kern, Stephen. 1983. *The Culture of Time and Space, 1880-1918*. Cambridge: Harvard University Press.

Klemperer, Victor. 1996. *LTI, La langue du IIIe Reich*. Paris: Éditions Albin Michel.

Kr má ová, Jana. 2009. "E.O. Wilson's Concept of Biophilia and the Environmental Movement in the USA." *Klaudyán: Internet Journal of Historical Geography and Environmental History* 6(1-2):4-17.

Kropotkin, Petr. 1901. *Fields, Factories, and Workshops*. 2nd edition. London: Swan Sinnenschein.

Laban, Rudolf, and Frederick Charles Lawrence. (1947) 1974. *Effort: Economy of Human Movement*. London: MacDonald and Evans.

Laban, Rudolf. 2003. *La Danse moderne educative*. Brussels-Paris: Éditions Complexe et Centre nationale de la danse.

Landau, Royston. 1985. "A Philosophy of Enabling: The Work of Cedric Price." *AA Files* 8:3-7.

Latour, Bruno. 1991. *Nous n'avons jamais été modernes. Essai d'anthropologie symétrique*. Paris: Éditions La Découverte.

——. 1996. “On actor-network theory. A few clarifications.” *Soziale Welt* 47:369-382.

Lefebvre, Henri. 1972. *Espace et politique: le droit à la ville* II. Paris: Éditions Anthropos.

——. 1974. *La production de l'espace*. Paris: *Éditions Anthropos*.

Leff, Enrique. 1998. *Saber ambiental*. Mexico City: Siglo XXI.

Leloutre, Géry. 2017. “Le Park System d'Anderlecht. Construction d'un espace public pour la couronne verte bruxelloise.” *Bruxelles Patrimoines* 22-23:114-129.

——. 2020. “La transformation moderne de Bruxelles. Processus d'agencement de l''espace urbain bruxellois entre 1949 et 1979.” PhD dissertation. Université Libre de Bruxelles.

Lemke, Thomas. 2011. *Biopolitics: An Advanced Introduction*. New York-London: New York University Press.

——. 2016. “Rethinking Biopolitics: The New Materialism and the Political Economy of Life.” In *Resisting Biopolitics: Philosophical, Political, and Performative Strategies*, edited by S.E. Wilmer and Audrone Zukauskaite, 57-73. New York: Routledge.

Lenel, Emmanuelle. 2013. “La mixité sociale dans l'action publique urbaine à Bruxelles: Projet ou langage politique?” *Brussels Studies* 65. doi.org/10.4000/brussels.1129.

Leopold, Aldo. (1949) 1966. *A Sand County Almanac*. New York: Sierra Club/Ballantine Books.

Léveillé, Alain. 1987. “1935: il piano direttore di Ginevra. Un piano decisamente modern.” *Urbanistica* 89:20-32.

Lévy, Jacques, and Michel Lussault. 2003. *Dictionnaire de la géographie et de l'espace des sociétés*. Paris: Belin.

Logan, William Bryant. 1995. *Dirt: The Ecstatic Skin of the Earth*. New York: Riverhead Books.

Lomi, Egidio, and Amos Masé. 1979. “Note per una lettura delle trasformazioni urbane tra urgenza edilizia e luogo architettonico.” In *Housing in Europa*. Bologna: Edizioni Luigi Parma.

López-Durán, Fabiola. 2018. *Eugenics in the Garden: Transatlantic Architecture and the Crafting of Modernity*. Austin: University of Texas Press.

Lootsma, Bart. 1999. “Now Switch Off the Sound and Reverse the Film...Koolhaas, Constant and Dutch Culture in the 1960s.” *Hunch* 1:154-173.

Lynch, Kevin A. 1960. *The Image of the City*. Cambridge: MIT Press.

Maniaque, Caroline. 2021. *L'aventure du Whole Earth Catalog*. Paris: Les Production du Effa.

Manner, Eeva-Liisa. (1956) 1992. *Counterpoint*. In *A Way to Measure Time*, edited by Bo Carpelan, Veijo Meri, and Matti Suurpää. Helsinki: Finnish Literature Society.

Marc, Franz. 2007. *La seconda vista*. Milan: Abscondita.

Marfaing, Jean-Loup, ed. 2009. *Architecture et Urbanisme Toulouse 45-75*. Portet-sur-Garonne: Éditions Loubatières.

Margat, Claire. 2003. “Ensauvager nos jardins.” *Les carnets du paysage* 9-10.

Marzocca, Ottavio. 2020. *Biopolitics for Beginners*. Milan-Udine: Mimesis.

Matoré, Georges. 1976. *L'Espace humain. L'expression de l'espace dans la vie, la pensée et l'art contemporains*. 2nd edition. Paris: Nizet.

McKaye, Benton. 1928. *The New Exploration: A Philosophy of Regional Planning*. New York: Harcourt Brace.

Menin, Sarah, and Flora Samuel. 2003. *Nature and Space: Aalto and Le Corbusier*. London: Routledge.

Mirbeau, Octave. (1899) 1991. *Le jardin des supplices*. Paris: Gallimard.

Mitchell, Timothy. 2013. *Carbon Democracy: Political Power in the Age of Oil*. London: Verso.

Montgomery, David R. 2007. *Dirt: The Erosion of Civilizations*. Berkeley-Los Angeles-London: University of California Press.

Moretti, Franco. 1997. *Atlante del romanzo europeo (1800-1900)*. Turin: Einaudi.

Moretti, Luigi. 2019. *“Spazio”. Gli editoriali e altri scritti*. Milan: Marinotti.

Morin, Edgar. 2020. “En finir avec les malheurs de l'écologie.” *Libération*, February

2. Accessed August 5, 2023. https://www.liberation.fr/debats/2020/02/02/en-finir-avec-les-malheurs-de-l-ecologie_1776814/.

Mumford, Eric. 2000. *The CIAM Discourse on Urbanism, 1928-1960*. Cambridge: MIT Press.

Naess, Arne. 1973. "The Shallow and the Deep, Long-Range Ecology Movement: A Summary." *Inquiry: An Interdisciplinary Journal of Philosophy and the Social Sciences* 16:95-100.

——. 2008. *The Ecology of Wisdom. Writings by Arne Naess*. Edited by Alan Drengson and Bill Devall. Berkeley; Counterpoint.

Nelson, Cary. 1997. *Manifesto of a Tenured Radical and Revolutionary Memory: Recovering the Poetry of the American Left*. New York-London: New York University Press.

Nikula, Riitta. 1993. *Architecture and Landscape: The Building of Finland*. Helsinki: Otava.

——. 1998. *La città negli scritti di Alvar Aalto*. In *Alvar Aalto, Visioni urbane*, edited by Pierre-Alain Croset. Milan: Skira.

Norri, Marja-Ritta. 1994. "Heroes and Matter: Notes on the 1950s." In *Heroism and the Everyday: Building Finland in the 1950*, edited by Marja-Ritta Norri. Helsiki: Museum of Finnish Architecture.

——, ed. 1994. *Heroism and the Everyday: Building Finland in the 1950*. Helsinki: Museum of Finnish Architecture.

Nuti, Franco. 1979. "Evoluzione delle tipologie abitative in rapporto ai sistemi costruttivi industrializzati." In *Housing in Europa*. Bologna: Edizioni Luigi Parma.

Osborne, Thomas, and Nikolas Rose. 1999. "Governing Cities: Notes on the Spatialisation of Virtue." *Environment and Planning D: Society and Space* 17(6):737-760.

Pancake, Breece D'J (Dexter John). 1983. *The Stories of Breece D'J Pancake*. Boston: Little, Brown.

Panerai, Philippe, Jean Castex, and Jean-Charles Depaule. 1977. *Formes urbaines: de l'îlot à la barre*, Paris: Éditions Dunod.

Pantzar, Mika. 2013. "'What are we to do with our new affluence?' Anticipating, framing and managing the putative plenty of post-war Finland." In *Coping With Excess: How Organizations, Communities and Individuals Manage Overflows*, edited by Barbara Czarniawska and Orvar Löfgren. Cheltenham-Northampton: Edward Elgar.

Peleman, David, Paola Viganò, Martina Barcelloni Corte, and Elsbeth Ronner, eds. 2022. *The Project of the Soil, Oase* 110.

Pelluchon, Corine. 2020. *Réparons le monde: Humains animaux nature*. Paris: Éditions Payot & Rivage.

Pépion, Ludovic. 2022. "Architecture ou destruction. La question de la durée dans le projet architectural et urbain à travers la modernité." PhD dissertation. Paris: PSL Université.

Perec, Georges. 1974. *Espèces d'espaces*. Paris: Éditions Galilée.

Perrocheau, Christophe, ed. 2012. *"Rendre possible». Du Plan construction au Puca : 40 ans de réalisations expérimentales*, Ministère de l'Écologie, du Développement durable et de l'Énergie Ministère de l'Égalité des Territoires et du Logement Direction générale de l'aménagement, du logement et de la nature, Plan urbanisme construction architecture.

Pevsner, Nikolaus. 1936. *Pioneers of the Modern Movement*. London: Faber.

Piccinato, Giorgio, Vieri Quilici, and Manfredo Tafuri. 1962. "La città-territorio: verso una nuova dimensione." *Casabella-Continuità* 270:16-25.

Pirandello, Luigi. 1926. *Uno, nessuno, centomila*. Florence: Bemporad.

Pisecki, Graciela S. 2007. "La mixité urbaine à Bruxelles: Interprétation locale à travers le discours." PhD dissertation. Université Libre de Bruxelles.

Pope, Albert. 1996. *Ladders*. New York: Princeton Architectural Press.

Precourt, Walter. 1983. "The Image of Appalachian Poverty." In *Appalachia and America. Autonomy and Regional Dependence*, edited by Allen Batteau. Lexington: University Press of Kentucky.

Preston-Dunlop, Valerie. 2003. Postface to the French edition of *La Danse moderne éducative*, by Rudolph Laban. Brussels-Paris:

Editions Complexe et Centre nationale de la danse.

Purdy, Jedediah. 2015. *After-Nature: A Politics for the Anthropocene*. Cambridge: Harvard University Press.

Rabinow, Paul. 1989. *French Modern: Norms and Forms of the Social Environment*. Cambridge: MIT Press.

Rancière, J. 2000. "Biopolitique ou politique?" *Multitude* 1:88-93.

Raffinot, Francois. 2014. "Des corps et des flux dans l'espace." In *Secrets de Fabriques*, edited by Elisabeth Essaïan and Marc Dilet. Paris: Editions Matière Première/ENSAPV.

Rashidzadeh, Kaveh. 2014. "The Geography of Evils in the Paris Region." PhD dissertation. Iuav University Venice.

Rautsi, Jussi. 1988. "The Alternative: Alvar Aalto's Urban Plans, 1940-1970." *HABITAT Intl.* 12(1):5-21.

Revel, Judith. 2014. "Tra Politica ed Etica." *Euronomade*. November 3. Accessed April 14, 2024. https://www.euronomade.info/politica-ed-etica-la-questione-della-soggettivazione/

Roukonen, Ria. 1994. "Landscape Design in Tapiola." In *Heroism and the Everyday: Building Finland in the 1950*, edited by Marja-Ritta Norri. Helsiki: Museum of Finnish Architecture.

Rowntree, B. Seebohm. 1910. *Land and labour. Lessons from Belgium*. London: MacMillan.

Saarikangas, Kirsi. 1993. *Model Houses for Model Families*. Helsinki: SHS.

Saarikoski, Pentti. (1983) 1992. *The Obscure Dances*. In *A Way to Measure Time*, edited by Bo Carpelan, Veijo Meri, and Matti Suurpää. Helsinki: Finnish Literature Society.

Saarinen, Eliel. 1958. *The City: Its growth, Its Decay, Its Future*. New York: Reinhold.

Salstrom, Paul, 1994. *Appalachia's Path to Dependency: Rethinking a Region's Economic History, 1730-1940*. Lexington: University Press of Kentucky.

Schaut, Christine. 2017. "Tout au Nord des tropiques: Une architecture moderne à Bruxelles." *CLARA* 4(1):203–218.

Schwab, Andreas, and Claudia Lanfranchi, eds. 2001. *Senso della vita e bagni di sole. Esperimenti di vita e arte al Monte Verità*. Ascona: Fondazione Monte Verità.

Scimemi, Gabriele. 1968. "Il ruolo delle teorie nell'urbanistica." In *Teoria della progettazione architettonica*, edited by Giuseppe Samonà. Bari: Edizioni Dedalo. Collection of lectures for the IUAV 1965-1966.

Sebald, Winfried G. 2009. *Storia naturale della distruzione*. Milan: Adelphi.

Secchi, Bernardo. 1986. "Progetto di suolo." *Casabella* 520/521:19-23.

——. 2000. *Prima lezione di urbanistica*. Rome-Bari: Laterza.

——. 2005. *La città del ventesimo secolo*. Rome-Bari: Laterza.

——. 2013. *La città dei ricchi e la città dei poveri*. Rome-Bari: Laterza.

——. 2014. "A tradição europeia do planejamento: culturas e políticas." In *Tempos e escalas da cidade e do urbanismo: quatro palestras, XIII Seminario de Historia da Cidade e do Urbanismo (Shcu)*, edited by E. Ribeiro Peixoto, M. F. Derntl, P.P. Palazzo, and R. Trevisan. Brasilia: Facoltà di Architettura e Urbanistica.

Secchi Bernardo, and Paola Viganò, et al. 2010, "Bruxelles et ses territoires, Plan Régional de Développement Durable. Elaboration d'une vision territoriale métropolitaine à l'horizon 2040 pour Bruxelles, first report."

Secchi Bernardo, and Paola Viganò. 2011. *La ville poreuse*. Geneva: MétisPresses.

Sennett, Richard. 1994. *Flesh and Stone: The Body and the City in Western Civilization*. London-New York: W.W. Norton.

——. 1998. *The Corrosion of Character: The Personal Consequences of Work in the New Capitalism*. London-New York: W.W. Norton.

Serres, Michel. 1980. *Hermès V, Le passage du Nord-ouest*. Paris: Éditions de Minuit.

Sica, Paolo. 1985. *Storia dell'Urbanistica, Il Novecento*. Rome-Bari: Laterza.

Smets, Marcel. 1986. "La Belgique ou la banlieue radieuse." *Paysages d'architectures*, 33–35. Brusells. Exhibition catalogue.

Söderqvist, Lisbeth. 2011. "Structuralism in Architecture: A Definition." *Journal of Aesthetics & Culture* 3.

Soja, Edward S. 1989. *Postmodern Geographies: The Reassertion of Space in Critical Social Theory*. London: Verso.

——. 1996. *Thirdspace: Journeys to Los Angeles and Other Real-and-Imagined Places*. Cambridge: Blackwell.

——. 2000. *Postmetropolis: Critical Studies of Cities and Regions*. Hoboken: Wiley-Blackwell.

——. 2009. "La ville et la justice spatiale." *Justice spatiale/Spatial Justice* 1.

Sterken, Sven. 2013. "Bruxelles, une capitale en mouvement? 50 ans d'architecture et d'urbanisme." In *Bruxelles Patrimoines*, edited by Arlette Verkruyssen, 187-203.

Stone, Christopher. 1972. "Should Trees Have Standing? Toward Legal Rights for Natural Objects." *Southern California Law Review* 45: 450-501.

Strauven, Francis. 1985. *René Braem: les aventures dialectiques d'un moderniste flamand = the dialectical adventures of a flemish modernist*. Brussels: Archives d'Architecture Moderne.

Swyngedouw, Eric. 2004. *Social Power and the Urbanization of Water: Flows of Power*. Oxford: Oxford University Press.

Tafuri, Manfredo. 1973. *Progetto e Utopia. Architettura e sviluppo capitalistico*. Rome-Bari: Laterza.

——, ed. 1980a. *Vienna Rossa*. Milan: Electa.

——. 1980b. *La sfera e il labirinto*. Turin: Einaudi.

Thaler, Richard H., and Cass R Sunstein. 2008. *Nudge: Improving Decisions about Health, Wealth, and Happiness*. London: Penguin.

Tschumi, Bernard. 2005. *Architettura e disgiunzione*. Bologna: Pendragon.

Tsing Lowenhaupt, Anna. 2015. *The Mushroom at the End of the World: On the Possibility of Life in Capitalist Ruins*. Princeton: Princeton University Press.

Tuomi, Timo. 1992. *Tapiola: A History and Architectural Guide*. Espoo: Espoo City Museum.

Turner, Jonathan, and Alexandra Maryanski. 1979. *Functionalism*. Menlo Park: Benjamin Cummings.

Valencia Torres, Angélica, Chetan Tiwari, and Samuel F. Atkinson. 2021. "Progress in Ecosystem Services Research: A Guide for Scholars and Practitioners." In *Ecosystem Services* 49:2.

Van Criekingen, Mathieu. 2013. "La gentrification mise en politiques." *Métropoles*. https://doi.org/10.4000/metropoles.4753.

Vattimo, Gianni. 1985. *La fine della modernità*. Milan: Garzanti.

Venturi, Robert. 1966. *Complexity and Contradiction in Architecture*. New York: Museum of Modern Art. [MoMA Papers on Architecture No. 1]

Vicari, François. 1984. "Biographies." In *Archithese: In zweiter Linie/ En deuxième Ligne, Genève 1929-1949*, March-April.

Vidal de la Blache, Paul. (1903) 1979. *Tableau de la géographie de la France*. Facsimile edition.

Viganò, Paola. 1999. *La città elementare*. Milan: Skira.

——. 2008. "Water and Asphalt: The Project of Isotropy in the Metropolitan Region of Venice." *Architectural Design* 78: 34-9.

——. 2010. *I territori dell'urbanistica. Il progetto come produttore di conoscenza* [*Territories of Urbanism: The Project as Knowledge Producer*]. Rome: Officina. English translation 2016. Chicago: EPFL.

——. 2012a. "Elements for a Theory of the City as Renewable Resource." In *Recycling City, Lifecycles, Embodied Energy, Inclusion*, edited by Lorenzo Fabian, Emanuel Giannotti, and Paola Viganò Paola. Pordenone; Giavedoni Editore.

——. 2012b. "Idiografia dell'agricoltura." *Territorio* 60: 73-80.

——. 2014a. "Evolving Narratives." *Topos* 88, *The Narrative of the Landscape*.

——. 2014b. *Territorialism*. Cambridge: Harvard GSD.

——. 2016a. "Della possibilità di un Progetto." In *Italia 1945-2045: Urbanistica prima e dopo. Radici, condizioni, prospettive*, edited by

SIU, Stefano Munarin, and Luca Velo. Rome: Donzelli Editore.

——. 2016b. "Suolo. Note per una ricerca sulla città contemporanea." In *Suolo. Letture e responsabilità del Progetto*, edited by Monica Bianchettin Del Grano. Rome: Officina.

——. 2018a. "De l'archive à l'espace." In *L'architecture. Entre pratique et connaissance scientifique*, edited by Jean-Louis Cohen. Paris: Éditions du Patrimoine.

——. 2018b. "The Urbanism of Hope." In *Urbanisme de l'Espoir. Projeter des horizons d'attente*, edited by Panos Mantziaras and Paola Viganò. Geneva: MetisPresses.

——. 2019. "Il grande mistero. Verso una ricerca su Appalachia." In *Territorio e Produzione*, edited by Cristina Bianchetti. Macerata: Quodlibet.

——. 2020a. "Why NO CAR ? Dessiner la ville autrement." In *Dessiner la transition: Dispositifs pour une métropole écologique*, edited by Panos Mantziaras, Roselyne de Lestrange, Bernard Desclève, and Hélène Gallezot. Geneva: MetisPresses.

——. 2020b. "Territorio-soggetto/ Territoire-sujet." In *Territori della post-ruralità/ Territoires Post-Ruraux*, edited by Marta De Marchi and Hamed Khorasani Zadeh. Rome: Officina Edizioni.

——. 2021. "Life as a Common: Space for a New Biopolitical Project." *New Geography* 12.

Viganò, Paola, Bernardo Secchi, and Lorenzo Fabian, eds. 2016. *Water and Asphalt. The Project of Isotropy*. Zürich: Park Books.

Viganò, Paola, Chiara Cavalieri, and Martina Barcelloni Corte, eds. 2018. *The Horizontal Metropolis. Between Urbanism and Urbanization*. New York: Springer.

Viganò, Paola, and Claire Guenat. 2022. "Our Common Soil." In *The Project of the Soil*, edited by David Peleman, Paola Viganò, Martina Barcelloni Corte, and Elsbeth Ronner. *Oase* 110.

Viganò, Paola, Bertrand Plewinski, Guillaume Vanneste, and Nicolas Willemet. 2023. "Peterbos – Living in the Park, Inhabiting the City." in *Urban Living Lab for Local Regeneration: Beyond Participation in Large-Scale Social Housing Estates*, edited by Nele Aernouts, Francesca Cognetti, and Elena Maranghi. New York: Springer.

La ville à livre ouvert, Regard sur cinquante ans d'habitat. 1980. Paris.

Whiteley, Nigel. 2002. *Reyner Banham, Historian of the Immediate Future*. Cambridge: MIT Press.

Whitman, Walt. 1900. *Leaves of Grass*. Philadelphia: D. McKay.

Wigley, Mark. 1998. *Constant's New Babylon: The Hyper-Architecture of Desire*. Rotterdam: 010 Publishers.

Wilson, Edward O. 1984. *Biophilia*. Cambridge: Cambridge University Press.

Woods, Shadrach. 1960. "Stem." *Architectural Design* 5. Republished 1961 in *Le Carré bleu, Feuille internationale d'Architecture* 3.

——. 1962. "Web." *Le Carré bleu, Feuille internationale d'Architecture* 3.

——. 1975. *The Man in the Street: A Polemic on Urbanism*. London: Penguin.

Woudstra, Ian. 1997. "Jacobus P. Thijsse's Influence on Dutch Landscape Architecture." In *Nature and Ideology, Natural Garden Design in the Twentieth Century*, edited by Joachim Wolschke-Bulmahn. Washington DC: Dumbarton Oaks.

Zevi, Bruno. 1948. *Saper vedere l'architettura*. Turin: Einaudi.

——. 1960. *Saper vedere l'Urbanistica. Ferrara di Biagio Rossetti, la prima città moderna europea*. Turin: Einaudi.

Paola Viganò, architect and urbanist, is Full Professor in Urban Theory and Urban Design at the EPFL Lausanne where she directs the Habitat Research Centre and the Laboratory of Urbanism; she is also Professor at IUAV University of Venice.

She received the Grand Prix de l'Urbanisme in 2013, the title of Doctor Honoris Causa by the UCLouvain in 2016 in the frame of "Utopia for our Time", the Flemish Culture Award for Architecture in 2017, and the Golden Medal for the Career of Milano Triennale in 2018. In 2022, she received the Schelling Prize for Architectural Theory.

Together with Bernardo Secchi, she founded Studio (1990-2014) working on numerous projects and visions in Europe. Since 2015, StudioPaolaViganò has worked on the ecological and social transition of cities, landscapes, and territories designing urban and territorial projects and realizing public spaces in Europe (the new public park in Dessel Nuclear Research Center, Belgium, Marie Janson Plein in Brussels, together with VVV, the Parc Crombez-bus station-Rue Royale in Tournai, Belgium), is completing the Zac de la Courrouze in Rennes (France) and the Flaminio neighbourhood masterplan together with the public space definitive design in Rome. StudioPaolaViganò has also won the competition for the realization of the municipal plan (PdCom) of Lugano (Switzerland), just completed, and is a consultant of the City of Geneva for its municipal plan (PdCom). StudioPaolaViganò is finally coordinating the Strategic Scheme for the recovery of the Vesdre Valley (Belgium) after the flooding catastrophe of 2021 summer. In 2019, her work was exhibited at the Shenzen Biennale, and in 2021 at the Venice Biennale.

The Biopolitical Garden
Spaces, Lives and the Transition.

Published by
Actar Publishers, New York, Barcelona
www.actar.com

Author and Editor
Paola Viganò

Editor
Actar Publishers

Graphic Design
Sofia Sandoval
Marga Gibert, Actar Publishers

Translations into English
Rebecca Milner

Proofreading
Walter Ancarrow

Printing and Binding
Gràfiques JOU, Barcelona

Distribution
Actar D, Inc. New York, Barcelona.

New York
440 Park Avenue South, 17th Floor
New York, NY 10016, USA
T +1 2129662207
E salesnewyork@actar-d.com

Barcelona
Roca i Batlle 2-4
08023 Barcelona, Spain
T +34 933 282 183
E eurosales@actar-d.com

Indexing
ISBN: 978-1-63840-120-9
Library of Congress Control Number:
2023949608

Printed in Europe
Publication date: July, 2024
Cover image: © Paola Viganò